The Idea of Public Journalism

The Guilford Communication Series

Editors
Theodore L. Glasser, *Stanford University*
Marshall Scott Poole, *Texas A&M University*

Recent Volumes

The Idea of Public Journalism, *Theodore L. Glasser, Editor*

Communicating Across Cultures, *Stella Ting-Toomey*

Communications Policy and the Public Interest:
The Telecommunications Act of 1996, *Patricia Aufderheide*

The Business of Children's Entertainment, *Norma Odom Pecora*

Case Studies in Organizational Communication 2: Perspectives
on Contemporary Work Life, *Beverly Davenport Sypher, Editor*

Regulating Media: The Licensing and Supervision of Broadcasting
in Six Countries, *Wolfgang Hoffman-Riem*

Communication Theory: Epistemological Foundations, *James A. Anderson*

Television and the Remote Control: Grazing on a Vast Wasteland,
Robert V. Bellamy Jr. and James R. Walker

Relating: Dialogues and Dialectics, *Leslie A. Baxter
and Barbara M. Montgomery*

Doing Public Journalism, *Arthur Charity*

Social Approaches to Communication, *Wendy Leeds-Hurwitz, Editor*

Public Opinion and the Communication of Consent, *Theodore L. Glasser
and Charles T. Salmon, Editors*

Communication Research Measures: A Sourcebook, *Rebecca B. Rubin,
Philip Palmgreen, and Howard E. Sypher, Editors*

Persuasive Communication, *James B. Stiff*

Reforming Libel Law, *John Soloski and Randall P. Bezanson, Editors*

Message Effects Research: Principles of Design and Analysis, *Sally Jackson*

Critical Perspectives on Media and Society, *Robert K. Avery
and David Eason, Editors*

Mass Media and Political Transition: The Hong Kong Press in China's Orbit,
Joseph Man Chan and Chin-Chuan Lee

The Journalism of Outrage: Investigative Reporting and Agenda Building
in America, *David L. Protess, Fay Lomax Cook, Jack C. Doppelt,
James S. Ettema, Margaret T. Gordon, Donna R. Leff, and Peter Miller*

The Idea
of Public Journalism

Edited by Theodore L. Glasser

Foreword by Cole C. Campbell

The Guilford Press
New York   London

© 1999 by The Guilford Press
A Division of Guilford Publications, Inc.
72 Spring Street, New York, NY 10012
http://www.guilford.com

Printed in the United States of America

This book is printed on acid-free paper.

Last digit is print number: 9 8 7 6 5 4 3 2 1

Library of Congress Cataloging-in-Publication Data

The idea of public journalism / edited by Theodore L. Glasser.
     p. cm. — (The Guilford communication series)
   Includes bibliographical references (p.) and index.
   ISBN 1-57230-460-X
   1. Journalism—Social aspects. 2. Journalistic ethics.
3. Journalism—Objectivity.   I. Glasser, Theodore Lewis.
II. Series
PN4748.I33 1999
302.23—dc21   99-12844
                                                            CIP

For Mun, m.l.

Contributors

Cole C. Campbell is editor of the *St. Louis Post–Dispatch*. He has been active in the American Society of Newspaper Editors, the American Press Institute, the Project on Public Life and the Press, the Virginia Press Association, and the Mid-America Press Institute. He was a John S. Knight Fellow at Stanford University. He began his career as a reporter at *The Chapel Hill Newspaper*, worked as a reporter and an editor at *The News & Observer* in Raleigh and the *Greensboro News & Record*, and was editor of *Tar Heel: The Magazine of North Carolina*. As editor of *The Virginian-Pilot* in Norfolk, Virginia, he collaborated with reporters and editors to incorporate the principles of public journalism in daily coverage.

James W. Carey is a professor of journalism in the Graduate School of Journalism, Columbia University, New York. He has published more than 100 essays, monographs, and reviews on the history of journalism, journalism ethics, press and politics, and the technology of communication from the printing press to computers, along with three books: *Media, Myth and Narratives: Television and the Press* (1988), *Communication as Culture: Essays on Media and Society* (1989), and *James W. Carey: A Critical Reader* (1997). He serves on the Board of Trustees of the Illinois Humanities Counsel, the Advisory Board of the Poynter Institute for Media Studies, and the Board of Directors of the Public Broadcasting Service.

Steven H. Chaffee is the Janet M. Peck Professor of International Communication and chair of the Department of Communication at Stanford University. His publications include articles in *Journalism Quarterly*, *Journal of Communication*, *Journal of Social Issues*, *Communication*

Research, American Behavioral Scientist, Public Opinion Quarterly, and *Human Communication Research.* He has also written and edited several books, including *Political Communication* (1976), *Television and Human Behavior* (1978), *Handbook of Communication Science* (1987), *Communication Concepts 1: Explication* (1991), and *To See Ourselves: Comparing Traditional Chinese and American Cultural Values* (1994).

Clifford G. Christians is a research professor of communication and director of the Institute of Communications Research at the University of Illinois at Urbana–Champaign. His primary areas of interest are communication ethics, philosophy of technology, and the philosophy of social science. His scholarship links communication issues with ethical theory and aims to construct a normative discourse for applied ethics. His book with John Ferré and P. Mark Fackler, *Good News: Social Ethics and the Press,* was published in 1993. With Michael Traber, he edited *Communication Ethics and Universal Values* (1997).

Theodore L. Glasser is a professor of communication and director of the graduate program in journalism at Stanford University. His research, commentaries, and book reviews have appeared in a variety of periodicals, including the *Journal of Communication, Journalism and Mass Communication Quarterly, Critical Studies in Mass Communication, The Quill, Nieman Reports,* and *The New York Times Book Review.* With James S. Ettema he wrote *Custodians of Conscience: Investigative Journalism and Public Virtue* (1998), and with Charles T. Salmon he edited *Public Opinion and the Communication of Consent* (1995).

Hanno Hardt is John F. Murray Professor Journalism at the University of Iowa and a professor of communication at the University of Ljubljana, Slovenia. He is the author of numerous articles in scholarly journals in the United States and abroad and several books, including *Critical Communication Studies: Communication, History, and Theory in America* (1992); *Newsworkers: Toward a History of the Rank and File,* edited with Bonnie Brennen (1995); and *Interactions: Critical Studies in Communication, Media, and Journalism* (1998). His work as a documentary photographer has appeared in exhibitions, magazines, and books.

Thomas C. Leonard is associate dean of the Graduate School of Journalism, and director of the mass communications program at the University of California, Berkeley. He is also the associate editor of the *American National Biography.* He is the author of *The Power of the Press: The Birth of American Political Reporting* (1986) and *News for All: America's Coming of Age with the Press* (1995), which includes a discussion of issues surrounding public journalism. His articles have appeared in *Media Studies Journal, Reviews in American History, Journal of American History,* and several other scholarly journals.

Michael McDevitt is an assistant professor in the Department of Communication and Journalism at the University of New Mexico, where he teaches courses on news writing and political communication. His research focuses on how communication-based campaigns can stimulate citizenship among people who are otherwise disengaged from the political process. He has evaluated successful interventions in the context of political socialization and public journalism.

John J. Pauly is chairman of the Department of Communication at Saint Louis University. His research on the history and sociology of mass communication has appeared in a variety of journals, including *Critical Studies in Mass Communication, Communication Research, Journalism Monographs,* and *American Quarterly.* He is writing a book tentatively titled *News and the Dream of an Information Society,* on the history of the American campaign to reform the daily newspaper.

John Durham Peters is an associate professor in the Department of Communication Studies at the University of Iowa. His work on the public sphere, public opinion, and media ethics has appeared in various journals and books. In 1995 he was awarded a fellowship from the National Endowment for the Humanities and is currently working on two books: *Communication and Mass Communication in Modern Thought* and *Political Philosophy and the Media.* His interest in public journalism grows out of his research on democratic political philosophy.

Jay Rosen is an associate professor of journalism and mass communication at New York University. From 1993 to 1997, he was the director of the Project on Public Life and the Press, a foundation-funded program designed to further the spread of public journalism. He has written in both scholarly and popular journals on the press, politics, and public life. He is completing a book on the rise of public journalism.

Michael Schudson is a professor in the Department of Communication at the University of California, San Diego. He writes on sociology of culture with two primary emphases: the American news media and collective memory and the relationship of history to social science theory. His primary research interest is now political communication. He is the author of *Discovering the News: A Social History of American Newspapers* (1978); *Advertising, the Uneasy Persuasion* (1984); *Watergate in American*

Memory: How We Remember, Forget, and Reconstruct the Past (1992); *The Power of News* (1995); and *The Good Citizen: A History of American Civic Life* (1998).

Barbie Zelizer is an associate professor in the Annenberg School for Communication at the University of Pennsylvania. She has written several articles on journalism as cultural practice and is the author of *Covering the Body: The Kennedy Assassination, the Media and the Shaping of Collective Memory* (1992) and *Remembering to Forget: Holocaust Memory through the Camera's Eye* (1998), for which she was awarded a Guggenheim Fellowship and a Research Fellowship from Columbia University's Freedom Forum Center for Media Studies in 1995.

Contents

PART II. The Challenge *for* Public Journalism

APPENDICES

Journalism as a Democratic Art

Cole C. Campbell
St. Louis Post–Dispatch

When people come together to talk about their lives, their families, their neighborhoods, their communities, their cultures, their country, they repeatedly return to one pressing question.

We face all sorts of challenges, they say. What can we do—that works?

That question marks the intersection that ought to link citizens and professionals, journalists and academicians, doers and thinkers.

Rarely do citizens, professionals, journalists, and academicians work together. Mostly, we stay within our own ranks. When we connect across the public domain, we often bring only part of what it takes to make a rich conversation.

Citizens may bring their demands, but not their hopes.

Professionals may bring their expertise, but not their vulnerability.

Journalists may bring their information, but not their ignorance.

Academicians may bring their critical acumen, but not their wonder.

Doers may bring their deeds, but not their failures.

Thinkers may bring their ideas, but not their imagination.

Demands, expertise, information, criticism, deeds, ideas—these are the grit of most public dialogue. Hopes, vulnerability, professed ignorance, wonder, failure, imagination—these are lost or derided or treated in passing.

The conversation is incomplete.

We face all these challenges.

What can we do—together—that works?

How can we—as familiar strangers, as a democratic culture, as a political community—have better conversations?

This volume addresses these questions. What can citizens expect of professionals, journalists, and academicians? What can each of these practitioners expect of citizens? In particular, how can academicians—the authors of these chapters—collaborate more effectively with journalists—the object of these essays—in dealing with the challenges facing democracy, culture, community, and craft?

I come to this discussion as a journalist, as you can tell from my constricted idiom—shorter words, abrupt sentences, and paragraphs that fatten in twelve-pica columns but flatten in this expanse of vellum.

We journalists have some beliefs that need reconsideration if we want to help our communities work through the problems confronting them. We believe, in the phrase of Alabama-born journalist William Bradford Huie, that we are in "the truth business."[1] We believe that our product is information, offered up with a dash of entertainment. And we believe, as is noted elsewhere in this volume, that journalism has nothing to do with philosophy.

Having listened to citizens talk about their lives and their newspapers for more than 20 years, I've come to three different beliefs:

- Journalism is in the problem-solving business, not the truth business.
- Journalism's product is a contribution to understanding (but not a fully finished state of understanding). Therefore, journalism is as much about models for understanding the world as it is about information about the world.
- Journalism *is* philosophy—a philosophical construct of what is worth paying attention to and how best to pay attention to it.

Citizens want us to do a better job helping them and their communities address tough problems. They turn to us as one source, but not necessarily an exalted one, in piecing together their sense of the world. And they can see in what we publish and broadcast, despite our protestations that we only cover what's before us, that we have an underlying philosophy directing us to cast our coverage nets in one direction and not another.

Journalism is in disrepute because we are not living up to citizens' expectations. What would it be like if we took these ideas—journalism as problem solving, as contributing to understanding, and as a philosophy of attentiveness—seriously?

Journalism as Problem Solving

E. J. Dionne Jr. of *The Washington Post* calls on his colleagues to reconnect with citizens by focusing on the problems we all face:

> With the country passing through a series of crises, journalism's primary task ought to be to engage citizens in the quest for paths forward. That will involve understanding the alternatives and weighing them for their faithfulness not only to the facts but also to the values and moral commitments that supposedly underlie them. It involves debate experienced not simply as combat but also as conversation. In this telling, journalism's role of providing information is only the beginning of its task.[2]

Too often, we journalists disavow any responsibility for our coverage. We pretend that news is a concrete thing that we merely collect and present, albeit with artful grace. We disavow any notion that we construct news by selecting which facts warrant attention and in what context. And we absolve ourselves further by saying our highest objective is the pursuit of truth. We are, in short, seekers of an already extant truth for which we cannot be held accountable for merely sniffing out.

And yet the esteem for such truthhounds, in the eyes of the people we serve, continues to drop.

Philosopher Richard Rorty says that the highest aim of all forms of inquiry should not be truth. Truth is ineffable, Rorty says, ever receding before shifting definitions of what is true and shifting standards for testing truth. Instead, he argues, the highest aim of all inquiry should be problem solving, a far more practical and rewarding pursuit.[3]

Even though Rorty makes his argument in the nearly ineffable language of academic philosophy, he speaks to the same imperative that Dionne addresses. And in a survey commissioned by the American Society of Newspaper Editors in 1997, citizens said they want newspapers to help them solve problems in their communities and to put energy into identifying solutions as well as problems.[4] A 1994 survey by the Times–Mirror (now Pew) Center for the People and the Press, cited elsewhere in this volume (Chapter 9), noted that nearly three-quarters of the respondents see the press as getting in the way of society solving its problems.[5]

We journalists have a great opportunity if we make problem solving the raison d'être of our news report. That could recast how we cover everything, moving the discussion away from who wins or loses power to what problems we ought to solve and how we might tackle them. For example, rather than cover students' falling scores on standardized tests as an indictment of the current school administration, we could cover it as a problem to be solved by everyone with a stake in the issue—students, parents, teachers, neighbors, as well as school boards, superintendents, and principals. If any part of the community whose participation is crucial to the solution, including, but not limited to, the school administration, doesn't help develop and implement a solution, then we hold that part accountable.

Academicians can help us think through ways of identifying and describing problems and ways to help political players—citizens as well as official actors—solve them.

Journalism as Contributing to Understanding

In the 1960s and 1970s, scholars determined that the mass media couldn't tell people what to think but could tell people what to think about.[6] Over the past decade, many scholars and practitioners have warned of the debilitating prospect of "information overload," "information anxiety," "the information explosion," and the like.[7]

Edward O. Wilson, the Harvard sociobiologist, projects into the next millennium:

> In the twenty-first century the world will not be run by those who possess mere information alone. Thanks to science and technology, access to factual knowledge of all kinds is rising exponentially while dropping in unit cost. It is destined to become global and democratic. Soon it will be available everywhere on television and computer screens. What then? The answer is clear: synthesis. We are drowning in information, while starving for wisdom. The world henceforth will be run by synthesizers, people able to put together the right information at the right time, think critically about it, and make important choices wisely.[8]

Will we journalists merely swamp people with information, or will we help people achieve synthesis? If we want the world to be run by democrats in the next millennium, shouldn't as many people as possible master the skills of synthesis? How can news media as mass media help secure that mastery?

Merely pumping more information through the fire hoses of news reports, or aiming those fire hoses at more issues, does not lead to synthesis. People also need more useful ways of processing the information. Journalists, working with academicians, can give people better models and tools.

Alfred R. Oxenfeldt, professor emeritus of business at Columbia University, writes:

> Few of the models governing our actions are based on careful study and reflection. As a result, they are likely to be only partially correct and could be seriously flawed. Faulty beliefs, both conscious and unconscious, rather than limited information, explain most poor decisions and misguided actions.[9]

Flawed models and faulty beliefs, not limited information. Oxenfeldt continues:

> Valid models are extremely valuable intellectual tools. They convey and embody basic understanding of and insight into complicated phenomenon. Such understanding enables executives to know what information to collect and how to interpret it. Facts alone usually are ambiguous and bewildering.[10]

Substitute for "executives" any of those we are talking about—citizens, professionals, journalists, academicians—and the conclusion holds up.

We need to reexamine many of our existing models of how the world works, which, as deadlines loom, we reflexively use to funnel new facts into old wineskins. Mark Silk of *The Atlanta Journal–Constitution* reminds us that ancient Greek rhetoricians called these devices *konoi topoi*, or "commonplaces." He cites a list of "Basic Religion Stories" compiled by Peter Steinfels of *The New York Times*:

- Religious leader reveals feet of clay (or turns out to be scoundrel).
- Ancient faith struggles to adjust to modern times.
- Scholars challenge long-standing beliefs.
- Interfaith harmony overcomes inherited enmity.
- New translation of sacred scripture sounds funny.
- Devoted members of a zealous religious group turn out to be warm, ordinary folks.[11]

Any careful reader can spin out similar *topoi* for all kinds of news coverage: the indefatigable entrepreneur who beats the conglomerate at its own game, the fearsome athlete/rock star/police officer who volunteers to work with disadvantaged children, the public official who—can you believe it—really means what she says.

Unfortunately, stories that don't fit these commonplace models often don't get covered. And many journalistic *topoi* in fact don't describe reality. Scholar after scholar has documented journalists' pro-

clivity to rely on set story lines that don't fit the facts. Political scientist
Thomas E. Patterson challenges the journalistic *topoi* that presidents'
campaign promises are smokescreens for their real intentions. He documents that presidents pursue almost all of their campaign promises
while the news media fixate on the few deviations, which may be driven
by any number of factors beyond sneakiness.[12] Historian David Thelen
challenges the *topoi* of Olliemania by contrasting news coverage of the
Iran–Contra hearings with citizens' correspondence to the House committee holding the hearings.[13]

It's time to reexamine lots of basic models that journalists employ.
Among them:

• The model that power corrupts and therefore must always be
constrained. Under what circumstances should power be increased? In
1925, Mary Parker Follett argued that "genuine power is capacity,"[14]
and in the 1990s Jay Rosen and others have argued that the press could
play a role in increasing the capacity of citizens and communities to act
to solve the problems facing them.[15]

• The model that conflict is a win–lose proposition and best seen
through a juxtaposition of extremes. Follett and others note that there
are lots of ways conflict can be resolved to satisfy the interests of all
parties,[16] while Richard Harwood and others argue that it helps to
attend to the tensions that underlie staked-out positions. And they
argue that most people aren't at the extremes on any issue. Instead,
they are distributed along a continuum of positions, or they are ambivalent rather than resolved about where they stand.[17]

• The marketplace model, used to explain all kinds of non-
economic activity, including elections, and blamed for all kinds of
problems in journalism itself.[18] (It's easier to blame capitalists and
bosses than to reexamine the routines of thought we all use; on the
other hand, as a journalist, I can change the way I think and act more
easily than I can restructure the media economy.) What if we conceived
of elections not as a swap of promises for votes but as a time for performance appraisals of incumbents and a job selection process for all aspirants to office?[19] These metaphorical constructs are just as accurate
and give new dimensions to coverage.

Jay Rosen, Richard Harwood, and others already have developed
some new tools for journalists to use, including the constructs of *framing stories* to incorporate within the frame possible ways of responding
to a problem, *positioning citizens* as political actors and not just as spectators,[20] and *mapping* ways to tap into layers of knowledge within communities.[21] Journalists around the country are experimenting with

other tools, from community conversations to deliberative polling to more sophisticated open-ended interviewing techniques. (Some, as advocated elsewhere in this volume, are even using coupons to engage citizens.) Others are exploring tools to measure and report on the health of their communities along a number of dimensions: physical, social, civic, and political.[22]

These tools are more than epistemological devices. They are also means of sorting for relevance and meaning, of helping citizens engage more effectively in public life so that they can more effectively synthesize information and, in Wilson's phrase, "make important choices wisely." Over time, some tools may prove as durable and long-lasting as a handsaw, whereas others will appear as curious and marginal as kitchen gimmick-gadgets touted in midnight television commercials.

But we should proceed in moving toward the "understanding" or "meaning" business with humility. Richard Harwood and his colleagues at the Harwood Group, which specializes in studying the public realm, have documented that citizens don't turn to the news media for understanding per se, but for input. They place journalistic input alongside their own life experience and input from families, friends, coworkers, and neighbors. They sort through all this to come to an understanding of the world, to complete their own acts of synthesis.[23]

In that sense, they see journalism as a raw material, or a refined commodity, more than as a finished, complete product. If we strengthen the models we use to describe the world, and give citizens better tools, we may increase our value. But we should recognize that we will always be contributors to understanding and never providers of it.

Journalism as a Philosophy of Attentiveness

Saul Bellow, novelist and Nobel laureate, is the kind of person we'd like to think loves newspapers—given our self-image as windows to the world, mirrors of society, defenders of free expression. If that's what we thought, we would be wrong, as Bellow made clear in "The Distracted Public," a 1990 address at Oxford University. He estimates that an average weekday *New York Times* contains more information than an Elizabethan would have acquired in a lifetime. "What good is such a plethora of information?" he asks. "It simply poisons us."[24]

He continues:

> Newspapers must be read cautiously, cannily, defensively. You know very well that journalists cannot afford to tell you plainly what is going on.

There are dependable observers who believe that the press cannot give Americans anything like a true picture of the world. The written word is untrustworthy and the spoken word (radio and TV) irresponsible. . . . The government does not seem able to understand or to explain its authority, the grounds for its decisions. Its antagonist, the press, interprets the government's operations in such a way as to destabilize public judgment. The jargon used by both antagonists excites, it thrills, it bewilders, it frightens, it confuses, it annihilates coherence, it makes comprehension utterly impossible.[25] . . .

Of course, the ceaseless world crisis, otherwise known as the chaos of the present age, is not the work of the communications industry and its Information Revolution; but for our peculiar pseudoknowledge of what is happening, for the density of our ignorance, and for the inner confusion and centerlessness of our understanding, for our agitation, the communicators are responsible. Intellectuals and universities, from the ideological side, also have much to answer for.[26]

Bellow's solution: "Writers, poets, painters, musicians, philosophers, political thinkers, to name only a few of the categories affected, must woo their readers, viewers, listeners, from distraction." A novelist who demonstrates "a distinct and human quality . . . more musical than verbal," he says, "has power over distraction and fragmentation, and out of distressing unrest, even from the edge of chaos, he can bring unity and carry us into a state of intransitive attention. People hunger for this."[27]

Too often, journalism settles for distraction, whether labeled celebrity news, entertainment, sensationalism or "tabloidization of the news." If we cast journalism as a philosophy of attentiveness—a system of thinking about what to pay attention to and how to pay attention—we begin to see its real, enduring value. Our main contribution is not information or understanding but a kind of ordering of topics worthy of contemplation, conversation, and further inquiry.

Ronald A. Heifetz has put forward a new model of leadership, and a systematic explanation of how it works, that centers on adaptive change. His model begins with, and frequently returns to, paying attention. Journalists could model much of what we do around it.

Heifetz contrasts the notion that "leadership means influencing the community to follow the leader's vision" with "leadership means influencing the community to face its problems."[28] Effective leaders do the latter, he says. Specifically, effective leaders do the following:

1. *Direct attention.* "Getting people to pay attention to tough issues rather than diversions is at the heart of strategy."[29]

2. *Test reality.* "Because authorities are expected to know, they are given *access to information*. . . . Authority figures are supposed to be agents of reality testing: they are supposed to investigate problems more objectively than people in the problems' grasp. By virtue of their authority, they are given a special *vantage point* from which to survey and understand the situation. They can compare different sources of evidence" (emphasis in the original).[30]

3. *Manage information and frame issues.* "People are more likely to pay attention to arguments and perspectives about which they feel some urgency. Urgency, well framed, promotes adaptive work." If only a few see an important issue as urgent, "the strategic challenge will be to find ways to generate more generalized urgency, and thus ripen the issue."[31]

4. *Orchestrate conflicting perspectives.* "Pieces of the puzzle—information about the problem—lie scattered in the hands of stakeholders across divisions, interest groups, organizations and communities. Not only is the information scattered, but the solution requires adjustments in the attitudes and behaviors of many people across boundaries. Hence, an authority who excludes stakeholders from defining and solving the problem risks developing an incomplete solution or a solution to the wrong problem."[32]

5. *Choose the decision-making process.* "Adaptive situations . . . tend to demand a more participative mode of operating to shift responsibility to the primary stakeholders. Because the problems lie largely in their attitudes, values, habits, or current relationships, the problem solving has to take place in their hearts and minds. One produces progress on adaptive problems by working the conflicts within and between the parties."[33]

This is an equally powerful blueprint for effective journalism. We don't want to influence citizens to follow our vision of what ought to be done. We do want to influence citizens to face their own problems by helping them identify and rank them. (Why else are we writing about them?) Paralleling effective leaders, effective journalists do these things:

1. *Direct attention*—by bearing witness to what matters most: the great themes of life and the great issues of the day, as well as the daily urgencies and insurgencies that shape the worlds of the people and communities we serve.

2. *Test reality*—by the same process available to leaders: access to

information and a vantage point free of self-interest, open to weighing various sources of information.

3. *Manage information and frame issues*—to make them urgent and ripe for discussion. We call these "news pegs" and "nut grafs," designed to explain why an issue needs attention now.

4. *Air conflicting perspectives*—moving beyond both-sides-of-the-story narrowness to a wide-ranging exploration that helps citizens understand not only their own stake in an issue but also the stakes of others.

5. *Describe the decision-making process*—and hold all parties (including citizens, as political actors and not passive spectators) accountable for their part in it.

In this model, neither leaders nor journalists take away power or responsibility from the community. Rather, they help order the discussion to ensure that communities face their problems.

This is a pragmatic process by which we journalists can give life to our philosophy of attentiveness. This can be our contribution to the rich philosophy of public life as communication, as conversation, put forward by John Dewey in the 1920s, enriched by James Carey and Jay Rosen in recent years and described and critiqued in this volume.

Journalism as Fact-Finding, Storytelling, and Conversation Keeping

Over the years, I have come to appreciate two traditions of journalism: fact finding and storytelling. The fact-finding tradition treats citizens as clients and helps create something akin to what John Dewey called "pragmatic intelligence."[34] Its most energetic expression has been muckraking, investigative journalism, and explanatory journalism; its weakest is what Ross Perot popularized as "gotcha journalism." The storytelling tradition treats citizens as an audience and, through something akin to what Gerald Early calls "the power of aesthetic experience,"[35] delivers epiphanies of understanding or emotional catharsis. Its most energetic expression has been human interest journalism, New Journalism, and literary journalism. Its weakest expression is gossip mongering and celebrity obsession.

Only by paying attention to the philosophical drivetrain of Dewey–Carey–Rosen[36] have I come to recognize and appreciate a third tradition—the conversation-keeping tradition. The conversation-keeping tradition treats citizens as partners and helps them be part of something akin to what Ralph Ellison called "the reflective consciousness"[37] of our culture. Its most energetic expression has been the synergy between print and talk that has characterized the expansion of democracy to ever-widening circles of Americans.

Historian Robert H. Wiebe writes that the extraordinary energy needed to sustain and transform democracy in the early 19th century was produced by a blend of newspaper reading and conversation. The emerging network of newspapers inspired citizens—restricted then, in terms of full voting rights, to white male adults—to make themselves literate in order to stay connected to public debate. Norms for public discussion changed, creating "a lightly polished everyday language" that "served nationally as a medium for democratic discussion."[38]

Participation, Wiebe writes, was the essence of democracy:

> Democratic politics was a vibrant public process: marching, chanting, disputing, debating, voting. People entered this process by demanding a place. The anger at secrecy, the demand for openness, was a functional response to situations that made democracy impossible. Without access, citizens have no role; private dealings paralyzed them. . . . The fact that citizens were "perpetually acting" in public life did not, as several Europeans suggested, signal a nationwide nervous disorder. Americans were keeping their democracy alive. At rest everything disappeared.[39]

Unfortunately, in the early 20th century, journalists changed sides. We took to heart the world view of Walter Lippmann, whose book, *Public Opinion,* James Carey calls "the founding book of modern American journalism."[40] Carey summarizes Lippmann's view, and the current practice of our craft:

> Journalists primarily served as conduits relaying truth arrived at elsewhere, by the experts—scientists in their laboratories, bureaucrats in their bureaus. The truth was not a product of the conversation or debate of the public or the investigations of journalists. Journalists merely translate the arcane language of experts into a publicly accessible language for the masses.[41]

Lippmann saw a need for "the hot light of publicity," which kept the experts from being "altogether ruthless." The problem, Carey argues, is that this "democratic politics of publicity and experts . . . confirmed the psychological incompetence of people to participate in it. Again, it evolved a political system of democracy without citizens."[42]

As a result, Carey concludes, we have a debased journalism:

We developed a journalism that was an early-warning system but one that kept the public in a constant state of agitation or boredom. It is a journalism that reports a continuing stream of expert opinion, but because there is no agreement among experts it is more like observing talk-show gossip and petty manipulation than like bearing witness to the truth. It is a journalism of fact without regard to understanding through which the public is immobilized and demobilized and merely ratifies the judgments of experts delivered from on high. It is, above all, a journalism that justifies itself in the public's name but in which the public plays no role, except as an audience; it is a receptacle to be informed by the experts and an excuse for the practice of publicity.[43]

The fights between the press and its sources are mostly over sources erecting "ever more complicated veils of appearance over events" and journalists trying "ever more assiduously to pierce the veil."[44] The public has become increasingly bored, alienated, and cynical, "learning to distrust appearances mounted by both elites and journalists and, most damagingly, to distrust all language, to look at language as a mere instrument of interest and obfuscation."[45] The result:

Today, Americans have lost interest in politics.
. . . Above all, the press lost credibility and respect; it was no longer believed. As poll after poll showed, journalists had earned the distrust of the public and were increasingly seen as a hindrance to, rather than an avenue of, politics and political reform.[46]

If we don't want to further debase democracy, we need to reinvigorate journalism's conversation-keeping tradition. We journalists can contribute ideas and information to that conversation, but mostly we must heed what ordinary citizens are saying, invite them back into the political dialogue we cover and reflect that in our newspapers and broadcasts. We can help order the flow of what's worth discussing immediately and what might wait for another day, as long as we see ourselves as partners with, and not cleverer than, the people and communities we serve.

What Do We Do Now?

There is much that we as journalists and academicians can work on to increase our own effectiveness and contribute to increasing citizens' and professionals' effectiveness. Academicians must help create new models and tools, not merely critique them, because these models and tools need to be alloys of practice and theory, ideas and action.

Here's a beginning list of things we need to do:

- Write more expressively about public life, using the experiences and aspirations of citizens less as illustrative anecdotes and more as compelling narratives.
- Learn more about the process of problem solving, so we can fashion more helpful news reports that address problems and devising solutions to them.
- Create new models and tools for our own work and for citizens and professionals to use in their work.
- Learn more about attentiveness from all the disciplines of attention, whether cognitive psychology or Zen Buddhism.
- Incorporate the lessons of adaptive change in the way we frame news reports, to help keep pressure on political communities and political actors (including citizens) to work through the problems confronting them.
- Widen and deepen our understanding of dialogue, deliberation, and conversation, so that our journalism can better reflect it, contribute to it, and, as appropriate, help order it. We need to include the emotional and intuitive components of conversation, as well as the rational elements.
- Recognize that public life is expressed not only through public discourse but also through public work—when citizens come together to create real and lasting institutions. We can cover this better, as well.
- Bring newsrooms into universities and universities into newsrooms, to increase collaboration and learning on both sides.
- Strengthen and integrate the three traditions of fact finding, storytelling, and conversation keeping.

There is also revolutionary work to be done, if we dare.

Here are two ways we could radically transform our journalism—as journalists.

1. What if we reoriented our journalism away from the sources of news and toward the recipients of news? Instead of building our beats around institutions and agencies, what if we built them around the troubles and joys in people's lives? Instead of a City Hall beat, we might have a political participation beat that tracks what's happening at City Hall in a way that helps citizens directly influence it. Instead of covering doctors and medical breakthroughs using patients as illustrations of what health care professionals can accomplish, suppose we covered patients and used doctors and medical breakthroughs as illustrations

of problem solving. What if we thought of institutions and agencies not as *sources of news* but as *resources for problem solving* that citizens could tap and work with?

2. What if we reoriented our journalism away from description of the present and toward imagination of a better alternative? Maxine Greene, an education professor at Columbia University, has come to "concentrate on imagination as a means through which we can assemble a coherent world" in part because "imagination is what, above all else, makes empathy possible. It is what enables us to cross the empty spaces between ourselves and those we teachers have called 'other' over the years. . . . of all our cognitive capacities, imagination is the one that permits us to give credence to alternative realities."[47] She goes further:

> We also have our social imagination: the capacity to invent visions of what should be and what might be in our deficient society, on the streets where we live, in our schools. As I write of social imagination, I am reminded of Jean-Paul Sartre's declaration that "it is on the day that we can conceive of a different state of affairs that a new light falls on our troubles and our suffering and that we decide that these are unbearable" (1956, pp. 434–435). That is, we acknowledge the harshness of situations only when we have in mind another state of affairs in which things would be better. . . . And it may be only then that we are moved to choose to repair or to renew.[48]

We cannot give up description of the present; it is essential to directing attention, testing reality, and framing issues. But we should not let it dominate our mind-set and our type set and our studio sets. We should make equal room for conceiving of alternative ways of living in a just world.

In offering these more radical ideas, I am mainly calling on us to continue the experimentation this volume discusses in detail. It is true to our democratic history, in which little is fixed and everything seems always at risk. As Jean Bethke Elshtain has written:

> From Jefferson's bold throwing down of the gauntlet to the British Empire, not knowing whether the upshot would be "hanging together or hanged separately," to Lincoln's "nation so conceived and so dedicated," to Martin Luther King's dream of an essentially pacific democratic people who judge their fellow citizens by the content of their character not the color of their skins, democratic culture has been a *wager*, not a frozen accomplishment.[49]

Our job as journalists and academicians, as citizens and professionals, is to keep anteing up—and to keep democratic culture a worthy bet. That's the culture I want to pass on, reenergized, to the next generations. We must perpetually act to keep democracy alive. At rest, everything disappears.

Notes

1. Conversation with E. Culpepper Clark, dean of the College of Communication and Information Sciences, University of Alabama, in Tuscaloosa, Alabama, April 22, 1998. The university's Center for Public Television and Radio produced a documentary on Huie whose title, *I'm in the Truth Business,* was a direct quotation from him. Huie is best known from his reporting about the Emmitt Till murder, the trial and execution of Private Eddie Slovak, and the novel that was the basis of the movie *The Americanization of Emily.*
2. E. J. Dionne Jr., *They Only Look Dead: Why Progressives Will Dominate the Next Political Era* (New York: Simon & Shuster, 1996), pp. 258–259.
3. Richard Rorty, "Is Truth a Goal of Inquiry?: Donald Davidson versus Crispin Wright," in *Truth and Progress: Philosophical Papers* (Cambridge, UK: Cambridge University Press, 1998), pp. 19–42.
4. "Leveraging Newspaper Assets," a report prepared for ASNE and NAA by Clark, Matire & Barolomeo Inc. (Reston, VA: American Society of Newspaper Editors, April 1998).
5. "The People, the Press and Politics: The New Political Landscape" (Washington, DC: Times–Mirror Center for the People and the Press, 1994).
6. See, for example, James Carey, "The Chicago School and the History of Mass Communication Research," in *James Carey: A Critical Reader,* eds. Eve Stryker Munson and Catherine A. Warren (Minneapolis: University of Minnesota Press, 1997), pp. 14–33.
7. See, for example, William J. Donnelly, *The Confetti Generation: How the New Communications Technology Is Fragmenting America* (New York: Holt, 1986), and Richard Saul Wurman, *Information Anxiety* (New York: Doubleday, 1989).
8. Edward O. Wilson, *Consilence: The Unity of Knowledge* (New York: Knopf, 1998), p. 269.
9. Alfred R. Oxenfeldt, "Models for Executive Decisions," *Decision Economics* (Menlo Park, CA: Crisp, 1997), pp. 17–18.
10. Oxenfeldt, "Models for Executive Decisions," p. 18.
11. Mark Silk, *Unsecular Media: Making News of Religion in America* (Urbana, IL: University of Illinois Press, 1995), pp. 49–55. Steinfels's list is on pages 53 and 54.
12. Thomas E. Patterson, *Out of Order* (New York: Vintage Books, 1994).
13. David Thelen, *Becoming Citizens in the Age of Television: How Americans Challenged the Media and Seized Political Initiative during the Iran–Contra Debate* (Chicago: The University of Chicago Press, 1996).
14. Mary Parker Follett, "Power," in *Mary Parker Follett: Prophet of Management,* ed. Pauline Graham (Boston: Harvard Business School Press, 1995), p. 111.

15. Jay Rosen, "Getting the Connections Right: What Public Journalism Might Be," presentation to the Project on Public Life and the Press, American Press Institute, June 13, 1994, p. 10.

16. Follett, "Constructive Conflict," in *Mary Parker Follett,* cited above at note 14, pp. 67–87.

17. "Meaningful Chaos: How People Form Relationships with Public Concerns," a report prepared for the Kettering Foundation by The Harwood Group (Dayton, OH: Kettering Foundation, 1993).

18. See, for example, John H. McManus, *Market-Driven Journalism: Let the Citizens Beware?* (Thousand Oaks, CA: Sage Publications, 1994), and David Pearce Demers, *The Menace of the Corporate Newspaper: Fact or Fiction* (Ames: Iowa State University Press, 1996).

19. Cole C. Campbell, "Solving Problems, Listening to Local Voters," *Nieman Reports,* L, 2 (Summer 1996): 15–17.

20. Jay Rosen, "Public Journalism as a Democratic Art," in Jay Rosen, Davis Merritt, and Lisa Austin, *Public Journalism: Theory and Practice: Lessons from Experience* (Dayton, OH: Kettering Foundation, 1997). Framing is discussed on pages 8 through 12 of a typescript of this chapter, and positioning is discussed on pages 14 and 15.

21. Richard C. Harwood, *Tapping Civic Life: How to Report First, and Best, What's Happening in Your Community* (Washington, DC: Pew Center for Civic Journalism, 1996).

22. See Arthur Charity, *Doing Public Journalism* (New York: Guilford Press, 1995), for a good baseline summary of these activities. See also Davis Merritt, *Public Journalism and Public Life: Why Telling the News Is Not Enough* (Hillsdale, NJ: Lawrence Erlbaum Associates, Publishers, 1995). The Pew Center for Civic Journalism has published some studies of projects, including *Civic Journalism: Six Case Studies,* eds. Jan Schaffer and Edward D. Miller (Washington, DC: Pew Center for Civic Journalism, 1995), and *Civic Lessons: Report on Four Civic Journalism Projects,* Esther Thorson and Lewis A. Freidland, evaluators, and Peggy Anderson, report writer (Washington, DC: Pew Center for Civic Journalism, 1997).

23. See in particular Richard C. Harwood, *America's Struggle Within: Citizens Talk about the State of the Union* (Washington, DC: Pew Center for Civic Journalism, 1995), pp. 13–15.

24. Saul Bellow, "The Distracted Public," in *It All Adds Up: From the Dim Past to the Uncertain Future* (New York: Viking, 1994), p. 157.

25. Bellow, "The Distracted Public," p. 157.

26. Bellow, "The Distracted Public," p. 160.

27. Bellow, "The Distracted Public," pp. 167, 168.

28. Ronald A. Heifetz, *Leadership without Easy Answers* (Cambridge, MA: Belknap Press of Harvard University Press, 1994), p. 14.

29. Heifetz, *Leadership without Easy Answers,* p. 113.

30. Heifetz, *Leadership without Easy Answers,* pp. 114f.

31. Heifetz, *Leadership without Easy Answers,* p. 116.

32. Heifetz, *Leadership without Easy Answers,* p. 118.

33. Heifetz, *Leadership without Easy Answers,* p. 121.

34. Gerald Early, "Decoding Ralph Ellison," *Dissent*, 44, 3 (Summer 1997): 114–118.

35. Early, "Decoding Ralph Ellison," pp. 114–118.

36. Most of my understanding of Dewey comes through other commentators, including Carey and Rosen. The best starting point to tackle Dewey is John Dewey, *The Public and Its Problems* (New York: Holt, 1927). Carey's work is compiled in two sources: James W. Carey, *Communication as Culture: Essays on Media and Society* (New York: Routledge, 1989), and *James Carey: A Critical Reader*, cited earlier at note 6. The best introduction to Rosen's work is Jay Rosen, *Getting the Connections Right: Public Journalism and the Troubles in the Press* (New York: Twentieth Century Fund, 1996). His contribution to this volume, "The Action of the Idea: Public Journalism in Built Form" (Chapter 2) is not only the latest extension of his ideas but also, in its endnotes, the source of a great bibliography of relevant work. For his most comprehensive discussion, see Jay Rosen, *What Are Journalists For?*, forthcoming from Yale University Press.

37. Early, "Decoding Ralph Ellison," pp. 114–118.

38. Robert H. Wiebe, *Self-Rule: A Cultural History of American Democracy* (Chicago: The University of Chicago Press, 1995), pp. 67–68.

39. Wiebe, *Self-Rule*, p. 68.

40. Carey, *James Carey: A Critical Reader*, p. 245.

41. Carey, *A Critical Reader*, p. 246.

42. Carey, *A Critical Reader*, p. 246.

43. Carey, *A Critical Reader*, p. 247.

44. Carey, *A Critical Reader*, p. 247.

45. Carey, *A Critical Reader*, p. 248.

46. Carey, *A Critical Reader*, pp. 248, 249.

47. Maxine Greene, *Releasing the Imagination: Essays on Education, the Arts, and Social Change* (San Francisco: Jossey-Bass, 1995), p. 3.

48. Greene, *Releasing the Imagination*, p. 5.

49. Jean Bethke Elshtain, *Real Politics: At the Center of Everyday Life* (Baltimore: Johns Hopkins University Press, 1997), p. 363.

Preface and Acknowledgments

This book began as a symposium held at Stanford University on April 26, 1996. Then and now, the idea was to focus on the *idea* of public journalism. This meant stepping back from the newsroom projects that have taken on the label "public" or "civic"[1] journalism to try to provide some perspective and context for them. It meant examining, critically but constructively, public journalism's claims about itself as well as its claims about the democratic practices it hopes to reinvigorate. And it meant raising related questions about how best to judge the quality of American journalism.

The level of sympathy and support for public journalism varies somewhat from chapter to chapter, but all the work presented in this volume at least begins with, though moves quickly beyond, a basic understanding of what public journalism wants: Public journalism calls on the press to take seriously its commitment to democratic participation and public debate. It asks journalists to help develop the means by which citizens can engage each other and thus create for themselves a sense of community defined by something stronger than a mere aggregation of personal preferences and private interests. Above all else, public journalism strikes a hopeful tone. It invites the press to embrace a kind of "good news," to invoke the title of a recent and relevant study of press ethics,[2] which conveys optimism about the future and confidence in our ability to get there. Public journalism, therefore, stands as a corrective to a language of despair and discontent; it tries to resist the corrosive cynicism that summons derision, not indignation.

The continuing debate over public journalism concerns not only the challenge public journalism poses but, of course, the challenge it faces. Accordingly, the material in this book is divided, though not entirely evenly, between assessments of the challenge *of* public journalism, which focus on the questions public journalism raises and the answers it provides (Part I); and assessments of the challenge *for* public journalism, which focus on the questions public journalism fails to raise or the ones it leaves unanswered (Part II). These discussions are complemented by three appendices. The first examines the difficulties of evaluating the practice of public journalism. The second reviews several books on and about public journalism. And the third is an annotated bibliography of material relevant to the issues and ideas examined in this volume.

*   *   *

Organizing a symposium and producing a book from it requires assistance and good counsel from any number of friends and colleagues. The symposium itself came together under the guidance of a planning committee of former and current graduate students (Anne Chappell Belden, Adrienne Russell, Mary Lou Korba, Stephanie Craft, Michael McDevitt, and Joseph Graf) and two Knight Fellows (Tom Hamburger and Marcia Stepanek). We were aided by the helpful staff of Stanford's Department of Communication, notably Barbara Kataoka, Terese Weinlader, and Lola Romero. Elissa Lee, then a Stanford undergraduate and now a PhD student, prepared an annotated bibliography for distribution among symposium participants. Others volunteered their time as moderators and discussion leaders: Steven Chaffee, Arthur Charity, Lewis Friedland, Jonathan Krim, Sally Lehrman, Marion Lewenstein, Peter Leyden, and Donald Roberts. David Broder delivered the annual Carlos McClatchy lecture at the close of the symposium. Joann Byrd and James Ettema spoke eloquently at the symposium but were not, unfortunately, able to prepare material for this book.

Funding for the symposium came mostly from an endowment created in memory of Carlos McClatchy, an early builder of the McClatchy Newspapers; the Peninsula Press Club, Stanford's John S. Knight Fellowship Program and New York University's Project on Public Life and the Press generously contributed additional funds. The Ford Foundation provided funds for the book.

Karin Wahl-Jorgensen and Michael McDevitt, both PhD students at the time, provided invaluable editorial advice and assistance as the book manuscript slowly began to take shape; they also helped Elissa Lee with the version of the annotated bibliography that appears here. Deanne Corbett and Karin Wahl-Jorgensen prepared the index. Donald Roberts and Steven Chaffee, chairs of the Department of Communication during, respectively, the organization of the symposium and the preparation of the book manuscript, made available a variety of resources that added up to precisely the kind of support faculty want but seldom receive.

Finally, the contributors to this volume deserve a special thanks for taking the time to transform their symposium comments into publishable chapters. Anyone familiar with a transcript of a "talk" knows how much work it takes to turn it into a carefully crafted essay. Except for parts of Hanno Hardt's review (Appendix B), which first appeared in the *Journal of Communication,* all the material in this book was prepared originally for this book.

THEODORE L. GLASSER
Stanford University

Notes

1. Although the terms "civic" and "public" journalism denote much the same set of claims, I prefer the latter because, as Jim Carey reminds us, it resonates with the history and rhetoric of modern American journalism: "Insofar as journalism is grounded, it is grounded in the *public.* Insofar as journalism has a client, the client is the *public.* The press justifies itself in the name of the *public*: It exists—or so it is regularly said—to inform the *public,* to serve as the extended eyes and ears of the *public,* to protect the *public's* right to know, to serve the *public* interest. The canons of journalism originate in and flow from the relationship of the press to the *public.* The *public* is totem and talisman, and object of ritual homage." James W. Carey, "The Press and Public Discourse," *The Center Magazine* (March/April 1987): 5; emphasis added.
2. Clifford G. Christians, John P. Ferré, and P. Mark Fackler, *Good News: Social Ethics and the Press* (New York: Oxford University Press, 1993). For an interesting and detailed example of "good news" as it applies to urban affairs reporting, see James S. Ettema and Limor Peer, "Good News from a Bad Neighborhood: Toward an Alternative to the Discourse of Urban Pathology," *Journalism and Mass Communication Quarterly,* 73 (Winter 1996): 835–856.

Introduction

Chapter 1

The Idea of Public Journalism

Theodore L. Glasser

Stanford University

There is no shortage of references to David Broder of *The Washington Post* as an early and eager supporter of the kind of press reform public journalism wants to bring about. In a nationally syndicated column published in the *Post* on January 3, 1990, under the headline "Democracy and the Press," Broder assailed the press for its dismal coverage of political campaigns and elections: "We cannot allow the 1990 elections to be another exercise in public disillusionment and political cynicism." This was not entirely the fault of the press, Broder acknowledged, but only the press could be counted on "to step forward to police the campaign process, very much as we try to catch cheating and chicanery in government":

> That means that we must be more assertive than in the past on the public's right to hear its concerns discussed by the candidates—in ads, debates and speeches—and far more conscientious in reporting those discussions when they take place. We have to help reconnect politics and government—what happened in the campaign and what happens afterward in public policy—if we are going to have accountability by our elected officials and genuine democracy in this country.

Feisty and forthright, Broder called on his colleagues in the press, reporters and editors alike, "to become activists, not on behalf of a particular party or politician, but on behalf of the process of self-government. It is time to expose the threats to that process and support the efforts to get rid of them."[1]

Six years later, however, at the Stanford symposium on which this book is based, Broder made it a point to distance himself from public journalism and its brand of activism. The activism that appealed to Broder was journalistic, not political; what he envisioned was the "very old fashioned kind of shoe leather reporting . . . knocking on doors, walking precincts, talking to people in their homes, paying heed to what they were saying." Specifically, Broder wanted journalists to better equip their readers, viewers, and listeners to "sort through" the manipulative techniques of political consultants; the press needed to find ways to combat—or at least compensate for—these "new bosses of American politics" who "knew how to use polls and media and all these other modern communications devices to manipulate public opinion and produce the desired results on election day."

With an explanation that pleased some and disappointed others, Broder separated politics and the press in the most traditional of ways. He wanted journalism to improve, of course, but at the same time he wanted to maintain the "still fundamental" distinction between "what journalists do and what civic leaders or politicians do." The "essence of politics," Broder explained during a question-and-answer period, is "getting people engaged." You win elections by bringing people into the campaign, Broder said with reference to the "great lesson" of John F. Kennedy's victory over Richard Nixon in 1960. If winning elections is what politicians do, then it follows, Broder insisted, that the "function of the journalist" cannot be to "organize the polity of the community." As much as he wanted to see more people engaged in the political process, Broder said in response to a question aimed at getting him to clarify his position on public journalism, "I honestly believe that once we take on the responsibility of being the agent for engaging them, that we are in politics."[2]

Broder's commitment to campaign reform—"policing the campaign process," as he puts it—would not, then, involve the press *in* campaigns or *in* the electoral process but would rather position the press in its time-honored "watchdog" role: As guardians of the political order, journalists would alert the community to problems, but they would not involve themselves in the search for solutions. This is obviously a considerable departure from the claims of public journalism, which at a minimum define the press in terms of promoting and indeed improving, and not merely reporting on or complaining about, the quality of public or civic life.

The loss of Broder as what was once thought to be a champion of public journalism means that Jay Rosen, among others, can no longer read Broder's "Democracy and the Press" column as an acknowledgement by "perhaps the nation's most respected political reporter" that journalists "are not merely chroniclers of the political scene, but players in the game who can (and should) try to shape the outcome."[3] More than that, it signals a symbolic loss as damaging to the prestige of public journalism as the symbolic "gain" public journalism endured when the Gannett newspaper chain took out a front-page advertisement in *Editor and Publisher* to promote its support: "We believe in 'public journalism'—and have done it for years."

No one, obviously, can control who rejects and who endorses the idea of public journalism, but the juxtaposition of Broder's rejection and Gannett's endorsement raises interesting questions about what in principle public journalism represents and what in practice it hopes to achieve. Answers to these questions could fill a book—and have in fact filled several—but, significantly, they do not add up to a coherent and comprehensive account of what public journalism wants and how it plans to get it. Indeed, the available answers to key questions about the nature of public journalism are themselves the source of considerable confusion, a confusion only compounded by the proliferation of critiques not of public journalism in any recognizable form but, too often, of someone's crude caricature of it.

Without an authoritative account of what it is and what it is not, just about anything can be construed as public journalism, as Michael Gartner, editor of the Ames (Iowa) *Daily Tribune* and a former president of NBC News, illustrated not too long ago when, incredibly, he claimed to understand the decision by *The New York Times* and *The Washington Post* to publish the Unabomber's "manifesto" as "public journalism run amok." Gartner could not define public journalism but, in the spirit of Justice Potter Stewart's famous "I know it when I see it" definition of obscenity, he was confident that he was "beginning to see it everywhere." And he was just as confident that what he was seeing was "just awful."[4]

The Genesis of Public Journalism

Remarkably and perhaps unavoidably, public journalism emerged in a way that invites Gartner and other critics to imagine their worst fears. Virtually every effort to explain and promote public journalism, from Rosen's many essays to Buzz Merritt's *Public Journalism and Public Life* and Art Charity's *Doing Public Journalism*, celebrates the absence of clear and precise definitions. Charity's "panoramic view" of public journalism, for example, shifts the responsibility for precision and specificity from the author to the reader: "Journalism's proper role in support of democracy is a case-by-case question, determined by circumstances and taste."[5] Merritt, too, wants to avoid any attempt to "codify a set of public journalism rules" because that would be an "arrogant exercise, a limiting one." Merritt would prefer that the practice of public journalism develop on its own: "Journalists who accept the challenge of the philosophy will, as journalists always have, develop their own rules over time and through experience. Giving more concreteness to the ideas expressed in this book would, by that very act, limit the possibilities."[6]

Eager not to prejudge its potential for reform, Rosen made it a point to introduce public journalism as a work in progress. In his presentation to a roomful of journalists and a handful of academics, myself included, at the American Press Institute in 1994, for example, Rosen began by disclaiming any canonical conception of public journalism: "The most important thing anyone can say about public journalism I will say right now: we're still inventing it. And because we're inventing it, we don't really know what 'it' is."[7] Rosen acted strategically and prudently when, during his frequent visits to newsrooms, he abandoned his theoretical framework in favor of a more pragmatic approach to explaining how public journalism works and what it might accomplish:

> I used to be a media critic, and here's how I worked: I would observe what the press does, filter it through my theoretical framework—essentially, my dissertation—and then write about the results. You can discover a lot that way, but there's a problem. Journalists haven't read your dissertation; they don't have your framework. So whatever you discover is of little interest to them. After all, they have deadlines to meet. . . .
>
> I now employ a different method: I operate almost completely through the medium of conversation. My theoretical framework becomes whatever is needed to keep the conversation progressing. Public journalism is something journalists themselves must carry forward. What I think it should be doesn't matter as much as the version of it that I can share with reporters, editors, and news executives around the country.[8]

More than a nice gesture, the decision by Rosen, Merritt, Charity, and others to keep the "theory and practice" of public journalism open-ended and experimental probably accounts for the rapid diffusion of a variety of interesting and often important newsroom projects aimed at, as Charity had hoped, making the press "more relevant to people as citizens."[9] But it also probably accounts for public journalism's disarray as a normative theory of the press.

As an idea, public journalism endures the ignominy of neglect. Seldom do its chief architects argue among themselves; too little has been written about what distinguishes public journalism from other plans, some now forgotten, to craft a public purpose for a private press; and no one has taken up the challenge of reconciling public journalism's optimistic claims for the betterment of public life with what James Carey bluntly describes as one of the chief sources of its impoverishment: "the ruthlessly privatizing forces of capitalism."[10] By substituting examples for explication, too much of the literature on public journalism glosses over inconsistencies and even contradictions in its premises and principles. If everyone writing in support of public journalism agrees, passionately but vaguely, that public life needs to improve and the press needs to redefine and reinvigorate its commitment to democracy and democratic participation, few agree on what "democracy" means, where "public life" exists, or should exist, what constitutes "participation"—and what role the press should play in making it all work.

From among the more important questions about public journalism, at least from the perspective of the *idea* of public journalism, three separate but related areas of confusion and controversy stand out: press responsibility, political power, and constitutional reform. What follows illustrates, rather than examines, some of the key issues by selecting, without good reason, one comparatively simple question in each of the three areas:

- Concerning press responsibility: What are the consequences of a press wedded to a strictly procedural role?
- Concerning political power: What will convening the community accomplish?
- Concerning constitutional reform: What view of the First Amendment best supports the ideal of democratic deliberation?

Public Journalism and Press Responsibility: A Strictly Procedural Role for the Press?

One of public journalism's most underdeveloped sets of claims concerns the notion of the press, in a phrase usually attributed to Merritt, as a "fair-minded participant in a community that works." In a section of his book called "The Fair-Minded Participant," quoted here almost in its entirety, Merritt uses a sports analogy, referring particularly to the role of the referee, to underscore the importance of a detached but not disinterested press:

> The function of a third party—a referee or umpire or judge—in sports competition is to facilitate the deciding of the outcome. Ideally, the official never impinges on the game; if things go according to the rules, he or

she is neither seen nor heard. Yet the presence of a fair-minded participant is necessary in order for an equitable decision to be reached.

What he or she brings to the arena is knowledge of the agreed-upon
rules, the willingness to contribute that knowledge, and authority—that is,
the right to be attended to. The referee's role is to make sure that the process works as the contestants agreed it should. In order to maintain that
authority, that right to be heard, the referee must exhibit no interest in
the final score other than it is arrived at under the rules. But, both for ref-
erees and contestants, that is the ultimate interest.

It is important to remember that the referee doesn't make the rules.
Those are agreed on by the contestants—in this case, the democratic public. The referee, rather, is the fair-minded caretaker.

What journalists should bring to the arena of public life is knowledge
of the rules—how the public has decided a democracy should work—and
the ability and the willingness to provide relevant information and a place
for that information to be discussed and turned into democratic consent.
Like the referee, to maintain our authority—the right to be heard—we must
exhibit no partisan interest in the specific outcome other than it is arrived
at under the democratic process.[11]

The press as a fair-minded participant thus rests on the proposition that an activist role for the press must be nonpartisan and apolitical. Charity makes this clear when he cautions journalists to steer clear
of substantive proposals for reform and to concentrate instead on "trying to create the as-yet-missing place where citizens can meet and talk
with one another in a realistic and constructive way."[12] Likewise, Rosen
calls on the press to create the capacity for a community to discover
itself, including its problems and the ways to solve them: "I do not
believe journalists should be solving problems. I think they should be
creating the capacity within the community to solve problems."[13] What
Rosen, Merritt, and Charity seem to share, then, at least with regard to
the ideal of fair-mindedness, is a fundamentally *liberal* view of democracy and an entirely "procedural" role for the press. Indeed, Charity's
"golden rule" for public journalism positions the press as a champion
of democratic means but not of democratic ends, "*Journalism should
advocate democracy without advocating particular solutions.*"[14]

Just as Rosen, Merritt, and Charity want the press to confine its
activism to improving democratic means, not democratic ends, democratic theory in the liberal tradition views democracy in terms of what
is *right to do* and generally not in terms of what is *good to achieve*. Liberalism assigns a priority to individual liberty and deals with the "common good," to borrow part of the title of Clifford Christian's chapter,
as a mere by-product of the free choices individuals make; it posits a
democratic order in which questions about what is right must be

answered independent of, and ordinarily prior to, questions about what is good. If now and then Rosen approvingly cites Michael Sandel,[15] a prominent critic of liberalism, the literature on public journalism seldom retreats from liberalism's central premise, summarized succinctly by one of its leading theoreticians, John Rawls: "It is not our aims that primarily reveal our nature but rather the principles that we would acknowledge to govern the background conditions under which these aims are to be formed and the manner in which they are to be pursued."[16]

Rawls nonetheless tempers his brand of liberalism with a "thin" theory of the good, a set of principles designed to guard against the erosion of certain "preeminently desirable" values.[17] For what Rawls recognizes, and what finally distinguishes liberalism from libertarianism, is that a "properly ordered" society—a *just* society—cannot be understood solely in terms of process or procedure. Put a little differently, liberalism requires an independent and prior conception of the right (i.e., principles concerning *what justice is*), but this requirement does not preclude complementary conceptions of the good (i.e., principles concerning *what justice demands*).[18] If in the United States, to use a handy illustration, the importance of a "fair trial" is usually understood with reference to what justice *is* (due process, rules of evidence, impartial juries, etc.) and not with reference to what justice *demands* (a particular verdict), the U.S. Constitution, an unmistakably liberal document, nonetheless proscribes, no matter how fair the trial, "cruel and unusual" punishment.

Public journalism, however, offers not even the thinnest of a thin theory of the good. It presents no conception of what justice demands. Unchecked, I fear, its constricted view of fair-mindedness can easily render the press incapable of promoting social change.

Leaving aside the question of what Merritt and others mean by "*the* democratic process" (emphasis added) and whether—and on what grounds—a "fair-minded" press can challenge it ("the referee," Merritt reminds us, "doesn't make the rules"), public journalism fails to contend with the consequences of a press wedded to a strictly procedural role. It fails, specifically, to address the predicament newsrooms face, to take an uncomfortably familiar scenario, whenever communities act intolerantly. What does a "fair-minded" press do when a community consensus calls for a book burning? What is an appropriate response from a "fair-minded" press when a popular vote yields a racist mayor? Does public journalism, which famously favors "connections" over "separations," expect newsrooms to separate their editorial agenda from their news agenda by condemning on one page the very activity or outcome they facilitated and now describe on another page? When Rosen calls on the press to develop a "vision of the community as a better place to live,"[19] is it a vision of only better means to unknown ends? Are there no ends themselves, not even the tiniest *telos*, public journalism wants to embrace?

Public Journalism and Political Power: What Will Convening the Community Accomplish?

Public journalism's preoccupation with procedure makes it difficult for journalists to join forces—to "connect," in the parlance of public journalism—with any part of the community associated with political or "partisan" interests. This effectively limits public journalism's partners to "foundations, broadcasters, universities, civic groups,"[20] and other politically benign organizations and institutions; and it effectively excludes trade unions, political parties, professional associations, local reform movements, and other special interest groups. Unwittingly or not, then, public journalism's fear of advocacy isolates the press from the very centers of power that are likely to make a difference locally, regionally, nationally, and even globally. In the name of impartiality and fair-mindedness, public journalism denies journalists an opportunity to broaden and even redirect a political infrastructure too often focused narrowly on settling, if not always reconciling, the competing claims of private parties pursuing their private ends.

Public journalism avoids partisan interests by disregarding the realities of political power and by appealing instead to a republican ideal which locates politics in a common discussion open and accessible to all interested citizens. Understandably, its democracy by dialogue attracts journalists, politicians, and others who would prefer a diffusion of power consistent with a direct, participatory democracy. But on most issues in most communities a democracy of a very different kind prevails. With or without public journalism's efforts to create for citizens a deliberative process of their own, power typically resides where resources, usually wealth, serve to obfuscate, if not entirely circumvent, public debate.

If in fact public journalism hopes to alter American democracy fundamentally by "orienting people to common goods beyond their private ends," as Sandel describes the principal goal of the republican, as opposed to the liberal, democratic tradition,[21] then "convening the community" might bring about only the illusion of reform. Worse, public journalism might become, as Ed Baker fears, "a technique of co-optation or legitimation that creates a false sense of participatory involvement without challenging entrenched elite interests."[22] Focus groups, town meetings, salons, and other attempts to convene the community amount to at best a contrived and artificial response to the need to cultivate citizenship. They create at most an ad hoc venue for discussion, a small and temporary site for a debate managed by and too often only for the press. Without the means to sustain these discussions over time and the conviction to broaden the range of topics they cover, the press cannot claim to have established much in the way of a *tradition* of civic participation.

Besides, creating new and better opportunities for public debate begs the bigger question: What are these debates intended to accomplish? Are they an end in themselves? If not, of what extrinsic value are they? The obvious and familiar answer, given that so many public journalism projects focus on campaigns and elections, is that they prepare citizens for their role as wise and responsible voters. But unless public journalism confuses a plebiscite with a democracy, this is at best a partial answer. Voting takes place maybe once a year; democracy, in contrast, requires constant and continuous renewal—and, notably, an opportunity to influence the resolution of issues on which citizens do not formally vote.

Beyond their occasional vote, citizens can involve themselves in the affairs of their community principally, though not exclusively, through the associations they keep and the groups they form. Understood as the beginning of a "continuum of activity," to use Benjamin Barber's apt phrase,[23] on which democratic participation depends, these groups and associations can sustain democracy in two important ways. First, they can strengthen the affective ties among individuals with shared interests, values, customs, and traditions; they can provide, in other words, a social setting in which a sense of self and a sense of belonging are mutually constituted. Second, they can enable individuals to position themselves collectively; they can develop, therefore, into the very *publics* whose opinions matter more than the untested, often unfounded, and essentially private opinions of individuals whose anonymous responses to polling questions end up mistakenly labeled as "public" opinion.[24]

That, realistically, individuals form *publics* and not *a* public is precisely the point Nancy Fraser makes when she warns against theorizing away "structural relations of dominance and subordination" by assuming "a single, over-arching public sphere" which stands open and accessible to everyone. Without discounting the possibility of an egalitarian *and* multicultural society that might some day exist in the United States—and the prospects for a unitary public arena for it—Fraser poses a challenge for public journalism, though not with reference to it, when she recognizes that the goal of "participatory parity" can be better achieved today through a "plurality of competing publics."[25]

Rather than expecting individuals to "reach across their social and ideological differences to establish common agendas and to debate rival approaches," as Todd Gitlin recently described the unlikely circumstances of a unitary public sphere, a multiplicity of publics—what Gitlin calls "sphericules"—invites participation through the "development of distinct groups organized around affinity and interest."[26] Better understood as the first of a "tier of publics," to return to Fraser's conceptualization, these comparatively small and relatively homogeneous groups—often the very groups public journalism is disinclined to engage—enlarge the opportunities for participation by setting aside a space for individuals whose identities and interests might have been ignored or slighted in the structured setting in which they live their lives. In part, then, these groups provide "spaces of withdrawal and regroupment," as Fraser puts it—an opportunity, that is, for individuals to express themselves on topics and in ways that might not be welcome elsewhere. This, in turn, creates the conditions for what Fraser calls "discursive contestation"; by serving as "bases and training grounds for agitational activities directed toward wider publics," these "counterpublics" enable individuals to achieve together a degree of participation they could have never achieved alone.[27]

Public Journalism and Constitutional Reform:
First Amendment Protection for Public Debate?

One potentially important but neglected ally in public journalism's campaign to redefine and revitalize American journalism is the Supreme Court, which Lee Bollinger insightfully describes as the "primary arbiter and definer" of the press's identity.[28] Not that the press cannot operate independent of the Court's conception of it, but the judiciary's image of a free press—and its rationale for it—can add some constitutional luster, and more than a little legitimacy, to the claims journalists make about their roles and responsibilities. Thus it might be of some consequence for public journalism that the Supreme Court continues to place a higher priority on the principles of self-expression and the conditions for individual autonomy than on the principles of self-government and the conditions for public deliberation.

Particularly since the Court's 1964 decision in *New York Times v. Sullivan,* a case heralded as the end of the legacy of seditious libel and the beginning of a new and important constitutional appreciation for "robust and uninhibited" expression, "a jurisprudence of and for the press," as Bollinger puts it, has emerged that protects journalists by insulating them from politics and politicians and by rendering them essentially "unaccountable" to any form of official authority.[29] To be sure, *Sullivan* and its progeny promote what Bollinger calls a "model of journalistic autonomy," a celebration of certain styles of journalism that "breathes life" into "a press conceived in the image of the artist . . . who lives (figuratively) outside society, beyond normal conventions, and who is therefore better able to see and expose its shortcomings."[30] Given this attention to the importance of keeping the press separate and independent from the individuals and institutions it covers, it should come as no surprise that Rosen finds that when it comes to articulating "what *attaches* the journalist to the citizenry, our political tradition and First Amendment doctrine provide few useful notions."[31]

Carey nicely sums up the challenge for public journalism when he recalls the tradition of American jurisprudence, now largely ignored by the courts, rooted in the works of Louis Brandeis and Alexander Meiklejohn. Their work, Carey writes,

> should provide our basic understanding of the press. The press exists not as the surrogate holders of the rights of the public but as an instrument which both expresses the public and helps it form and find its identity. The press, then, as an institution must support the maintenance of public space and public life; it must find ways in which the public can address one another, and it must enhance those qualities of discourse such as decent manners and formal social equality that allow public space to develop and to be maintained.[32]

Meiklejohn's work in particular provides a serious and sustained argument in support of the proposition that public expression deserves constitutional protection not because it advances the interests of individuals but because it enables citizens to "understand the issues which bear upon our common life."[33] This fundamentally reverses the usual order of First Amendment priorities by accentuating the need to cultivate citizenship—even, at times, at the expense of individual liberty. When Meiklejohn observes, "What is essential is not that everyone shall speak, but that everything worth saying shall be said," he means that the First Amendment, properly conceived, provides for "the common needs of all members of the body politic" and has, comparatively, "no concern" for the needs of individuals to express themselves.[34] Meiklejohn thus shifts the analysis from one that understands the individual in mostly psychological terms to one that understands society in mostly political terms.

A Meiklejohnian perspective on freedom of expression distinguishes itself from conventional First Amendment theory in much the same way market metaphors distinguish themselves from models of discourse built on the deliberative ideal of the town meeting. Whereas one presupposes the rationality of *self*-interest when individuals, acting alone or in "private" association with others, are free to choose from among competing policies, platforms, and politicians, the other presumes, to shift to the vernacular of Jürgen Habermas, the "mutual enlightenment" of a "public" committed to "critical–rational" debate on issues of *general* interest.[35] As crudely sketched in Table 1.1, Meiklejohn's view of the First Amendment rests on the importance of the community's "right to know" rather than on an individual's "right to be heard"; it substitutes a "positive" for a "negative" view of freedom by affirming self-governance, not self-expression, as the principal justification for First Amendment liberties; and it seeks to facilitate a certain "quality" of debate by protecting the *content* of expression—even when that protection amounts to a restriction on *individual* expression.

By calling attention to the need to concern ourselves with the *quality* of public debate, Meiklejohn reminds us of the inevitable difference between a "responsible and regulated discussion" and the "unregulated

TABLE 1.1. First Amendment Theories

	Theories that assign a priority to the individual	Theories that assign a priority to the community
Define freedom . . .	Negatively	Positively
Protect . . .	Individual expression	Content of expression
Are modeled on . . .	The marketplace	The town meeting/ public sphere
Say the press's role is . . .	To promote self-expression	To promote self-government
Accommodate . . .	A variety of ideas[a]	A diversity of ideas[a]
Say the press's responsibility is . . .	To inform the public	To manage public deliberation
Say the First Amendment's goal is . . .	The right to be heard	The right to know

[a]"Variety" denotes a range of ideas in accordance with popular demand and consumer choice; it accommodates what individuals, treated as an aggregation, *want*. In contrast, "diversity" denotes a range of ideas in accordance with shared interests and common goods; it accommodates what individuals, treated as a community, *need*. For a related discussion of the distinction between "wants," defined psychologically in terms of personal preference and private gratification, and "needs," defined culturally in terms of general welfare and public purpose, see the several references to these terms in Daniel Bell, *The Cultural Contradictions of Capitalism* (New York: Basic Books, 1976).

talkativeness" that takes place when individual expression receives protection without regard for what it contributes to the larger debate.[36] Because marketplace models of discourse can only justify the "survival" of an idea that has proven itself popular, Meiklejohn rejects them as inadequate for the needs of democratic debate.[37] To better accommodate a genuinely diverse range of points of view, as opposed to the mere variety of opinion that market forces ordinarily tolerate, Meiklejohn advocates a "structure of authority" that Robert Post fairly terms "managerial."

The "quandary of democratic dialogue," Post writes in his recent critique of work focused on, quoting an essay by Stephen Holmes, the First Amendment's *"positive* purpose of creating an informed public capable of self-government," concerns the proper "management of deliberation."[38] Post strains valiantly to reach a compromise between the "ascription of autonomy," which he regards as the "axiomatic and foundational principle" of First Amendment law, and the "managerial authority" of the state, which he regards as legitimate only under "intolerable conditions of private power and domination."[39] What Post does not explore, however, is the less controversial "managerial authority" of the press, a role that preserves press autonomy and at the same time assigns to journalism the responsibility to promote what Post acknowledges is now widely seen as the "essential objective" of the First Amendment: "a rich and valuable public debate."[40]

The constitutional challenge for public journalism, then, and one for which there is considerable scholarly support,[41] is not how to justify a role for the state in the management of deliberation but how to justify a role for the state in strengthening the *press's* role in the management of deliberation. The distinction is an important one, for it assigns to the press, not the state, the responsibility to manage deliberation; it assigns to the state *only* the responsibility to make it possible for the press to do so. A First Amendment jurisprudence consistent with the principles of public journalism expects the state, particularly jurists and legislators, to recognize and indeed to insure a free and independent press not as an end in itself but, to quote Meiklejohn one last time, as the best available means "to give to every voting member of the body politic the fullest participation in the understanding of those problems which the citizens of a self-governing society must deal."[42] This means that the press can call on the state for protection and subvention only when it can show that its role as a manager of deliberation is being threatened or subverted. It matters not whether the threat or subversion comes from the state, where traditional First Amendment theory focuses its attention, or from, in Post's phrase, "conditions of private power and domination," which are generally ignored by traditional

First Amendment theory. What matters is the state's, especially the judiciary's, commitment to a press capable of sustaining the conditions of self-government.

Notes

1. David S. Broder, "Democracy and the Press, *The Washington Post,* January 3, 1990, p. A15.
2. David S. Broder, "Journalism and Real Life," 26th Annual McClatchy Lecture, Department of Communication, Stanford University, April 26, 1996.
3. Jay Rosen, "Politics, Vision, and the Press: Toward a Public Agenda for Journalism," pp. 1–33 in *The New News v. The Old News: The Press and Politics in the 1990s* (New York: Twentieth Century Fund, 1992), p. 8.
4. Michael Gartner, "Give Me Old-Time Journalism," *Quill* (November/December 1995): 68.
5. Arthur Charity, *Doing Public Journalism* (New York: Guilford Press, 1995), p. 14.
6. Davis Merritt, *Public Journalism and Public Life: Why Telling the News Is Not Enough* (Hillsdale, NJ: Erlbaum, 1995), p. 124.
7. Jay Rosen, "Making Things More Public: On the Political Responsibility of the Media Intellectual," *Critical Studies in Mass Communication,* 11 (1994): 363–388. See also Theodore L. Glasser and Stephanie Craft, "Public Journalism and the Search for Democratic Ideals," pp. 203–218 in *Media, Ritual and Identity,* eds. Tamar Liebes and James Curran (London: Routledge, 1998), p. 206.
8. Jay Rosen, "A Scholar's Perspective," pp. 14–26 in *Imagining Public Journalism: An Editor and Scholar Reflect on the Birth of an Idea,* eds. Davis Merritt and Jay Rosen, Roy H. Howard Public Lecture, IN University, Bloomington, Indiana, April 13, 1995, p. 23. See also Jay Rosen, "Public Journalism: A Case for Public Scholarship," *Change* (May/June 1995): 38.
9. Charity, *Doing Public Journalism,* p. 14.
10. James W. Carey, "The Press, Public Opinion, and Public Discourse," pp. 373–402 in *Public Opinion and the Communication of Consent,* eds. Theodore L. Glasser and Charles T. Salmon (New York: Guilford Press, 1995), p. 374.
11. Merritt, *Public Journalism and Public Life,* pp. 94–95.
12. Charity, *Doing Public Journalism,* p. 151.
13. Jay Rosen, personal correspondence, March 16, 1999.
14. Charity, *Doing Public Journalism,* pp. 144, 146, emphasis in the original.
15. See, for example, Rosen, "Making Things More Public," p. 382; and "Politics, Vision, and the Press," p. 10. Rosen cites Michael Sandel, *Liberalism and the Limits of Justice* (New York: Cambridge University Press, 1982).
16. John Rawls, *A Theory of Justice* (Cambridge, MA: Harvard University Press, 1971), p. 560. See also *Political Liberalism* (New York: Columbia University Press, 1993).
17. Rawls, *A Theory of Justice,* p. 62.

18. For a worthwhile use of the distinction between "what justice is" and "what justice demands," see Stephen White, *The Recent Work of Jürgen Habermas* (New York: Cambridge University Press, 1988).

19. Jay Rosen, "Public Journalism: First Principles," pp. 6–18 in Jay Rosen and Davis Merritt Jr., *Public Journalism: Theory and Practice* (Dayton, OH: Kettering Foundation, 1994), p. 15. For a discussion of the consequences of a "political agenda lacking substantive moral discourse," see Michael J. Sandel, *Democracy's Discontent: America in Search of a Public Philosophy* (Cambridge, MA: Harvard University Press, 1996), pp. 323–324.

20. Jay Rosen, *Community Connectedness: Passwords for Public Journalism* (St. Petersburg, FL: Poynter Institute for Media Studies, 1993), p. 9.

21. Sandel, *Democracy's Discontent*, p. 117.

22. C. Edwin Baker, *The Media That Citizens Need*, unpublished manuscript, University of Pennsylvania, p. 34.

23. Benjamin Barber, *Strong Democracy: Participatory Politics for a New Age* (Berkeley: University of California Press, 1984), p. 235.

24. This point is developed in Charles T. Salmon and Theodore L. Glasser, "The Politics of Polling and the Limits of Consent," pp. 437–458 in *Public Opinion and the Communication of Consent*, eds. Theodore L. Glasser and Charles T. Salmon (New York: Guilford Press, 1995). For an application of this critique to public journalism, see Glasser and Craft, "Public Journalism and the Search for Democratic Ideals," pp. 210–211.

25. Nancy Fraser, "Rethinking the Public Sphere: A Contribution to the Critique of Actually Existing Democracy," pp. 109–142 in *Habermas and the Public Sphere*, ed. Craig Calhoun (Cambridge, MA: MIT Press, 1992), p. 122.

26. Todd Gitlin, "Public Spheres or Public Sphericules?," pp. 168–174 in *Media, Ritual and Identity*, ed. Tamar Liebes and James Curran (London: Routledge, 1998), p. 173.

27. Fraser, "Rethinking the Public Sphere," p. 124. See also Salmon and Glasser, "The Politics of Polling," pp. 451–452.

28. Lee C. Bollinger, *Images of a Free Press* (Chicago: University of Chicago Press, 1991), p. 133. Commenting on the Court's many First Amendment decisions in the last few decades, Bollinger writes, "Certainly the process of developing a set of constitutional protections has been accompanied by the development of a *conception* of the social role of the press that is thought to justify them. And, though it was not necessary that the underlying, theoretical conception of the First Amendment embody a normative judgment about what a *good* press is, there is little doubt that that is what has occurred" (p. 43).

29. For a worthwhile review of the significance of the *Sullivan* case, see, in addition to Bollinger, Anthony Lewis, *Make No Law: The Sullivan Case and the First Amendment* (New York: Random House, 1991).

30. Bollinger, *Images of a Free Press*, p. 55.

31. Rosen, "Public Journalism: First Principles," p. 11. For an interesting assessment of the gap between what roles public journalism wants the press to play and what roles for the press the courts are inclined to protect, see Clay

Calvert, "Clashing Conceptions of Press Duties: Public Journalists and the Courts," *Communication Law and Policy*, 2 (Autumn 1997): 441–475.

32. James W. Carey, "Community, Public, and Journalism," pp. 1–15 in *Mixed News: The Public/Civic/Communitarian Journalism Debate*, ed. Jay Black (Mahwah, NJ: Erlbaum, 1997), pp. 12–13. Except for the Supreme Court's anomalous decision in 1969, in *Red Lion v. FCC*, where the court found that, on balance, the listeners' right to hear was more important than the broadcasters' right to be heard, the judiciary continues to defend freedom of expression in terms of individual autonomy and self-fulfillment.

33. Alexander Meiklejohn, *Political Freedom: The Constitutional Powers of the People* (New York: Oxford University Press, 1965), p. 75.

34. Meiklejohn, *Political Freedom*, pp. 26, 55.

35. See Jürgen Habermas, *The Structural Transformation of the Public Sphere: An Inquiry into a Category of Bourgeois Society*, Thomas Burger, trans. (Cambridge, MA: MIT Press, 1989).

36. Meiklejohn, *Political Freedom*, pp. 25–26.

37. Even ardent supports of marketplace models acknowledge that market forces tend to discriminate against minority and unpopular ideas. See, for example, Bruce Owen, *Economics and Freedom of Expression* (Cambridge, MA: Ballinger, 1975).

38. Robert Post, "Managing Deliberation: The Quandary of Democratic Dialogue," *Ethics*, 103 (July 1993): 654–678. See also Stephen Holmes, "Liberal Constraints on Private Power? Reflections on the Origins and Rationale of Access Regulation," pp. 21–65 in *Democracy and the Media*, ed. Judith Lichtenberg (Cambridge, UK: Cambridge University Press, 1990), p. 47.

39. Post, "Managing Deliberation," pp. 672–673.

40. Post, "Managing Deliberation," p. 654.

41. See, for example, Zechariah Chafee, *Government and Mass Communications*, Vol. 2 (Chicago: University of Chicago Press, 1947); Jerome A. Barron, *Freedom of the Press for Whom?* (Bloomington: Indiana University Press, 1967); Thomas I. Emerson, "The Affirmative Side of the First Amendment," *Georgia Law Review*, 15 (Summer 1981): 795–849; Cass R. Sunstein, "Preferences and Politics," *Philosophy and Public Affairs*, 20 (1991): 3–34.

42. Quoted in Michael J. Sandel, *Democracy's Discontent: America in Search of a Public Philosophy* (Cambridge, MA: Harvard University Press, 1996), p. 79.

Part 1

The Challenge
of Public Journalism

Chapter 2

The Action of the Idea
Public Journalism in Built Form

Jay Rosen
New York University

Public journalism is an idea that "happened," which is to say that not all ideas do.

It happened because certain journalists around the country did what they did and said what they said. It happened because certain professors and writers thought what they thought and wrote what they wrote. It happened because some foundations and think tanks decided it was an enterprise worthy of support. It happened because the American press took note and made "news" of public journalism. Because other civic groups, not connected to the press, noticed what was happening, public journalism happened with them, too. It happened in the public lives of communities across the land, from Portland, Maine, to Portland, Oregon. It happened in newsrooms, conference rooms, hotel ballrooms, and even barrooms, over drinks. It happened in dozens of different ways, and this rich variety of events—what we might call the *action* of the idea—is what makes it more than an idea.

I look at public journalism as a concept with a career, an abstraction that became an adventure within and around the American press. The notion is evacuated, drained of much intellectual excitement, unless it somehow incorporates the action into the abstraction. This is not a simple matter of recognizing how theory got applied in practice, for it is just as correct to say that practice was applied to theory. If we are going to understand the thing that goes by the name "public journalism," we have to see it as many things going on simultaneously. The idea is hiding somewhere in that simultaneity, and my aim in this chapter is to find it there.

Now if all this sounds a bit cryptic, hang on. It should become clearer as I proceed. If I were asked to craft a short definition of public journalism (and I have been asked, many times), it might go something like this:

> Public journalism is an approach to the daily business of the craft that calls on journalists to (1) address people as citizens, potential participants in public affairs, rather than victims or spectators; (2) help the political community act upon, rather than just learn about, its problems; (3) improve the climate of public discussion, rather than simply watch it deteriorate; and (4) help make public life go well, so that it earns its claim on our attention. If journalists can find a way to do these things, they may in time restore public confidence in the press, reconnect with an audience that has been drifting away, rekindle the idealism that brought many of them into the craft and contribute, in a more substantial fashion, to the health of American democracy, which is the reason we afford journalists their many privileges and protections.

Definitions are useful, as far as they go. But this one does not go very far, for if the idea is summed up by the definition, we miss a lot of what happened when it went public—that is, began to have its own public life—beginning around 1993. Taking it public was a key feature of the idea when it emerged in what architects call "built form," meaning, the way it stands after it's been constructed and inhabited. Thus, another way of defining public journalism (also called civic journalism) is to understand it in at least five ways:

• Public journalism as an *argument,* a way of thinking about what journalists should be doing, given their own predicament and the general state of public life in America. The argument is more or less what I wrote earlier in my attempt at a definition.

• Public journalism as an *experiment,* a way of doing journalism that corresponded to the argument and was tried in hundreds of communities across the country, as journalists attempted to break out of established routines and make a different kind of contribution to public life.

• Public journalism as a *movement,* a loose network of practicing journalists, former journalists who wanted to improve their craft, academics and researchers with ideas to lend and studies that might help, foundations and think tanks that gave financial assistance and sanctuary to the movement, and other like-minded folk who wanted to contribute to a rising spirit of reform.

• Public journalism as a *debate,* an often heated conversation within the press and with others outside it about the proper role of the press at a time of trouble—in newsrooms and in American democracy. This debate was about the idea, sort of, but because it was largely a production of the press itself, it revealed in its content and tone the very habits of mind that public journalism was trying to question in the first place. Which—if you're starting to get it—was part of the point of going public with the idea. In the debate that emerged about the notion, the notion was put into a shape others wanted it to have; it was vivified for their use, whether that meant writing news stories about public journalism as a "trend," objecting to it as an assault on values held dear, or arranging for a controversy between "believers" and "skeptics." All these acts *by* journalism upon the thing called public journalism contributed to the edifice of the idea, even when they were hostile in spirit, as some were.

• Public journalism as an *adventure,* an open-ended and experimental quest for another kind of press. The adventure had no fixed goal, no directing agency, no clear formula for success, no sharp boundary between itself and many other varieties of civic work, (including academic work) and no limits on who might join in. Most of all, no one really knew where the quest might lead. Of course, I am being somewhat romantic when I call it an "adventure," but there was romance in the idea, too. Among certain journalists, love of craft met a renewed love of democracy. The two hit the road together, not knowing what they would find.

When I refer, then, to the action of the idea, I mean, in part, what the philosopher Hannah Arendt meant by "action." For Arendt, to act is to "take an initiative . . . to set something in motion." Action is further illuminated by Arendt's distinction between acting and behaving. We behave when we conform to organizational pressures and lose ourselves in automatic routines, neglecting the essence of the human condition, which is "natality," the capacity to start something new.[1] My suggestion is that an idea can be improved when a good number of people act with and on it. Together, they set something in motion, break out of established routines, and go forward with a different sense of what's possible. They hazard a guess about what the world will accept and let the world do its work on their guess. Arendt always said that action was unpredictable, and this proved true for the adventure of public journalism.

The Public Adventure of Public Journalism

Seen as an argument, an experiment, a movement, a debate, and a kind of adventure, public journalism looks a good deal more complicated—more interesting, I hope—than my quick definition suggests. Now let me try a third way of defining public journalism, by describing some of the things that happened during its emergence into built form.

Before there was anything called public journalism there was the imagination of it, floating around among a group of scholars and critics, many of whom are still writing, some of whom are long departed. The world's shortest definition of public journalism is actually three words: "what Dewey meant." I refer, of course, to John Dewey, who in 1927 wrote an important book on the general theme, called *The Public and Its Problems*. What James Carey meant by calling the public the "god term" of journalism in several of his powerful essays; what Clifford Christians, John P. Ferré, and P. Mark Fackler meant when, in a groundbreaking book, they wrote of a journalism conducted in the common good; what Theodore Glasser meant in describing communication as the "cultivation of citizenship"; what Michael Schudson meant in noting that the "news media necessarily incorporate into their work a certain view of politics, and they will either do so intelligently and critically or unconsciously and routinely"; what Edmund B. Lambeth meant in calling for a "committed journalism"; what Rob Anderson, Robert Dardenne, and George Killenberg meant in arguing that "the prime role of journalism . . . is to take responsibility to stimulate public dialogue on issues of common concern to a democratic public."[2] My list could go on, and that is exactly the point. A raft of scholars have written on this theme and thus contributed to the idea.

Now my point continues: Public journalism is what Buzz Merritt of *The Wichita Eagle* meant by altering his election coverage in 1990; what the staff at *The Charlotte Observer* meant by following his example in 1992; what Jeremy Iggers meant when he and a few others started the "Minnesota's Talking" roundtables at the *Star Tribune;* what Wisconsin Public Radio, Public Television, and the *Wisconsin State Journal* meant by forming their "We the People" project, which brought deliberative discussions among citizens to a statewide television audience, what *The Virginian-Pilot* in Norfolk meant by bringing together the reporters who had covered local politics and calling them the "public life team," which wrote its own mission statement "knowing that a lively, informed, and most of all, engaged public is essential to . . . newspapers."[3]

But it's also what the Kettering Foundation had in mind by convening a series of discussions about citizens, democracy, and the press involving journalists and a few academics in the years 1990–1992, before there was a name for that discussion. It's what the Knight Foundation, Kettering, the American Press Institute, and New York University's department of journalism intended when they joined forces to create the Project on Public Life and the Press, which I had the privilege to direct from 1993 to 1997. It's what the Poynter Institute of Media Studies was doing by aiding *The Charlotte Observer* in its 1992 experiment and following up with other studies of what became public journalism. It's what the Pew Charitable Trusts did in 1993 by creating the Pew Center for Civic Journalism, giving it a lot of money to spend, and asking a veteran journalist, Edward M. Fouhy, to run it.[4]

Now stretch your imagination and realize that public journalism was also the *American Journalism Review* writing a feature on it, head-lined, "The Gospel of Public Journalism," in which the idea's propo-nents were described as traveling preachers staging a tent show. It was Michael Gartner, former president of both NBC News and the Ameri-can Society of Newspaper Editors, giving a speech on public journal-ism to the Society of Professional Journalists, in which he described the thing as a "menace." It was Rosemary Armao, then the director of Investigative Reporters and Editors, a major professional group, calling the people involved in public journalism a "cult." It was the editorial page of *The New York Times* warning of the "damage" to the "credibility of the press" wreaked by "the fad for intellectually flaccid 'civic journal-ism.' "[5] When our image of public journalism begins to incorporate these responses (and the revealing metaphors they employ), we are coming closer to what I mean by the action of the idea.

The action is further visible in a 1997 report entitled, "Civic Jour-nalism and Local Government," issued by the International City/ County Management Association, a group of nonjournalists interested in what was happening. It is there in a special issue of the *National Civic Review*, published by the venerable National Civic League (begun dur-ing the Progressive era). The journal's title for its special issue is "Rethinking Journalism: Rebuilding Civic Life." It is there in an audit of *The Virginian-Pilot*'s news coverage, conducted by the local chapter of the League of Women Voters and intended to measure the paper's progress in one of its declared aims: positioning people as potential actors rather than victims. (The results were printed in the *Pilot,* along with an editor's column encouraging more such efforts to hold the paper accountable.) The action is there in the public libraries that cooperated with the *San Jose Mercury News* in holding a series of public forums that brought local citizens of different races together to deliber-ate on one of the most divisive issues of our time, affirmative action.[6]

All of this is "public journalism," but more to the point, all of it is part of the *idea* of public journalism in built form. For one of the design elements in the idea was a desire to move into the American public sphere with the claim that there could be a "more public" press: not just to make the claim, not just to write about it, and not just to act on it but also to do and think, speak and write, experiment and learn, and generally stir up trouble, in such a way that people within and without the press would react, and by reacting reveal something—or better yet, do something—that might somehow further the idea.

My shorthand for the paragraph above is to point out that public journalism has itself been "public" in its style of development. First, it grew from public dialogue about the press and its predicament.[7] Work done under its name was published or broadcast in the mass media: daily newspapers, newscasts, public radio programs. Scholarly inquiry into the idea was published—made public—in a different way.[8] In trade magazines and press reviews, journalism did journalism to public journalism, and that work was public.[9] As a "movement," public journalism moved, not only through the American press but through corners of the foundation world, the world of civic activists and community-builders, organizations like the National Civic League, and so on.[10] The idea insinuated itself into a wider conversation about democracy and its difficulties, and this too made it public in form.

Here's another (admittedly small) way that public journalism was itself made public. As director of the Project on Public Life and the Press, I insisted from the outset that all its events be recorded and thus "on the record." That phrase, familiar to every journalist, meant one thing in practical terms and another as symbol or totem. In practice, it meant that things said at the Project's seminars could be reviewed and quoted by others. They became a small part of the public record, preserved in documentary form and available to all.

Symbolically, to speak on the record is to address that elusive (but not entirely nebulous) entity: the public. On-the-record speech partakes of a certain spirit: the spirit of mutual dialogue, open conversation, communal storytelling, thinking aloud. Public journalism, I felt, should try to earn its adjective by employing a public language in public settings, by subjecting itself to public scrutiny and debate, by conveying through style and stance a confident respect for public life and for the "public as partner" in the quest for a better press.

"Infuse the means with the spirit of the end" is the way I phrased it one address to the Project's seminar participants. What does the phrase mean? Something like this: If what you are hoping for is a more engaged public and a journalism that helps it into existence, then one way to act on that hope is to proceed publicly—to speak in front of your colleagues, experiment in the pages of your newspaper, talk candidly with your fellow citizens, enter willingly into the ordeal of debate, and be grateful for the chance to lead a public, in addition to a professional, life. Plenty of journalists started behaving this way; they went public with their ideas, and their willingness to do so was part of the idea of public journalism.[11]

It helps to contrast this approach with what might be called "fortress journalism." In fortress journalism, the press is criticized by all, in conversation with none. Journalists rely on their professional culture—a peer culture—for approval and status. Liberty of the press, that ringing phrase, offers insulation more than inspiration. Journalism is what journalists do, not what democracy may need done. Conventions of the craft are defended as if they were first principles rather than familiar practices. Anxiety and alarm are occasionally permitted, rethinking and reform are not.

The journalist's understanding of the First Amendment is part of the culture's fortifications. That favorite newsroom battlecry, "hands off the press," often gets extended to any sort of threatening voice. As scholars Clifford Christians, John P. Ferré, and P. Mark Fackler observe, "Whenever challenged, the press thrusts the First Amendment forward as a fetish to ward off the spirits of responsibility."[12] Martin Linsky, who has experience as a journalist, scholar, and public official, notes that "the press is a substantial barrier to overcome" for those "attempting to move toward a richer, more participatory . . . dialogue on public affairs." People in journalism "want to believe that the nature and quality of dialogue about public issues is none of their business, that they just report the news," he writes. Linsky adds, "Most journalists interpret the First Amendment as freeing them from [a duty to society] in the ethical and community as well as the legal and constitutional senses."[13]

Michael Janeway, former editor of *The Boston Globe* and later a journalism school dean, notes how the culture of the press discourages thoughtful reflection. His remarks are a concise description of the intellectual attitudes in fortress journalism:

> The press says as a matter of professional identity, and I myself have said as a journalist, that our business is facts, the public has a right to know them, freedom has a price, we let the chips fall where they may, we are not in the philosophy business. . . . It says, no one got into this business to be loved, weighty reflection about our role is for journalism schools and op-ed pages, not for the reporter and the editor under the gun or on the trail of the next Watergate.[14]

If the fortress disavows "weighty reflection" on the proper task of the press, then this is another way to understand the idea of public journalism. You try to get inside the fortress and bring with you the weightiest terms you can smuggle through: democracy, participation, community, deliberation, public life. You start using these terms in odd or arresting ways, like Buzz Merritt did in a 1995 essay: "Public life,

according to the values of public journalism, requires shared information and shared deliberation; people participate in answering democracy's fundamental question of 'What shall we do?'"[15] Once inside, you
move from the vocabulary of public journalism to the vocation of it:
the real-world experiments and changes in practice that both illustrate
the idea and push it further. Now the thinking has to catch up to the
doing; theory has to accommodate itself to practice. Explain all this as
best you can to audiences in the press who wonder what's going on,
(and maybe don't like the sound of it) and fortress journalism begins
not to crumble but at least to rumble a bit. It reacts, making noises
about public journalism that say a lot about the need for it.

As a kind of action on the culture of the press, public journalism
provoked those inside the fortress to come out and fight—that is, to
fight for their own view of public life and the press. People said the
most remarkable things when they were disapproving of public journalism in the years 1993 to 1997, when it first got going. In a Sunday column on the subject, Max Frankel, the former editor of *The New York
Times,* wrote that although the movement makes some sense as a critique of lazy or sloppy practice, this "hardly justifies a new ideology in
journalism."[16] Remarkable! For what Frankel unwittingly acknowledged
is the existence of an established ideology, which, he implied, was working just fine.

As far as I know this is a first for a former editor of *The New York
Times*: sure, we have an ideology, and we don't need a new one.
Frankel's advice to public journalists was to "leave reforms to the
reformers." As Tom Wolfe might have said back in the days of New
Journalism, "Well, all right!" Frankel has said something provocative
here. He seems willing to disavow the long and glorious history of journalism done in pursuit of political reform—including, say, investigative
reporting's roots in the muckrakers of the early 20th century. Surely
Frankel doesn't mean that. He isn't willing to drop investigative reporting from his idea of heroic journalism. But he's willing to *say* it, "leave
reforms to the reformers," in order put forward a purified vision of the
press as fact finder only, unconcerned with any kind of reform.

Public journalism "helped" Frankel do this. Its emergence on the
radar screen of the press persuaded some in the press to turn thumbs
down on the idea. That was expected, part of the normal give-and-take
of public debate. But in doing so, the doubters put up on the screen
the image of "good journalism" they had in their heads. According to
the man who once ran *The New York Times,* good journalists just tell it
like it is, leaving all thought of reform to the reformers. Really? Is that
what they've always done? These questions can now be asked, which is
the action of the idea at work.

Shortly after Frankel's column appeared, I tried to extend the action. I sent the *Times* magazine a letter, which was not printed. There's nothing sinister about that; the paper prints only a tiny fraction of the mail it gets. So my letter did not become public through the normal route. Here it is, anyway.

To the editor:

Max Frankel's column, "Fix-it Journalism" (May 21), described the reform movement known as "public" or "civic journalism" in a way that suited the author's purposes (curt dismissal) but not the movement itself. Civic journalists, he writes, "want to tell it and fix it all at once." Actually, they want to tell it in a way that allows *communities* to do the fixing, and they don't mind acting as a catalyst or convener if that seems required. What is truly radical about public journalism is something Frankel ignores: the suggestion that journalists are implicated in the sad state our public life has reached, and have a duty to contribute to its repair. While Frankel and others in the elite press resist this message, journalists in places like Wichita, Norfolk and Charlotte are busy revising their routines. "Leave reforms to the reformers," Frankel writes. By doing just that, he forfeits his leadership position in a field that, as he admits, "sorely needs improvement."

One more thing: Frankel says that my own criticism of such "journalistic clichés" as objectivity "hardly justifies a new ideology" in the press. This suggests, intriguingly, an "old" or standard ideology that Frankel wishes to defend. If only he would do so, in terms that address the crisis in our public institutions—including the press. Then we would have a genuine debate.

Well, that was one debate I didn't have. But others did engage *Times* editors on the same point. Moved by a friendly nod to the idea in a book by James Fallows (former Washington editor of *The Atlantic Monthly*), the *Times*'s editorial page editor, Howell Raines, wrote a stinging, signed column, which went even further than Frankel did in denying any political identity to American journalism. The "ethical tradition" that mainstream journalism had developed since World War II "calls on reporters to forswear partisan advocacy, to be indifferent to the fortunes of individual candidates, to be agnostic as to public policy outcomes, to be dogged in the collection of information for its own sake," Raines wrote. Readers are poorly served by reporters who see themselves as "civic stenographers" (his term for public journalists) now "dedicated to promoting worthy policies and well-motivated politicians."[17]

Raines's argument drew an incredulous response from one of his peers, Richard Harwood, a longtime editor at *The Washington Post* who had lived the ethical tradition of mainstream journalism himself. In a column for the *Post*'s op-ed page, Harwood looked dubiously on any view of the press as "agnostic" and "indifferent" toward the outcome of public struggles. Such phrases, he noted, are "well established in the defensive rhetoric newspapers employ when the practices of contemporary journalism are brought into question." He recognized them as features of the fortress. "But if Raines is suggesting that these precepts are faithfully adhered to by the 'mainstream press' and its journalists, then he and I are living on different planets."

Serious about avoiding partisanship, journalists do try to keep their political leanings in check, Harwood said. But no newspaper can operate without "social and community values," which appear "in what it chooses to print and not to print." Howell Raines, a southerner, had made his mark reporting on the civil rights battles in the American South. No doubt Harwood had this in mind when he argued:

> It is simply not credible or intellectually defensible to argue that the reporters and news editors for the networks or for newspapers such as the New York Times were "indifferent" and "agnostic" about the policy outcomes of the civil rights struggles in the South in the 1960s, that they cared nothing about the outcome in Vietnam, or that they care nothing today about the outcomes of the quests of women, homosexuals and other groups for full acceptance in society.

This led him to public journalism, which he called a "work in progress." Who knows if any of it will succeed? "But there is nothing in the movement up to now that is necessarily subversive to good journalism. . . . " Journalists have always esteemed those newspapers that "took on slumlords, worker exploitation, rapacious monopolies and utilities, drug lords, the criminals of Teapot Dome and Watergate." Was this agnosticism? The *Times* itself "has been, in a journalistic sense, a leading patron and arbiter of high culture and the arts." Its "social and political values are easily discerned in its pages." That's not a scandal, Hardwood said. "Those are public-spirited things to do and are not inconsistent with the spirit of 'civic journalism.'"

Consciously or not, he added, critics of the movement often seem to suggest "that the only true and legitimate journalist is a strange species of citizen who betrays himself and his 'calling' if he harbors notions of civic responsibility or cares about the purpose and impact of his work." Fortunately for both journalism and democracy, such creatures are rarely seen, Harwood concluded. The title of his column in the *Post*: "The Legitimacy of 'Civic Journalism.'"[18]

Now here was some good action. The fortress is seen divided

within itself, arguing on its editorial pages not just about civic journalism but about the institution's self-understanding, the view of the press that reigned in its own citadels. The idea thus moved through the Fallows book into the journalism elite's exchanges with itself. And what were these exchanges about? Public life and the press, democracy and the figure of the journalist, the ethical traditions that were supposed to make sense of all this—but which also made barriers to sense, ideological cover for an institution unaccustomed to arguing about such weighty matters.

The Fallows to Raines to Harwood relay also illustrates what I mean by the "adventure" of public journalism. For who knew that this kind of discussion would break out? Personally, I was astonished to see Raines take such a hardened position: journalists as "agnostics." But I was also intrigued when he did, and even more intrigued when his column brought a sharp reply in *The Washington Post*. So if public journalism was an adventure within the press, for those who saw merit in the idea, it was also an adventure *for* the American press, which now had to cope with questions that for too long were the province of professors. Questions like these:

- If there are different ways of thinking about democracy, and each has implications for journalism, what model of democracy should journalists at this moment adopt?
- If journalism at its best addresses us in our capacity as citizens, which forms of journalism do address us that way and which do not?
- If the press is not only an observer of but a participant in our political life, what kind of participant should it be, playing what kind of role?
- What kind of relationship should there be between the political community and the journalists pledged to serve that community if it is not only journalism but also communities that are to thrive?
- And, my personal favorite, what are journalists for, anyway? What do they stand for? And what are they willing to stand up for, or defend, at this troubled moment in American democracy?

Whatever way American journalism decided to cope with these questions became part of the idea of public journalism, one goal of which is to widen the arena in which such questions were asked. For over the years the press had grown accustomed to silence on its fundamental aims and purposes. From the fortress no lively conversation *with* the democracy ensued about the travails of the democracy in which our press is embedded. Along with this distaste for "weighty reflection," a weak spirit of experiment prevailed within a profession that is itself a key part of the American experiment. Journalists did not often put their ideas about democracy, citizenship, and public life at risk, where they might be challenged by others who do not see the scene they way they do. They did not regularly explain to their communities what they were trying to accomplish by doing journalism the way they did it; more typically, they just did what they did, following the rules of their profession, and defined whatever they did as "journalism."[19]

Of course, there was a sense in which we professors did not put our ideas at risk either. We often kept them confined to the campus, to our professional journals and debates, where they faced every kind of challenge except the crucible of public life itself.[20]

Making Ideas Public

To take one prominent example, the work of German philosopher Jürgen Habermas on the "public sphere" has had a long and contentious life among academic critics, most of whom, despite their differences, join in the belief that democracy, the media, and public life could somehow be better. What "better" means they argue about. Or rather, "we" argue about it, for I am one of them. Habermas's idealized but forceful notion of a public sphere—where reason, discussion, and the force of the better argument prevail—has enriched the scholarly fields of social criticism, feminist thought, public opinion research, political theory, and media studies. By drawing students in those fields together, the philosopher's work created its own sphere, which is "public" in certain ways. Habermas and his thinking are open to debate, an item on the floor among a broad group of speakers and listeners, writers and readers, who share an understanding of the work and find many things problematic within it.[21]

Especially since the translation in 1989 of his important book, there has been an "academic public" for Habermas, if such a term makes sense. This public has been busy of late: sifting through the episodes in history where the public sphere could be said to exist, then questioning when it ever existed; conjuring with Habermas's image of a "structural transformation" of the public sphere, then applying it to politics in the media age. For several years now, the Habermas public has been extending, defending, and attacking his thesis, setting itself to task on an expanding agenda for thought—all of which arises from his

powerful book, *The Structural Transformation of the Public Sphere.* This is
how scholars do their work. They get busy debating the issues that
unite and divide them, trying to enrich an already productive body of
thought.

"Productive" for scholars, mostly. There's the fortress coming into
view. Behind its walls—made from language that gets technical and
dense very fast because Habermas himself is a dense and technical
thinker—much progress is made in ventilating Habermas, updating
Habermas, and correcting Habermas; in exposing his weaknesses, realizing his strengths, and reckoning with the work's relevance to our current problems. But whereas this movement of thought is increasingly
"public" in the academy's terms, open to a diverse group of students
and scholars, it is not open to many others outside the institution, who
might conceivably want a taste, if they could understand what was
being said.

The scholar's choice of language is fateful, if not fatal. For me, a
professor of communication with a "field" to master and monitor, getting into the debate over Habermas and the public sphere is well worth
the entry fee. For the fee goes toward a lively and sophisticated discussion, with important results in several scholarly domains. But it also
limits, for scholars, the *field of activity* in which our work gains significance. The universe of fellow inquirers lies within the borders of the
university. One has to master a lot of material, become familiar with
the lingo, to get into the game.

I want to be clear: There is nothing "off" or unworkable about a
scholarly debate in which the terms and references are obscure to
the outsider. This is how knowledge normally progresses when the
knowers in question are other academics. Here, for example, is a passage from an influential critique of Habermas by philosopher and literary theorist Nancy Fraser. In summing up her objections she
writes:

> I have shown that the bourgeois conception of the public sphere, as
> described by Habermas, is not adequate for the critique of the limits of
> actually existing democracy in late capitalist societies. At one level, my
> argument undermines the bourgeois conception as a normative ideal. I
> have shown, first, that an adequate conception of the public sphere
> requires not merely the bracketing, but rather the elimination, of social
> inequality. Second, I have shown that a multiplicity of publics is preferable
> to a single public sphere both in stratified societies and in egalitarian soci-
> eties. Third, I have shown that a tenable conception of the public sphere
> would countenance not the exclusion, but the inclusion, of interests and
> issues that bourgeois masculinist ideology labels "private" and treats as
> inadmissible.[22]

This is scholarship and its peculiar rhetoric at work. Fraser's essay is cogent and useful to others who want to get into the public sphere debate on campus. But they also limit the sphere of that debate—its publicness, as it were—to those who know the terms and can pay the fee. To wit:

- A "bourgeois conception" of the public, present in "late capitalist societies" is said to be inadequate.
- A better conception demands the "inclusion . . . of interests and issues that bourgeois masculinist ideology" leaves out.
- A genuine public sphere requires "not merely the bracketing, but rather the elimination, of social inequality."
- Fraser's argument "undermines" Habermas as a "normative ideal."

Language like this is both exacting in its attempt at theoretical rigor and excluding in its targeted appeal to readers with knowledge of "critical theory," one of the university's specialized domains and political clubs. Plenty of people know how to read and learn from Fraser's careful and suggestive essay, entitled "Rethinking the Public Sphere: A Contribution to the Critique of Actually Existing Democracy." But many others—including people who do practical work in the public sphere—do not.

For one of the results of the scholar's language is the scholar herself. Fraser fashions herself into an academic voice among similar voices; she is inside the fortress, where the public sphere is an issue alive among professors—and also reserved *for* professors by the density of the treatment. Terms such as "bourgeois masculinist ideology," which are common currency in contemporary theory, may have little valence outside it—where, following Fraser, we might locate the "actually existing" public sphere.

Journalists at the *Chicago Tribune*, a short train ride from Northwestern University, where she once taught, would have a hard time joining in the discussion Fraser conducts. But aren't they a part of it? And aren't producers at a public radio station, who "produce" the public sphere in audible form, included as well? What about members of the local League of Women Voters, who erect stages for debates in the public sphere? Or candidates concerned about the amount of money they need to raise to have a chance in the next election? Or citizens who watch as policy issues they care about get "systematically distorted" (Habermas's term) in the public arena or the news media. All these people have a stake in what kind of public sphere actually exists in say,

Chicago, the state of Illinois, or the United States. But academic work on Habermas and the public sphere is not made for their use.

Surely we can recognize this without saying there is anything "wrong" with such work. Its contribution simply lies elsewhere. Sophisticated thinking about the public sphere often works better, advances academic understanding more, when it is dense and theoretical (for the right reasons), when it is grounded in common texts that make for difficult but important reading, when it is committed to political goals such as the lessening of social inequality.

But there's a contribution that Fraser's mode of "rethinking the public sphere" cannot make. I know hundreds of thoughtful journalists concerned about democracy and public life. All of them operate in the American public sphere, such as it is. I barely know one who is well versed in critical theory, has absorbed even the outlines of Habermas's work, or could find the points where their own efforts to cultivate a better climate for public discussion meet up with some of Nancy Fraser's ideas.

Granted, it is unfair of me to pick out one author and one essay. Fraser has plenty of company, which is how it should be in the field of scholarly critics. I count myself among them, having written for an academic audience on the public sphere debate.[23] In 1992, MIT Press published an exciting and overdue collection of essays entitled *Habermas and the Public Sphere.*[24] This volume (which includes Fraser's article and a contribution by our Michael Schudson, one of the voices in this book) is an indispensable source for scholars. But it is not about Habermas *in* the public sphere, for he is not there. Meaning only that his work is not common currency among the public at large, or even that portion of it that is invested in democratic politics and keeps up with current debate in newspapers, magazines, and political talk shows.

And yet in another sense Habermas is "there," in the wider public culture, because his concerns are alive in the debates we have outside the academy. When we argue, as a nation, about campaign finance reform, or the performance of the press, what else are we arguing about but the prospects for the contemporary public sphere in a media-dominated age? But this broader discourse, as it appears on C-SPAN, in *The Washington Post, The Atlantic Monthly*, or National Public Radio, goes on at a considerable remove from our academic work on the same subject: until academic work goes public, that is, which leads me back to "public" journalism, understood now as an idea with academic roots, pulled up and replanted in civic soil outside the academy. To shift backward in my metaphors: Whereas breaking into the fortress of American journalism was one part of the idea's adventure, breaking out of the fortress of "critical theory" was another. For at some point in the academic public's debate about Habermas, a question may be put to the floor: When do we start doing academic work *in* public if what we seek is a better public sphere? How do we bring Nancy Fraser and her concerns to the *Chicago Tribune*, or the *Tribune's* taken-for-granted assumptions about politics, media, and public discussion into the sophisticated world of Habermas and his critics?

Jack Fuller, a former editorial writer and now the publisher of the *Tribune*, wrote a thoughtful and learned book on journalism called *News Values: Ideas for an Information Age*, published in 1996 by the University of Chicago Press.[25] It cites, among others, Plato, Herodotus, Montesquieu, Sigmund Freud, Simone de Beauvoir, and the contemporary philosophers William Barrett and Sissela Bok. As an intellectual and journalist, Fuller moves well beyond the fortress, but not toward Habermas or his interpreters, who certainly have "ideas for an information age." Why should this be?

Well, Habermas and Fraser are tough going, as we might say to undergraduate students in a political science course or master's degree candidates at a journalism school. Indeed, I have said exactly that, "Habermas is tough," to curious newspaper editors who have heard the name dropped. Maybe I was mistaken, but I felt they would get frustrated by the language and lose their appetite for dipping into a difficult literature.

On the other hand, I could often say to them, "Read this piece by James Carey," with some confidence that, if they did, their understanding would deepen in a way that met with their daily work. The journalist's curiosity about "theory," which was real, would be rewarded because Carey's work on the subject, especially the language in which it floats, is sufficiently close to the craft's own manner of thinking and talking that a thoughtful professional can, as we say, get into it.

Consider in this connection Carey's learned treatment of the classic exchange in the 1920s between Walter Lippmann and John Dewey on the nature of the modern public.[26] That debate was a source for Habermas, as Habermas is a source for Carey. And Carey is a good source for journalists—and professors—who want to bring the debate about "the public and its problems" forward to our present environment. The Lippmann to Dewey to Carey relay is capable of being run by people without PhDs, and this is part of what makes it "public" in character. As it turned out, the version of public sphere theory present in Lippmann and Dewey actually made its way into wider and wider arenas as a result of both the ferment surrounding public journalism and journalists who were reading the likes of James Carey.

Arguing about Lippmann and Dewey and the nature of the modern public thus became the business of people in the American press. They did it before an audience of their peers. They did it for a literate but nonacademic readership, the sort who subscribe to the *Atlantic* and buy hardcover books at Barnes & Noble or Borders. They did it for their own communities in the daily newspaper. If we can trace this longer relay of thought—out of the 1920s into Carey's work during our own time, then outward to debates among journalists in the 1990s—we have another opportunity to see the action of the idea unfold. Public journalism, I have been trying to say, *is* this action. And the idea of it should recognize that.

The relay begins with the publication in 1922 of Walter Lippmann's *Public Opinion*, followed by Dewey's response five years later in *The Public and Its Problems*. After languishing in the library for a good portion of the intervening years, this exchange has been interpreted and updated by a host of scholars interested in the press and democratic politics.[27] None has been more effective or persistent than Carey. I will offer an excerpt from one of Carey's treatments, then show how the same tension—between Lippmann's skeptical treatment of the citizen's capacities and Dewey's call to improve those capacities through the enrichment of public culture—has drawn the interest of journalists reflecting on the state of politics and democracy in the 1990s and the proper role of the press. All commented on the Lippmann–Dewey debate, at times by employing the work of Carey. Addressing different audiences in a variety of forums, these journalists went public with what had been an academic discussion. And Dewey and Lippmann went public through them.

Here, then, is Carey on the original exchange:

> Let me summarize Lippmann and Dewey. In Lippmann's view, an effective public opinion exists when the individual minds that make up the public possess correct representations of the world. The newspaper serves its democratic function when it transmits such representations to individual members of the public. An effective public opinion then can be formed as the statistical aggregation of such correct representations. This is at present impossible because of censorship, the limited time and contact available to people, a compressed vocabulary, certain human fears of facing facts, and so on. But the greatest limitation is in the nature of news, which fails to adequately represent, at best signals events, and implants and evokes stereotypes. . . .
>
> Dewey's response takes a number of turns. Public opinion is not formed when individuals possess correct representations of the environment, even if correct representations were possible. It is formed only in discussion, when it is made active in community life. Although news suffers from many of the deficiencies Lippmann cites, its major deficiency is

not its failure to represent. The line between an adequate image and a ste-
reotype is impossible to draw anyway. The purpose of news is not to represent and inform but to signal, tell a story, activate inquiry. Inquiry, in
turn, is not something other than conversation and discussion but a more
systematic version of it. What we lack is the vital means through which
this conversation can be carried on: institutions of public life through
which a public can be formed and can form an opinion. The press, by seeing its role as that of informing the public, abandons its role as an agency
for carrying on the conversation of our culture. We lack not only an effective press but certain vital habits: the ability to follow an argument, grasp
the point of view of another, expand the boundaries of understanding,
debate the alternative purposes that might be pursued.[28]

One journalist who read Lippmann, Dewey, and Carey was Cole
Campbell of *The Virginian-Pilot,* who in 1997 moved on to become editor of the *St. Louis Post Dispatch.* At a 1995 forum on public journalism
sponsored by the Pew Center in Washington, Campbell told his colleagues in the press:

> Four score and minus seven years ago, in 1922 our intellectual father Wal-
> ter Lippmann brought forth his contention, a new notion, skeptical about
> liberty and dubious of the proposition, that all men are equal to the task
> of self-government. Now we are engaged in a great newsroom war—testing
> whether Lippmann's notion or any notion so skeptical and dubious
> should still endure.
>
> Greetings from the *Virginian Pilot,* where circulation is relatively flat
> and profits are strong ... where objectivity is mostly intact and rascals
> still get driven from office by the newspaper, and where the editor is
> humbled daily.
>
> In *Public Opinion,* his seminal work on American media and politics,
> Lippmann declared, "The common interest very largely eludes public
> opinion entirely and can be managed only by a specialized class."
> Lippmann sharpened his view in his 1925 sequel, *The Phantom Public.*
> "Only the insider can make the decision, not because he is inherently a
> better man, but because he is so placed that he can understand and can
> act. The public must be put in its place so that each of us may live free of
> the trampling and the roar of a bewildered herd." ...
>
> Walter Lippmann was a rare presence in American journalism, a
> Harvard-educated intellectual who rose to power as an editor of popu-
> lar publications, including the *New Republic* and the editorial page of
> the *New York World.* ... Even today identification of journalists with
> professionals and insiders, as opposed to citizens, pervades newsroom
> cultures.
>
> Given Lippmann's intellectual legacy and our predilection not to
> reflect on it, there is little wonder many journalists scorn new initiatives
> to connect with citizens as pandering to the public.

This debate began 70 years ago when Lippmann was challenged by his contemporary and intellectual peer, John Dewey. Dewey argued that people talking to each other are capable of attending to common interests and public decisions. Dewey said, "The printed word is a pre-condition of the creation of a truc public, but it is not sufficient. People must engage each other in conversation about issues in the news."

This is the whole debate in a nutshell, according to James Carey of the Columbia School of Journalism. Carey says that: "To Lippmann, the journalist is an eyewitness trying to describe what the insiders are deciding to a passive public whose only real role is to vote the rascals in or out."

To Dewey, the journalist is, at her best, a catalyst of conversation, and insiders and citizens alike are active participants and partners in that conversation. The conversation in the end is the medium of democracy, not newspapers.

So what does all this theory have to do with life in the newsroom of the *Virginian Pilot*? Most fundamentally we believe that vital journalism cannot exist without vital democracy, and that vital democracy cannot exist without vital journalism. . . .

We have learned that, to improve our work and revitalize our craft, we must live in two worlds—the world of ideas and the world of action. We have begun to peel back the layers of our unexamined newsroom ideology to learn what frames our view of public life. We are coming to realize that deliberative democracy may hold more possibilities than representative democracy, and that covering democracy one way can be just as legitimate as covering it another.

We have gone immediately into the field reporting and writing our stories in new ways, not as special projects but as daily field tests. And we have begun to build a deliberative newsroom, where journalists are taking charge of their shared professional destiny.

We have discovered a more powerful kind of accountability, beyond the scared, deer-in-the-headlights, freeze-frame of the expose. We are learning to hold citizens accountable, not only in asking them during conversations to reconcile their beliefs with contradictory evidence, but also asking them to spell out what they believe to be their responsibility for the health of the community.

And we have begun to hold ourselves accountable to our communities by publicly explaining why we're covering stories the way we are. . . .

We have done all this in the pursuit of a big idea that was a gift to us from Davis Merritt, Jr., editor of the *Wichita Eagle*. Buzz Merritt defines a successful community as one in which the people know what's happening and take responsibility for it. This . . . is where a kind of a new idea enters the debate: We're all comfortable as journalists with the first half of that, which is making sure people know what is going on. What is new to us is exploring our role in how we can help people take responsibility for it. We use our story-telling and investigative skills to help citizens know what is going on, but we don't want them to feel like a passive audience or dependent clientele, so we are developing a third set of skills, the skills of conversation, deliberation and frankly democracy to help people take responsibility for what's happening. . . .

I'd like to close with John Dewey, who said something that was very powerful and really hard to get my mind around. In 1916 he said, "Society exists not only by transmission or by communication, but it may fairly be said to exist in transmission or in communication." In other words, our society exists only as we share it with one another, as we transmit its values, communicate its values and what is happening. If that profound thought is true, then I think we, as communicators, have a huge responsibility to reflect upon what our role is in that transmission, in that communication. And I daresay we cannot do it effectively from a detached position.[29]

And here is James Fallows, who, shortly after the publication of *Breaking the News*, left the *Atlantic* to become editor of *U.S. News & World Report*, one of the nation's major newsweeklies. Fallows wrote:

Dewey argued that a healthy *process* of democratic self-government was at least as important as an efficient result. Indeed, he said that unless citizens were actively engaged in the large decisions any society had to make, the results of those decisions would inevitably be flawed.

Therefore, Dewey contended, those in charge of both the government and the press had a responsibility to figure out how to engage the entire public in the decisions that would affect them all in the long run. If the public was confused, alienated, pessimistic, or hostile to government, that was only partly the public's fault. Dewey's work also indicated that the government and the nation's system of transmitting ideas—its educators but also its journalists—had not done their job of involving people in the ongoing process of democratic decision. . . .

Nearly seventy-five years after the appearance of *Public Opinion*, the argument between Lippmann and Dewey is the basic argument about the roles of government and the press. Some parts of Lippmann's analysis have stood up well. What was complicated about science and technology in the early 1920s—when there was no knowledge of DNA, nuclear bombs, or the transistor and the semiconductor chip—is a thousand times more complicated in the late 1990s. . . . Yet from the perspective of the end of the twentieth century, Dewey's analysis seems to hold up better than Lippmann's, and his recommendations are more useful in our times.

Today's journalistic establishment has tried harder to meet Lippmann's challenge—the need for expert accounts of complicated issues— than it has to accommodate Dewey's concern about the impact of journalism on democracy. Reporters operate as experts, or at least insiders, in their field, and they often act as if their real audience is made up of the other reporters or government officials they consider their peers. The system does not work with as much refinement as Lippmann would have hoped, but the public anger at journalism does not arise from the gap between today's journalism and Lippmann's ideal.

Instead, the anger comes from the problem that John Dewey identified: the public's sense that it is not *engaged* in politics, public life, or the discussion that goes on in the press. The media establishment seems to talk *at* people rather than with or even to them. When anchormen travel to the site of a flood or bombing or hurricane, when correspondents do standups from the campaign trail or the White House lawn, they usually seem to be part of a spectacle, competing to hold our attention for a moment, rather than part of a process that would engage us in solving or even considering shared problems.[30]

Now listen to Davis Merritt explain the contemporary relevance of the same debate to readers of *The Wichita Eagle* in a 1996 editor's column:

Many prophetic things were said by both men during their exchanges, but perhaps the most prophetic one given today's political atmosphere came from Dewey. He countered Lippmann's dreary evaluation of the public's potential with a warning: "The very ignorance, bias, frivolity, jealousy, instability which are alleged to incapacitate" ordinary citizens, he wrote, makes them less [likely] to passively submit to rule by a governing elite.

Lippmann's views, however, prevailed for decades, embodied in the reform movement that swept through governmental and social establishments. Experts would take care of things; citizens merely needed to stand by and occasionally decide whether or not they were happy. What happened, however, is that the information developed and possessed by the experts became confused in their minds as superior knowledge, and superior knowledge became misunderstood to be wisdom. A huge disconnect developed between the governing elite and ordinary citizens. . . .

For journalism, the inevitable consequence of Lippmann prevailing in the debate was an almost total, and in most ways calculated, disconnect between journalists and ordinary people.

Many journalists, particularly on the national scene, soon saw themselves as part of the elite, which inevitably disconnected them from ordinary citizens.

Public journalism, a different way of imagining journalism's role in a democracy, seek to repair that disconnect.[31]

Finally, here is E. J. Dionne of *The Washington Post*, a former political reporter (with a PhD from Oxford) who became a regular columnist on the paper's op-ed page. Writing in *They Only Look Dead*, his 1996 book on progressive politics, Dionne brings in Christopher Lasch, another scholar who wrote about Lippmann and Dewey (citing Carey along the way). Dionne observes:

Lippmann was skeptical of democracy because he believed that the citizens making the decisions had little information and little interest in acquiring it. Dewey had a more positive view of democracy precisely because he believed that the public debates democracy fostered helped to create a more enlightened public. As Lasch puts it, following Dewey, "it is only by subjecting our preferences and projects to the test of debate that we come to understand what we know and what we still need to learn." Lasch concludes:

> If we insist on argument as the essence of education, we will defend democracy not as the most efficient but as the most educational form of government, one that extends the circle of debate as widely as possible and thus forces all citizens to articulate their views, to put their views at risk, and to cultivate the virtues of eloquence, clarity of thought and expression, and sound judgment.

Lasch, of course, is describing an ideal to which democracy should strive, not the day-to-day workings of democracy in the United States. But nurturing the educational spirit that ought to lie at the heart of democracy is surely a central task of journalism in a free society. Journalism ought to be where facts, convictions and arguments meet.

With the country passing through a series of crises, journalism's primary task ought to be to engage citizens in the quest for paths forward. That will involve understanding the alternatives and weighing them for their faithfulness not only to the facts but also to the values and moral commitments that supposedly underlie them. It involves debate experienced not simply as combat but also as conversation. In this telling, journalism's role of providing information is only the *beginning* of its task. As James Carey puts it, "The press, by seeing its role as that of informing the public, abandons its role as an agency for carrying on the conversation of our culture." The press and television must find ways of keeping the public informed without shutting the conversation down or closing it off to all but the most inside of political insiders.[32]

Here, then, is an idea—actually a cluster of ideas—*becoming more public* as it moves out of academic circles into a wider sphere of discussion. This is precisely what happened to public journalism. But it is also happened because of public journalism, which recommended Carey, Lippmann, and Dewey to journalists seeking to redescribe the task of the press. Thus, Cole Campbell drew on the debate from the 1920s to explain what he and his staff were doing in Norfolk. (His remarks came at a conference where E. J. Dionne also spoke.) Fallows used the same exchange to introduce his book's discussion of public journalism—which in turn led to dueling views on the editorial pages of *The New York Times* and *The Washington Post*. Merritt told readers in Wichita what two thinkers from another era said about the press and public life, trying, like Campbell, to illuminate the aims of public journalism. Dionne then entered into the debate, employing Carey's work while touching on the central ideas in public journalism ("journalism's primary task ought to be to engage citizens in the quest for paths forward") without employing the term itself.

Note also how the different forms of publication in this climate of thought—scholarly articles, book chapters, editorial pages, a newspaper editor's column, the printed proceedings of a journalism conference—represent different public forums in a widening sphere of activity, which is more of what I mean by the action of the idea. That action helped bring "public journalism" into built form. What emerged was a lively, intelligent, and contemporary discussion that was not exclusively academic in orientation. Journalists (and, presumably, their readers) could join in because the language and entry fee were not so forbidding. Such an approach has its strengths and weaknesses, of course. Whatever may be lost in conceptual rigor or scholarly depth is offset by the greater "publicness" of the Lippmann to Dewey to Carey to journalism relay.

I would not leap to judge the gains as necessarily greater than the losses. That is something scholars can and should argue about. But if we are going to get a fix on public journalism, we should be willing to locate the idea in one of its more successful forms: an occasion for bringing debates about democracy, citizens, and the press out of the academy and into the mind of the craft, to encourage more thoughtful reflection on journalism's civic purpose—thus bringing journalists into the "philosophy business," as Michael Janeway called it.

With public journalism's appearance in built form, Lippmann and Dewey and Carey were now "in" the actually existing public sphere, alive among members of the working press, in a way that Jürgen Habermas and Nancy Fraser were not. This is not to say that Fraser and Habermas can't be taken public themselves. Perhaps one day they will be. If it happens it will be a welcome event—and, I have tried to suggest, a scholarly event, for it will require the synthesis of a third language, not the vocabulary of "critical theory" or the discourse we hear on C-SPAN but an intelligent passage found between the two.

Time to sum up. Public journalism is an idea that happened, I have said. It happened in a variety of ways. In this variety lies the scholarly, as well as the practical, significance of the idea. Indeed, the proposition that scholarly work is "practical"—and doable—for journalists is just one part of the idea. I have identified some others:

- Public journalism as a fivefold enterprise: an argument, an experiment, a movement, a debate, and a kind of adventure within the American press.

- The roots it claimed in academic exchanges from the 1920s to the 1990s.
- The journalists who contributed ideas and experiments to a widening field of activity, which touched their staffs, their peers, and their communities.
- The other institutions, themselves a part of the public sphere, that got involved: foundations, think tanks, civic associations, professional groups, etc.
- The journalism that was done about public journalism, revealing some of the habits and controlling metaphors the idea was intended to challenge.
- The debates that sprang up among journalists, and inside the citadels of the elite press, as public journalism became more widely known and people took a position on it.
- The mutual breakdown of "fortress journalism," a product of craft culture, and the academic fortress in which public sphere theory resided, an outcome of the university's preferred ways of knowing.

To understand the idea in "built form" is to look at all these items as load-bearing features, to continue the architectonic imagery. Some were design elements; others just happened at the edifice evolved. The "just happened" part is the adventure story I have tried to tell. If we incorporate all this action into the abstraction, then we emerge with a different view of what public journalism is "about." An alternative definition to the one I offered at the outset of this chapter would thus go something like this:

> Public journalism is a way of thinking about the business of the craft that calls on journalists, those who study democracy, politics and the media, and others who enter into public life to imagine a different kind of press, one that would: (1) address people as citizens, potential participants in public affairs, rather than victims or spectators; (2) help the political community act upon, rather than just learn about, its problems; (3) improve the climate of public discussion, rather than simply watch it deteriorate; (4) help make public life go well, so that it earns its claim on our attention and (5) speak honestly about its civic values, its preferred view of politics, its role as a public actor. If we can all find a way to act upon our hope for such a journalism; if we can air both our thoughts and our convictions in public settings, using a public language, and welcoming public debate, then we may in time restore our own confidence in the press as an instrument of democracy and democracy as the instrument of a free people.

In the difference between my first and second definitions of public journalism is "the action of the idea." This action leads outward from distinct and isolated cultures—in journalism, in politics, in the university, in civic life generally—toward a richer public culture, a shared world of concerns alive with intelligent talk, promising experiment, cooperative learning, genuine debate, and the possibility of reform.

Not a journalism for journalists but our hope for another kind, imagined by democrats for other democrats, is the idea of public journalism in its most potent—and most public—form.

Notes

1. On Arendt's understanding of action see Hannah Arendt, *The Human Condition* (Chicago: University of Chicago Press, 1988), p. 177; on action versus behavior see Ch. 6 of the same work. On Arendt's notion of "natality" see Margaret Canovan, *The Political Thought of Hannah Arendt* (London: Dent, 1974), pp. 58-59, 74.

2. See John Dewey, *The Public and Its Problems* (New York: Holt, 1927); James W. Carey, "The Press and the Public Discourse," *The Center Magazine* (March 1987): 4-16, and "The Press, Public Opinion and Public Discourse," pp. 373-402 in *Public Opinion and the Communication of Consent*, eds. Theodore L. Glasser and Charles T. Salmon (New York: Guilford Press, 1995); Clifford G. Christians, John P. Ferré, P. Mark Fackler, *Good News: Social Ethics and the Press* (New York: Oxford University Press, 1993); Theodore L. Glasser, "Communication and the Cultivation of Citizenship," *Communication*, 12 (1991): 235-247; Michael Schudson, *The Power of News* (Cambridge, MA: Harvard University Press, 1995), p. 222; Edmund B. Lambeth, *Committed Journalism: An Ethic for the Profession* (Bloomington: Indiana University Press, 1986); Rob Anderson, Robert Dardenne, and George Killenberg, *The Conversation of Journalism* (Westport, CT: Praeger, 1994), p. xx; emphasis removed.

3. On the initiatives in Wichita and Charlotte see John Bare, "Wichita and Charlotte: The Leap of a Passive Press to Activism," *Media Studies Journal,* 6 (1992): 149-160; Michael Hoyt, "The Wichita Experiment," *Columbia Journalism Review (July/August 1992): 43-47; Edward D. Miller, The Charlotte Project: Helping Citizens Take Back Democracy* (St. Petersburg, FL: Poynter Institute for Media Studies, 1994); Steve Smith, "Your Vote Counts: *The Wichita Eagle's* Election Project," *National Civic Review*, 80 (1991): 24-30. On Iggers and the Minnesota Roundtables, see Jeremy Iggers, "Minnesota's Talking: Readers Asked to Take Part in Issue Discussions," *Star-Tribune* September 1, 1992, pp. 1E-2E. On the Wisconsin "We the People" project, see Frank Denton and Esther Thorson, *Civic Journalism: Does It Work?* (Washington, DC: Pew Center for Civic Journalism, 1995); Jay Rosen, *Getting the Connections Right: Public Journalism and the Troubles in the Press* (New York: Twentieth Century Fund, 1996), pp. 52-54; Jan Schaffer and Edward D. Miller, eds., *Civic Journalism: Six Case Studies* (Washington, DC: Pew Center for Civic Journalism, 1995), pp. 12-21; on the public life team in Norfolk, see "Civic Journalism: Can Press Reforms Revitalize Democracy?" *CQ*

Researcher, 35,6 (September 1996): 822–823; Jay Rosen, "Public Journalism as a Democratic Art," pp. 10–11 in *Public Journalism, Theory and Practice: Lessons from Experience* eds. Jay Rosen, Davis Merritt, and Lisa Austin (Dayton, OH: Kettering Foundation, 1997).

4. On the Kettering discussions and the origins of the Project on Public Life and the Press, see Jay Rosen, "Making Things More Public: On the Political Responsibility of the Media Intellectual," *Critical Studies in Mass Communication,* 11 (1994): 363–388. On the Poynter Institute's work with *The Charlotte Observer,* see Miller, *The Charlotte Project.* On the Pew Center for Civic Journalism, see G. Bruce Knecht, "Why a Big Foundation Gives Newspapers Cash to Change Their Ways," *Wall Street Journal,* October 17, 1996, p. A1; "Civic Journalism: Can Press Reforms Revitalize Democracy?" *CQ Researcher,* 35,6 (September 1996): 831–832; see also various issues of the Center's newsletter, *Civic Catalyst,* starting in December 1994 (Washington, DC: Pew Center for Civic Journalism).

5. Alicia C. Sheppard, "The Gospel of Public Journalism," *American Journalism Review* (September 1994): 28–34; Michael Gartner, "Give Me Old-Time Journalism," *Quill* (November/December 1995): 66, 68–69; Rosemary Armao's remarks came at the Investigative Reporters and Editors Annual Conference, Miami, FL, June 8–11, 1995, during a panel entitled, "Public Journalism: Death or Savior for American Newspapers?"; "The Color of Mendacity," *New York Times,* July 19, 1996, p. A26.

6. *Civic Journalism and Local Government* (Washington, DC: International City/County Management Association, 1997); *National Civic Review,* 85,1 (Winter/Spring 1996); Cole C. Campbell, "League Takes Us at Our Word: Studies Our Effort to Serve Citizens Better," *Virginian-Pilot,* June 18, 1995, p. A2; Rob Elder, "Affirmative Reaction," *San Jose Mercury News,* October 22, 1995, p. 7F.

7. On this general point see Rosen, "Making Things More Public" and "Public Journalism: A Case for Public Scholarship," *Change* (May/June, 1995): 34–38. For an example of public discussion of the idea, see "Civic Journalism: Is Good Journalism or Pandering to the Public?," *The James K. Batten Symposium on Civic Journalism and Award for Excellence in Civic Journalism* (Washington, DC: Pew Center for Civic Journalism, 1995).

8. For two examples of scholarly treatment, see Edward B. Lambeth, "The News Media and Democracy," *Media Studies Journal,* 6 (1992): 161–175; Edward B. Lambeth and David Craig, "Civic Journalism as Research," *Newspaper Research Journal,* 7 (1995): 149–160.

9. For examples of trade journal and press review treatment, see Tony Case, "Public Journalism Denounced," *Editor and Publisher* (November 12, 1994): 14–15; Michael Hoyt, "Are You Now, or Will You Ever Be a Civic Journalist?" *Columbia Journalism Review* (September/October 1995): 27–33; Alicia C. Sheppard, "The Gospel of Public Journalism," *American Journalism Review* (September 1994): 28–34.

10. On the role of foundations, see Knecht, "Why a Big Foundation Gives Newspapers Cash to Change Their Ways," and the Winter 1992 issue of *Kettering Review,* published by the Kettering Foundation. On the interest of

other civic organizations, see, for example, "Rethinking Journalism and Rebuilding Civic Life," *National Civic Review*, 85 (1996); "Rebuilding Communities," *National Voter*, 45 (1995).

11. This passage is drawn from my introduction to *Speaking of Public Journalism: Talks from the Project on Public Life and the Press Seminars at the American Press Institute, 1993–1997* (Dayton, OH: Kettering Foundation, 1997), p. iii. On "infuse the means with the spirit of the end," see *Speaking of Public Journalism*, p. 80.

12. Christians, Ferré, and Fackler, *Good News*, p. 53.

13. Martin Linsky, "The Media and Public Deliberation," in ed. Robert Reich *The Power of Public Ideas* (Cambridge, MA: Harvard University Press, 1988), p. 211.

14. Michael Janeway, "The Press and Privacy: Rights and Rules," pp. 129–130, in *The Morality of the Mass Media*, ed. W. Lawson Taitte (Dallas: University of Texas at Dallas, 1993).

15. Davis Merritt, "Public Journalism—Defining a Democratic Art," *Media Studies Journal*, 9 (Summer 1995): 131.

16. Max Frankel, "Fix-It Journalism," *New York Times Magazine*, May 21, 1995, p. 28.

17. See James Fallows, *Breaking the News: How the News Media Undermine American Democracy* (New York, Pantheon, 1996), Chap. 6; Howell Raines, "The Fallows Fallacy," *New York Times*, February 25, 1996, sec. 4, p. 14.

18. Richard Harwood, "The Legitimacy of 'Civic Journalism'," *Washington Post*, March 8, 1996, p. A21.

19. On these themes, see Jay Rosen, "Losing the Thing You Love: Six Lessons about Change from an Inside–Outsider," pp. 8–13 in *Change: Living It, Embracing It, Measuring It* (Reston, VA: American Society of Newspaper Editors, 1997), 8–13; and Steve Smith, "Getting Down and Dirty with the Critics," *Civic Catalyst* (Washington, DC: Pew Center for Civic Journalism, January 1997), p. 3.

20. On this point, see Jay Rosen, "Making Things More Public: On the Political Responsibility of the Media Intellectual," *Critical Studies in Mass Communication* 11 (1994): 363–370.

21. See Jürgen Habermas, *The Structural Transformation of the Public Sphere*, Thomas Burger with Fredrick Lawrence, trans. (Cambridge, MA: MIT Press, 1989). See also two collections—*Habermas and the Public Sphere*, ed. Craig Calhoun (Cambridge, MA: MIT Press, 1992), and *The Phantom Public Sphere*, ed. Bruce Robbins (Minneapolis: University of Minnesota Press, 1993)—for a range of views on Habermas; and John Durham Peters, "Distrust of Representation: Habermas on the Public Sphere," *Media, Culture and Society*, 15,4 (1993): 541–571, for a view from a communication scholar.

22. Nancy Fraser, "Rethinking the Public Sphere: A Contribution to the Critique of Actually Existing Democracy," *The Phantom Public Sphere*, pp. 26–27. Originally published in *Habermas and the Public Sphere*.

23. See Jay Rosen, "Making Journalism More Public," *Communication*, 12,4 (1991): 267–284.

24. *Habermas and the Public Sphere.*
25. Jack Fuller, *News Values: Ideas for an Information Age* (Chicago: University of Chicago Press, 1996).
26. See, for example, James W. Carey, "The Press and the Public Discourse," *The Center Magazine* (March 1987): 4–16; James W. Carey, *Communication as Culture* (Boston: Unwin Hyman, 1989), Chap. 3; James W. Carey, "A Republic, If You Can Keep It," pp. 108–128 in *Crucible of Liberty: 200 Years of the Bill of Rights,* ed. Raymond Arsenault (New York: Free Press, 1991); James W. Carey, "The Press, Public Opinion and Public Discourse," in *Public Opinion and the Communication of Consent,* pp. 373–402.
27. Public Opinion (1922) (New York: Free Press, 1965); John Dewey, *The Public and Its Problems* (New York: Henry Holt, 1927). For some thoughtful interpretations, see Christopher Lasch, "The Lost Art of Argument," *The Revolt of the Elites and the Betrayal of Democracy* (New York: Norton, 1995), Ch. 9; John Durham Peters, "Democracy and American Mass Communication Theory: Dewey, Lippmann and Lazarsfeld," *Communication,* 11,3 (1989): 199–220; John Durham Peters, Revising the 18th-Century Script," *Gannett Center Journal,* 3,2 (Spring 1989): 152–167; Alan Ryan, *John Dewey and the High Tide of American Liberalism* (New York: Norton, 1995), pp. 201–218; Michael Schudson, *Discovering the News: A Social History of American Newspapers* (New York: Basic Books, 1978), pp. 122–134; Robert Westbrook, *John Dewey and American Democracy* (Ithaca: Cornell University Press, 1991), pp. 294–319.
28. James W. Carey, *Communication as Culture* (Boston: Unwin Hyman, 1989), pp. 81–82.
29. Campbell's remarks are in *The James K. Batten Symposium,* p. 22.
30. James Fallows, *Breaking the News: How the News Media Undermine American Democracy* (New York, Pantheon, 1996), pp. 237–238, 240.
31. Davis Merritt, "Democracy From the Bottom Up," *Wichita Eagle,* October 27, 1996, p. 23.
32. E. J. Dionne, *They Only Look Dead: Why Progressives Will Dominate the Next Political Era* (New York: Simon & Schuster, 1996), pp. 258–259. See also Christopher Lasch, "The Lost Art of Argument," *The Revolt of the Elites and the Betrayal of Democracy* (New York: Norton, 1995), Chap. 9.

Chapter 3

In Defense of Public Journalism

James W. Carey

Columbia University

The years since World War II have seen a number of efforts to reform American journalism. Public journalism is the first such effort to assume the shape of a social movement with a semblance of formal organization. Although normally suspicious of "movements," I remain a strong supporter of public journalism. The movement is not beyond criticism, but my intent here is not criticism. For the moment criticism is beside the point. In these unsettled times we do not have the luxury of standing by while commitments shaping the future of journalism are being made in both professional societies and corporate offices. Efforts at reform are, in the main, deserving of support, and public journalism needs defense against the two tendencies aimed at undermining those efforts. The most dangerous and pervasive is the attempt, true to the conservative temper of our times, to commit journalism to a naked "market model" in which all standards of practice are sacrificed to profit and "shareholder value." Here is one expression, from Stuart Garner, the president and chief executive officer of Thomson Newspapers, among many that might be cited:

> It is my utter conviction that newspapers are a business and, since their production is a team process, no department can be immune from the fact. They are expensive to equip and run and the only way to ensure their future is to make a healthy profit. For us that means an overall 20% profit margin. . . . Shareholders have to get good return on their investment and we do not want them to feel they could do better putting their funds elsewhere.[1]

The remarks are unexceptional, but they nakedly express a reversal of normal expectations. We used to believe that newspapers, for example, needed to make a profit to serve a public interest. In Garner's view, "public interest" and the rights and prerogatives that flow from it merely establish conditions for competition and the framework for maximizing profits. But if newspapers are solely a business, why do they need protection under the First Amendment, protections greater than those afforded other commercial enterprises? The Supreme Court, upholding the rights of journalists in case after case and simultaneously broadening the reach of protection for the press, has consistently justified such decisions not because newspapers are businesses but because they perform a public or civic function: to provide a check on the state and, more frequently, to constitute the conditions of democratic debate and discussion. Those who believe the market is the sole test of journalism also believe that the authority of professional practice is guaranteed by serving the needs of consumers. However, the link between the market and civic functions of journalism is merely circumstantial and, in every case, temporary. Furthermore, the rhetoric of markets has seeped so deeply into the rhetoric of journalism that it is becoming impossible to understand journalism in anything other than economic terms. Under this dispensation, the representative figure in journalism is no longer the citizen but the consumer, not the reporter or even the publisher but the shareholder.

The second resistance to reform is defense of the sanctity of traditional practice against any effort to alter it in light of contemporary politics and culture. Michael Gartner's blunt defense of historic practice, speaking at an annual meeting of the Society of Professional Journalists, is atypical only in its candor:

> Newspapers are supposed to explain the community, not convene it. News reporters are supposed to explore the issues not solve them. Newspapers are supposed to expose the wrongs, not campaign against them. Reporters and city editors are not supposed to write legislation or lead campaigns or pass moral judgments. They're supposed to tell the truth. And God knows that's hard enough to do all by itself.[2]

Again, the comment is unexceptional except that it denies everything journalists do. Can anyone seriously claim, given the heroic place of Watergate in the history of the press, that journalists do not convene and constitute communities of judgment, sort out virtue from vice, campaign against wrongs, pass moral judgments, direct the community toward needed legislation, and, incidentally, tell the truth along the way? Gartner here supports what Michael Schudson calls a trustee model of journalism.[3] Journalists "own" the First Amendment in the name of a "public" incapable of exercising its own prerogatives. As such, journalists decide what part of politics needs demystification, which institutions require reform, which truths need to be told while denying both their intentions and their deeds.

By contrast, and with all its limitations, public journalism represents an attempt to be honest about the role of journalists in contemporary life, to bring journalists into the "conversation of the culture," to align the ideology of journalists with the role they actually play among us. It recognizes that democracy is the sine qua non of journalism. Without journalism there is no democracy, but without democracy there is no journalism either. Against both the marketeers and trustees, public journalism claims as its first task the necessity of making public life possible and cultivating an ethic of citizenship rather than cults of information and markets. If that were all, one might dismiss public journalism as just another attempt, idealistic and well intentioned, at reform. But it is more, for the movement contains a particular understanding of the "actually existing conditions" with which journalism must deal.

Journalism and Politics

Let us approach the defense of public journalism, at the outset at least, in a formal and more or less theoretical way. Among the useful and instructive lessons taught us by Charles Darwin is the admonition to think ecologically: think always about the relations among species rather than treat them in isolation. All elements in the living world exist by complex modes of adaptation to an existing environment including species inhabiting common terrain. This admonition encourages attention to the complex spatial and temporal relations among species. To reduce this all to a slogan, it leads to this rule: Whenever you come upon a flower with a long stem, look for an insect with an extended proboscis as its adaptive partner. If we apply that metaphor to our subject—politics and journalism—the lesson is clear. Journalism and politics cannot be "thought" as two separate independent domains of activity. Rather, they are related actively, symbiotically; they can only be known via their mutual and active adaptations which are cooperative and antagonistic by turns; one can only be known in the light of the other.

To put this more formally, but without much distortion, every conception and practice of politics is simultaneously a conception of journalism and every conception of journalism is simultaneously a conception of politics. Democracy, for example, is constituted by particular media of communication and forms of expression through which politics is conducted: speech and the agora, the colonial newspaper and the precincts and taverns of Philadelphia, the omnibus daily and political parties in a national society, the television news report and the private home in an imperial nation. Similarly, a medium of communication is defined by the democratic aspiration of politics: a conversation among equals, the organ of political ideology, a watchdog on the state, an instrument of dialogue on public issues, a device for transmitting the information and propaganda of interest groups. These options are not in every case mutually exclusive, but the patterns of adaptation once formed are not easily broken because of their symbiosis.

To belabor the point: Politics takes many particular institutional forms, as does the practice of journalism. However, journalism and politics are always formed by mutual adaptation such that what we mean by democracy depends on the forms of journalism through we conduct politics; what we mean by journalism depends on the central impulses and aspirations of democratic politics.[4]

I put the matter this way because many journalists seem to believe that the press and politics are "things" independent of one another, governed by their own distinctive principles, not only antagonistic but estranged. I want to emphasize in contrast a mutual adaptation, a particular symbiosis between the press and politics, with which we have been living for the past 100 years. The challenge of the moment is that the symbiosis is breaking up, has been for the past 30 years or so, and nothing has adequately filled the resulting void. That is what gives a special urgency to public journalism, for something will fill this void and it would be nice to ensure that it be supportive of democratic politics. There are no guarantees, however. As Ralf Dahrendorf recently argued, when economic values dominate politics, as in the market model, "liberty is often at risk. The new economism of capitalists is no less illiberal than the old one of Marxists."[5] The tendency of the market model is toward authoritarianism, and the simple reassertion of trustee journalism will not provide a counterforce for the conditions supporting such journalism have evaporated. This has been apparent since the 1960s but is particularly evident in the years since the end of the Cold War.

We are not, let me quickly add, living in an "imaginative proximity to revolution," to adapt or misadapt Perry Anderson's clever phrase. But it is no longer business as usual; we are not practicing "normal journalism" but looking for the abnormal in practice. A while back Richard Harwood of *The Washington Post* reminded his readers: "We [journalists] tend to believe that our concepts and definitions of news and good newspapering were divinely inspired yet there are volumes of evidence suggesting that the people live on different planets so far as their interests and values as concerned."

Two things are important in this modest quotation: first, Harwood's admission that journalistic practices are not divinely inspired, are not embroidered into the genetic code of the craft. Rather, these practices come into existence at a particular historic moment as an adaptation, an attempt, unavailing or not, to deal with the particular problems of particular times. The practices so adapted generate in turn self-understandings among journalists: images journalists have of themselves and their craft. Because the culture of a group is as recalcitrant to change as the psychology of individuals, these self-understandings—these stories journalists tell themselves about themselves—hang on long after the originating conditions that gave rise to them have disappeared. Shorn from their historical origins, these practices seem to be preternatural, and to abandon them seems like an invitation to abandon the craft entirely. In other words, one has to convince journalists there is another way to practice the craft, consistent with their skills and interests, but better adapted to prevailing conditions of politics and contemporary life.

The second thing of importance in Harwood's quote is the admission of a third term to the equation: It is not only the press and politics that is formed symbiotically but the public as well. Press, public, and politics mutually constitute one another; they create spaces and roles in relation to one another, and, when any of the parties opts of the symbiosis, it necessarily breaks up. My contention is that a particular symbiosis, let us call it the modern one, has broken up because at least two of the parties have drifted away: The press has, as noted above, increasingly opted for a purely economic definition of its mission. The public has largely given up the entire enterprise as bootless and drifted off in either private life or in search of a new politics. The only question that remains is this: What will now replace the old synthesis of interest group politics, a watchdog press, and a spectator public? Some history might help us formulate an answer.

The Promise of Modern Journalism

Depending on whether we wish to emphasize origins or endings, we can describe the period between approximately 1890 and 1968 as the era of modern journalism. Both Jay Rosen and Michael Schudson call the form of journalism practiced during this period "trustee journalism," the spirit of which is expressed on a plaque presented to the

National Press Club in Washington on the occasion of its 50th anniversary:

> I believe in the profession of journalism. I believe that the public journal is a public trust; that all connected with it are, to the full measure of their responsibility, trustees for the public; that acceptance of a lesser service than public service is a betrayal of that trust.

Trustee journalism gradually replaced the partisan journalism that had been typical of the American press since the formation of political parties early in the republic. Under the partisan model, journalists gave expression to the ideology of political factions and pursued the interest of those factions. Partisan newspapers steadily loosened their ties to political parties during the 19th century and became increasingly dependent on circulation and advertising revenue (rather than political subsidies—direct or indirect) without loosening commitments to the ideology of parties as the basis of professional practice. Today when journals of opinion and faction—*The National Review, The American Spectator, The Nation, The American Prospect, Dissent, The New Republic*— are charitable institutions that exist only by generous benefaction, it is hard to remember that ideological papers could be profitable. Partisan journalism gave rise, nonetheless, to a faction-ridden public sphere, though one not to be despised on that account. The break from partisan to trustee journalism was, like most such breaks, overdetermined, but it is worth mentioning in passing one such cause.

During the period of reconstruction, race was a principal battleground of partisan politics. The Republican party was heavily dependent on the vote of newly enfranchised blacks in the southern states which formed the basis of its electoral support. Democrats, on the other hand, had an interest in diminishing the importance of black votes and voters. Partisan journalism featured, then, the vitriol of race. The "race card," and with it an undermining of confidence in the capacity of black citizens, was central to the electoral strategy of Democrats and it introduced into the iconography of American politics racial images—the feckless Negro and the kindly white benefactor—with which we have been living ever since. Trustee journalism, then, was in part a revolt against a public sphere polluted with poisonous stereotypes and racial antagonisms that passed all boundaries of reason and sympathy.[6]

There were, of course, good economic reasons for abandoning partisan journalism in search of a wider, less ideologically polarized reading audience. But what were the practices enshrined in trustee journalism? First, trustee journalism involved a declaration of independence, not independence from society but independence from political parties. Journalists aligned themselves with the "progressive movement" in the way Michael Schudson suggests: a shared antipathy to political parties and to conventional partisanship.[7] The road to truth and progress was no longer to be sought through ideological confrontation but by application of the methods of systematic inquiry and reporting to discover a truth beyond partisanship. Let me emphasize again: This was not only a declaration of independence from party politics but a declaration of allegiance to the independent voter, to the progressive movement, and to a public good realized through impartial inquiry. The press not only sided with the independent voter but thought of itself as the independent voter writ large: Someone who, despite a leaning toward one party or the other, would listen with a relatively unbiased mind to all arguments, search out information necessary to resolving disputes, and cast allegiance to whatever option the political system offered that was closer to the truth and in line with the requisites of progress so understood.

At the level of practice, trustee journalism gave rise to two characteristic forms of expression that always have been in uneasy tension and frequent contradiction. The first was "muckraking," which in its initial stages directed its attack against the "plutocracy" and the business class. Muckraking forged a tradition of journalism that took as its task the unmasking of power: to serve as a watchdog not only of the state but of the full range of interest groups which progressively displaced political parties as the major instrument of politics. It was a distinctively American form of journalism in a number of ways. First, muckraking was framed within the language of American democracy; that is, muckrakers took themselves to be representative of the people—protectors of the people's interests and not an independent, *avant garde,* intellectual class. Second, muckraking was straightforward, descriptive, and aimed at provoking public action rather than theoretical reflection. Third, although they aimed their efforts at unmasking the power of the business class, economic institutions, and business ideology, muckrakers examined concentrated power and propaganda in all its forms: labor unions as well as manufacturers' associations, universities, and businesses.

Muckraking eventually took up residence in newspapers, indeed in all journalistic media, under the banner of investigative reporting. But true to its origins, investigative reporting was not merely factual reporting but a form of moral discourse. It sought out wrongdoing and, therefore, had to have standards of right and wrong which it more or less adopted wholesale from the progressive movement. It attempted to empower the citizen against the "interests." It attempted to expose the wickedness of political machines and forms of graft and patronage in which they specialized. Eventually, in our own time, it attempted to expose moral laxity in general and supported strict standards of public and private behavior, even standards which journalists themselves regularly contradicted.

The second practice systematically instituted in modern journalism was the beat system, and this gave rise to the canons of objective reporting and a more continuous and systematic politics: the politics of daily life rather than the extraordinary event. Whereas investigative journalism, in principle at least, uncovered corruption in all institutions, beat reporting provided the daily journalistic watchdog of government. Reporters were stationed as listening posts at all the major institutions of the state: city hall, the courts, the police department, the school and sanitary boards, the party and campaign headquarters, wherever, in short, there were "public authorities." The beat system was a shadow map of government designed to produce an authoritative record of government activity beyond the official transcript supplied by the state itself. This record gave daily continuity to a life in politics and generated, in principle, the information by which citizens could evaluate public performance. Although there were other sections to the newspaper—sports, business, the arts—they were not places of real journalism for they uneasily mixed the press release and public relations with the news of these sectors. Together, the adversary and the watchdog were representative metaphors of modern journalism and produced by way of adaptation the characteristic practices of government: the handout and press release, public information and public relations officers, spin and stonewalling (a process in which the state erected ever more elaborate curtains behind which to practice interest group politics and journalists tried ever more assiduously to penetrate the veil).

This is the setting in which the traditions of modern journalism, particular conceptions of the media, democracy, and the public, formed themselves in mutual relief to the political state. The press, in effect, broke away from politics. It established itself, at least in principle, as independent of all institutions: independent of the state, independent of political parties, independent of interest groups. It became, as I said, the independent voter writ large; its only loyalty was to an abstract truth and an abstract public interest. In this rendition, a democratic press was the representative of the people, of people no longer represented by political parties and the state itself. It was the eyes and ears of a public that could not see and hear for itself or indeed talk to itself. It went where the public could not go, acquired information that the public could not amass on its own, tore away the veil of appearances that masked the play of power and privilege, set on a brightly lit stage what would otherwise be contained off stage, in the wings, where the real drama of political life was going on unobserved. The press seized hold of the First Amendment and exercised it in the name of a public that could no longer exercise it itself. The press became an independent profession and a collective institution: a true fourth estate that watched over the other lords of the realm in the name of those unequipped or unable to watch over it for themselves. Inevitably trustee journalism focused on the powers of the press rather than on the prerogatives of the public. Journalists would serve as agents of the public in checking an inherently abusive government. To empower it to fulfill such a role, the press had to possess special rights to gather news. Thus under the fourth estate model, a free press was equated with a powerful press possessing special privileges of news gathering.[8]

There was a downside to modern journalism, however. Ultimately the public became a passive observer in the theater state of politics. The public had to do no more than keep itself informed and exercise its power now and again in elections. The public was an observer of the press rather "participators in the government of affairs" and the dialogue of democracy. The active roles were reserved for the state, the press, and interest groups. The role of the citizen was not to participate in the formation of politics but to become a member of a veto group restraining decisions once they passed a certain boundary: a boundary marked by the investigative work of the press. The image of an active and continuous public of involved citizens fails to describe not only the reality of American politics but even a desirable state of affairs. The public's participation in politics was not protected beyond the periodic extension of the franchise; rather, it was the press that was the protected party. The individual citizen was seen as remote and helpless compared to the two major protagonists—government and the media.

The view of the press as the representative of the public and the effectiveness of its watchdog and adversary roles could only be sustained if the following conditions were met: (1) The public had to believe the press was authentically their representative and therefore in a responsible and fiduciary relation to it; (2) the public had to believe that the press was not in cahoots with the state, with the most powerful interest groups, or both; and (3) the public had to believe that the press was capable of representing the world, that is, of rendering a reasonable, unbiased, true, and factual account of it. In all these senses of "represent," the press and the state have been found wanting and the public has decided, for reasons both good and bad, that the game is not worth the candle.

My argument, then, is not that modern journalism was a failure; in fact, it was a resounding success and it served the country well during the major political crises—Depression, World War II, the Cold War, Vietnam, Watergate—of the modern era. Modern journalism was well adapted to the conditions that gave rise to it, met the major challenges on modern politics, and was deserving of all the protection the Supreme Court awarded it. But, like most things in life, it was undermined by its own success. To effectively resist the power of the modern state and deal with the conditions of the modern economy, the press had to effectively aggrandize its own size and power. To effectively represent the public, it had to increasingly distance itself from the very public it was representing. As a result, there have been periodic attempts over the last 50 years to reform it. The first reform effort came as a report on *A Free and Responsible Press,* by the Hutchins Commission.[9] The report was primarily aimed at the increased concentration of the press that was product of the rise of broadcasting. The organizations of broadcasting, primarily the radio and television networks, and the growth of newspaper groups that also held broadcasting interests generated a scope and convergence in the press such that the commission concluded that the state was not the only threat to liberty but had been joined by business interests in the mask of a free press. It also proposed a revision in our predominantly individualistic understanding of the First Amendment to deal with the increasingly collective character of contemporary life. The second reform attempt was at the level of practice. The New Journalism attempted to create new journalistic routines to eclipse the distance between the press and it audience. It did this by creating a more immediate and personal journalism, merging techniques of fiction and reportage. The beat system and the procedures designed to effect it seemed increasingly out of touch with both the characteristic events of contemporary life (e.g., the Vietnam War) and the sensibilities of an audience that was drawn to both protest and privatization simultaneously.[10] The third reform effort was the creation of the National News Council, designed to reconnect journalism to both the community and to the subjects of its reporting by creating modes of accountability outside the legal system.[11]

Public journalism is the fourth such effort at reform. This one, as opposed to the Hutchins Commission and the National News Council, originated within the craft and, unlike the New Journalism, was a self-consciously organized collective effort.

Public Journalism and Civic Republicanism

The origins of public journalism are conventionally traced to the aftermath of the 1988 elections, though we could just as easily trace it to the period between 1968 and 1972, between the Pentagon Papers and

Watergate. These two events mark the apogee of modern journalism. Watergate begins in beat reporting and ends in a formal investigation by journalists of the legitimacy of President Nixon, perhaps the most stunning, if often overblown, vindication of the power of an adversary and watchdog press. The Pentagon Papers decision powerfully affirmed this role by placing the burden of proof for the support of injunctions, even in cases of national security, on the state. The court insisted that the government demonstrate the threat to national security attendant to publication rather than merely await the concurrence of the court. At the same time, the court did not consider the fact that the papers themselves were stolen documents leading to Chief Justice Burger's powerful dissent asserting that an adversary press had removed itself from the burdens and responsibilities of normal citizenship.[12]

When Nixon waved good-bye from the steps of the helicopter transporting him from the White House for the last time, he might have been waving goodbye to his fiercest enemy, modern journalism. It was not so apparent at the time that Minerva's Owl was gathering flight once again at twilight, but the flowering of modern journalism was the prelude to its demise. Following Watergate, the public and the political system became progressively ideologized and privatized, though that would not be apparent until the presidency of Ronald Reagan. With public government, relatively speaking, in eclipse, the independent voter and with it an independent press became superfluous. Just as important, the watchdog press increasingly became the prisoner of whatever administration was in power. As Bob Woodward later admitted, Watergate was a prelude to the cooptation of journalism by power[13]: journalism lost its role as a representative of the people both because there were no more people to represent and because politics became, in Jürgen Habermas's memorable phrase, refeudalized.

The implications of these changes were evident in the election of 1988. Joan Didion memorably captured the theatrical politics, hermetically sealed away from the "real world" typical of that campaign:

> When we talk about the process, then, we are talking increasingly, not about "the democratic process," or the general mechanism affording citizens of a state a voice in its affairs, but the reverse: A mechanism seen as so specialized that access to it is correctly limited to its own professionals, to those who manage policy and those who report on it, to those who run the polls and those who quote them, to those who ask and those who answer the questions on the Sunday shows, to the media consultants, to the columnists . . . to the handful of insiders who invent, year in and year out, the narrative of public life. . . . What strikes one most vividly about such a campaign is precisely its remoteness from the actual life of the country.[14]

In the aftermath of the 1988 election there was widespread disgust with American politics and with the press itself, a disgust that muted the normal happiness of political victory and the end to yet another endless season of campaigning.[15] It was a monumentally smarmy campaign, reduced to a few slogans and brutal advertisements that produced yet another record low in voter turnout. The widespread disenchantment of the public with the spectacle of politics—with what Ms. Didion called "Insider Baseball," a game only for the players, not even the fans—was evident not only in low voter turnout but in the large, 9 percent, decline in the television audience for the political conventions. The conventions were saved only by commercial demography: as one advertising specialist put it, "the upscale target audience was there."[16] Following the election there were renewed calls for the press to reconstruct its approach to politics along with a predictable round of seminars and symposia decrying the "degradation of democratic discourse" and the immiserization of the press in horse race and gossip column journalism.

But thoughtful observers of that election recognized a much deeper erasure of the public interest. In 1988, the end of the Cold War was clearly in view and that election offered an opportunity to discuss both the foreign and domestic policies—liberal internationalism, the welfare state, the national security state—that had dominated American politics for a half century. In that campaign there was, as if by mutual agreement of the press and the candidates, no discussion or debate of any of the issues facing the nation. It did not occur in the campaign and it certainly did not occur in the press. An even greater failure of the press and the political system was the agreement, again almost conscious, to keep out of the campaign the plans afoot to bail out the banking system in the wake of the savings and loan crisis, the single greatest theft of the public treasury in the history of republics. If ever the public needed evidence that it could not rely on a watchdog press to either protect or represent its interests, the public found it in the savings and loan bailout.[17]

These were the actually existing conditions, as opposed to vague discontents and idealistic posturing, that led many journalists, reporters, and editors, notably Davis Merritt and David Broder, to conclude that journalism and politics had both become a mutually reinforcing sham. From this, and the crucial work of Jay Rosen, public journalism was born.

Public journalism focused in its origins on election coverage and, given the debacle of 1988, with good reason. Election coverage is the paradigmatic form of modern journalism: the event that best fits the talents of the craft. It is backed by a powerful meta-narrative enunciating the role of elections in democracy. It asks journalists to practice the craft under the most exhausting deadline conditions. Campaigns have clear time horizons. The presidential campaign begins in Iowa and New Hampshire and ends 18 months later on election day. Campaigns offer a structure for advance planning and a built-in dramatic structure of acts and denouement. Campaigns are unambiguous and have binary outcomes: One person, one party will win, the other will lose, and the decision is unequivocal. Campaigns allow journalists to play the role they like best, as handicappers, determining the odds and the gamble. Moreover, campaigns allow for both the structure of the beat and "scoops": journalism as both daily reporting of the surface of events and as police work investigating malfeasance, personal failings, moral corruption, and political compromise.

But election coverage is paradigmatic in a second sense. The forms of journalism developed to deal with campaigns spread to other forms of coverage and other sections of the newspaper and television report. Campaigns are the richest source for the norms of journalism. So, in selecting political campaigns as the first site of a new practice, public journalists chose the critical arena in which they had to establish themselves and from there innovations could spread to other forms of coverage.[18]

However, there is a deeper source for the impulse of public journalism than political campaigns and the events of the last 30 years. That source is the inclination to civic republicanism that is deeply within the American political tradition. Central to this tradition is a belief, namely, that freedom consists of something more than the protection of rights *against* the society and the preservation of freedom to choose our lifestyle as we do goods in a supermarket. The "more than" entails sharing in self-government, deliberating with fellow citizens about the common good, and working together to shape the destiny of the political community. It asserts that citizenship is more than rights and interests but also a matter of identity. This identity requires a sense of belonging, a concern for the whole, a moral bond with the community whose fate is at stake, and, naturally, knowledge of public affairs. Therefore, although republican government can be neutral toward many of the values and ends of its citizens, it must draw the line somewhere. Republican government must espouse and support certain values, namely, the good that inheres in the common life, in the possibility of the common good, in republican government itself. The political community cannot be a mere apparatus for satisfying individual desires and, although tolerant, the republican tradition cannot respect an oxymoron: the unencumbered citizen, bereft of moral and civic ties to the larger whole. Even more, republican theory asserts that the alternative form of democracy, what Michael Sandel calls "the procedural republic," cannot inspire the sense of community and civic engagement that liberty requires.[19] A paper like *The Wall Street Journal*, let us say, can attend to the interests of its readers. It can assume that its readers are citizens only in the guise of their financial interests and can unambiguously support privatized, interest group politics (though in fact it does not do those things exclusively), but the press in general must identify its readers not as consumers or investors but as citizens whose identity and freedom, not just their interests, is grounded, in part, in the civic life. And such a press must, therefore, support not only journalism but other civic institutions that cultivate the virtues of public engagement and a broader concern for the common life. There are dangers in this tradition, of course, and one need only remember the travesty of the title "citizen" in the Jacobin overachievement of the French Revolution to remind oneself of those dangers. Yet, the countervailing force of this tradition must be periodically renewed if American democracy is not to descend into the anarchy and authoritarianism (they can occur together) of "the market" and "the interests."

The civic republican impulse behind public journalism leads to the charges—they sound like charges, though why they should be is beyond me—that public journalism actively espouses "values," or, alternatively, "doing what we always should have been doing," or, in Michael Schudson's view, is deeply conservative. In making the charge—certainly a strange one to make against a tradition whose intellectual roots go back a couple of thousand years—Schudson notes that public journalism has failed to resolve the contradiction within progressivism between "empowering people" and "entrusting elites with public responsibility."[20] True enough. But, there was another contradiction within the progressive movement that contains the major key to both the aspiration and problems of public journalism.

The Progressive Movement, in the wing of it occupied by, say, Theodore Roosevelt, Walter Lippmann, and Herbert Croly, took the position that only by strengthening the power of national institutions and national elites could the power of corporate capitalism be contained. This meant, of course, undercutting the authority of local and intermediate institutions in the name of national standards, national politics, and a national culture. At the level of the nation, then, power was to be contained via the opposition of a centralized state and a centralized capitalist system. Other institutions—the press, labor, philanthropy, political parties—were necessarily nationalized and centralized to compete in this new forum dominated by the national state and the national economy.

This centralizing and nationalizing tendency carried the day against its opposition, namely, the decentralizing wing led by John Dewey and Louis Brandeis. They sought to oppose central power with decentralized and localized institutions. Rather than offsetting centralized economic power with ever stronger central government, the decentralizing progressives sought to contain this power through antitrust laws and the breaking up of centralizing forces. It sought to oppose economic democracy with political democracy and a national culture with a regionally diverse one. It is clear now who won this struggle and, because of the continuing problem of race, perhaps deserved to win.

But the question of the position of national, regional, and local institutions is now back on the table of debate. The resurgence of the economic model of journalism reflects the national and progressively global integration of the means of communication. These globalizing tendencies threaten now to undercut the nation state itself. In response, local and regional movements of autonomy and independence have been springing up all over the world. We are replaying the acts and choices of 100 years ago but playing them now on a global stage. How we deal with the new tendencies and directions in the economy and with it the new power of elites is as much our dilemma as it was the dilemma of progressive intellectuals 100 years ago. One route is surely to transcend the nation state and to construct ever more powerful and centralized global institutions of the state, law, and the polity to offset the globalization of capital. We will probably have to do precisely that. But we can also exert countervailing force by reviving the local and, particularly, the regional and the national. These are not mutually exclusive options and to pursue one without the other would be a recipe for disaster.

Beyond Liberty for the Press

Public journalism has committed itself, in my view, to the reawakening of an antecedent tradition of journalism and politics, one that emphasizes local democracy, the community of locale, and citizenship as against the distant forces that would overwhelm it. It is no accident, in my view, that the greatest insensitivities to traditions of American democracy are exhibited by international owners such as Thomson Newspapers and Rupert Murdoch or by American corporations, such as Disney, with fully articulated global interests. In its attempts to find a new expression of what journalism might mean and be, one consistent with the tradition of civic republicanism, public journalism performs a great service in reminding us of what is worth protecting. We can admit that this is a partial solution and one fraught with problems. But the question for critics is this: Do you have a better solution? The successes of public journalism, as local and erratic as they are, may not prevail against the aggrandizing and centralizing forces of history, but it is, at this moment, the only movement around that at least provides some oppositional force to the next wave in the global concentration of power and the tyranny of the market.

We would be remiss not to mention a new and ominous element in the current situation. It is perhaps worth reminding ourselves that republics are fragile. The founding fathers believed by their historical investigation that republics generally lasted 200 years. They believed republics fell because of their corruption—above all, their corruption from wealth.

Our understanding of journalism, both the partisan press and the independent press, has proceeded from idea, taken from the enlightenment, that the press is a basic institution of political liberty. Today the First Amendment is ceasing in the eyes of many to have that implication of a public trust held in the name of a wider community for the purpose of guaranteeing liberty. Increasingly, in the organization of our journalism, the First Amendment seems more to refer to a property right, establishing ground rules for economic competition. And lest you think this hyperbolic—listen to the thoughts on this by Rupert Murdoch, one of the new barons of the conglomerates. He says, in referring to Asia:

> Singapore is not liberal, but it's clean and free of drug addicts. Not so long ago it was an impoverished, exploited colony with famines, diseases, and other problems. Now people find themselves in three room apartments with jobs and clean streets. Countries like Singapore are going the right way. Material incentives create business and the free market economy. If politicians try it the other way around, with democracy, the Russian model is the result. Ninety percent of the Chinese are interested more in a better material life than in the right to vote.[21]

That is a new voice in the inversion of the historic commitments to the relationship of economic and political democracy. The problem is that political democracy does not follow from the presence of an effective market economy. And a politically free press does not follow from an economically free one.

The market can take quite illiberal forms. As Murdoch attests, modern economic developments seem to favor authoritarian rather than democratic regimes. As Ralf Dahrendorf reminds us, authoritarian does not mean totalitarian. For such regimes do not require a great leader nor an invasive ideology nor a permanent mobilization. Nor do they require a self-perpetuating public class. These are countries that can be quite nice for the visitor, predictable and undemanding for the natives, but for poets and journalists, they are "unbearable places to live."[22]

What has been added to the mix is a new experiment—an experiment that makes developments in Asia particularly interesting—as to whether you can have free markets without political democracy. For example, the concern that runs through the separation or the deseparation of the walls between journalism and business is this question precisely. Whether the historic meanings of political liberty and a free press can be preserved once the borders separating journalism and business, the corporation and the newsroom, are effectively breached is a central question of the American press today.

In the late 1930s, Harvard economist Joseph Schumpeter, a great lover of capitalism, wrote that he feared for capitalism's future because of what he called its process of creative destruction. Capitalism was such an innovative economic system, he thought, that it tended to destroy all things including itself. It did so by eating its own seed corn, by destroying the social and political bases that guarantees it.[23]

The issue today is whether the values of the republican tradition as embodied in the First Amendment are the foundation of political liberty that the organizations that own the press have an obligation to sustain or whether the First Amendment is seen largely as an economic right to enable a protection for those corporate organizations to sustain themselves.

Notes

1. From a public letter submitted and read to a forum of the Committee of Concerned Journalists, Harvard University, Cambridge, MA, May 22, 1998.
2. Michael Gartner, "Give Me Old-Time Journalism," *Quill* (November/December 1995): 68–69.
3. See Michael Schudson, Chapter 7, this volume, p. 119.
4. These comments paraphrase the arguments of an earlier essay: "The Press, Public Opinion, and Public Discourse," pp. 373–402, in *Public Opinion and the Communication of Consent*, eds. Theodore L. Glasser and Charles T. Salmon (New York: Guilford Press, 1995).
5. Ralf Dahrendorf, *After 1989: Morals, Revolution and Civil Society* (London: Macmillan, 1997), p. 99.
6. Richard Kaplan,
7. See Schudson, Chapter 7, this volume, p. 123.

8. Lee Bollinger, *Images of a Free Press* (Chicago: University of Chicago Press, 1991), Ch. 1.
9. Robert D. Leigh, ed., *A Free and Responsible Press* (Chicago: University of Chicago Press, 1947).
10. Tom Wolfe, *The New Journalism* (New York: Harper & Row, 1973).
11. Norman Isaacs, *Untended Gates* (New York: Columbia University Press).
12. Warren Burger, dissent in the Pentagon Papers case.
13. In an interview with William Greider on the PBS television program, *The Betrayal of Democracy*, Woodward commented that following Watergate, journalists like himself were "brought to the bosom of the establishment very quickly." Greider went on to comment, "Watergate ironically may have marked the high point for the media's independence. The press [following Watergate] made peace with rival powers both in government and business and turned into a much more reliable member of the ruling constellation." Woodward later asked himself this question: "What is our connection to the people we serve?" He meant "readers" and gave this answer: "We don't have a department that handles that. We don't have an assistant managing editor for the real world."
14. Joan Didion, "Insider Baseball," in *After Henry* (New York: Touchstone Books, 1993).
15. Jay Rosen and Paul Taylor, *The New News v. The Old News: The Press and Politics in the 1990s* (Washington, DC: Brookings Institute, 1992).
16. Didion, "Insider Baseball."
17. See William Greider, *Who Will Tell the People* (New York: Simon & Schuster, 1992)
18. Similarly, and reflexively, politics takes on the form of a continuous campaign. As Woodward comments on *The Betrayal of Democracy*, "He [Bush] conducts the presidency like a political campaign."
19. I here draw on two sources in defining the republican tradition: Michael Sandel, *Democracy's Discontent: American in Search of a Public Philosophy* (Cambridge, MA: Harvard University Press, 1996), particularly Chs. 1 and 2; and Bruce Smith, *Politics and Remembrance: Republican Themes in Machiavelli, Burke, and Tocqueville* (Princeton, NJ: Princeton University Press, 1985).
20. See Schudson, Chapter 7, this volume.
21. Quoted in Dahrendorf, *After 1989*, p. 98.
22. Dahrendorf, *After 1989*, p. 96.
23. Joseph Schumpeter, *Capitalism, Socialism and Democracy* (New York: Harper-Collins, 1962).

Chapter 4

The Common Good
as First Principle

Clifford G. Christians
University of Illinois–Urbana

The future of public journalism depends on the notion of the common good—on whether we can articulate it, justify it philosophically, establish its logic and rationale.[1] Public journalism aims at community formation. It seeks to invigorate the public sphere politically and sociologically. But activating the public will be directionless unless we can bring the idea of the common good into its own.

Public journalism is not merely a set of techniques for revitalizing journalistic practice. Rather, it recognizes the "fundamental connection between democracy and journalism" and insists that democracy "fulfill its historic purpose."[2] Davis Merritt asks that the critics of public journalism focus not on its early experiments but on its intellectual roots for "a truly useful and needed debate to occur. Public journalism is as much or more about public life than it is about journalism."[3] And as it establishes itself within the larger arena of democratic liberalism, coming to grips with the common good is paramount. Public journalism's goals presume a common good of some sort—providing a framework for healthy democracies, community connectedness, civic involvement, for example. The long-term vitality of public journalism is rooted in and sustained by the principle of the common good. Palm trees will not grow in saltwater oceans.

The common good is an important notion in Western political philosophy.[4] Aristotle's "common interest" is the basis for distinguishing defensible constitutions in the people's interest from illegitimate ones on the rulers' behalf.[5] For Cicero, an identifiable political entity, in principle, is not an ad hoc collection of individuals but "a partnership for the common good."[6] Thomas Aquinas insists on the common good as "the end of law and government."[7] In a similar vein, for Locke "the good of the people" along with peace and safety are the ends of political society.[8] Rousseau understood "the common good" as the object of the general will and the end of the state, in contrast to "particular wills."[9] In Habermas, discourse in the public sphere must be oriented "toward mutual understanding" while allowing participants "the communicative freedom to take positions on validity claims."[10]

Although political and moral philosophers have differed on the precise content of the common good and how to promote it, there is a core meaning that the welfare of all citizens, rather than that of factions or special interests, should be served impartially. Moreover, it is a normative principle, not just the majority results of an opinion poll or voting. The common good cannot be understood statistically but is a "fundamental concept of social morality."[11]

The individualism of liberal democracy has left the common good in tatters. We are still living off our inheritance, but it is fast being used up. The common good has become disoriented conceptually—vacuous, in fact. A broken educational system and a mainstream press disconnected from community life are both blameworthy. But neither can be redirected successfully unless the concept of the common good comes into its own conceptually. Citizenship, civic discourse, community activism, and grass-roots participation are only moralistic pleading unless they are grounded in a defensible notion of the common good.

The common good preoccupies the sociopolitical theory of Michael Sandel, Charles Taylor, and Carole Pateman. Contrary to the individual autonomy of democratic liberalism, they have argued for a communitarian paradigm that clears up the theoretical confusion.[12] From this perspective, the common good is the axis around which community formation revolves, and public journalism prospers in direct proportion to it.

Goods Instead of Rights

A liberal politics of rights entails a commitment to individual autonomy as the first principle. "Each person," says John Rawls, has an "equal right to the most extensive total system of basic liberties" compatible with similar liberty for all.[13] From the classical liberalism of Locke and Mill to the libertarian self-ownership of Robert Nozick, individual liberties have priority. We are constituted as selves antecedently, that is, in advance of our engagement with others. A sense of community describes a possible aim of individuated selves but is "not an ingredient of their identity."[14]

Liberal political theory presumes that people are distinct from their ends. For Sandel, however, the liberal picture of persons as separate from their conceptions of the good ignores the extent to which we are constituted by those conceptions themselves. "Who, the communitarian asks, is the shadowy 'person' that exists independently of, and able freely to choose, the ends that give her life meaning and value?"[15] Individual identities cannot be established in isolation from history and culture.

A voluntaristic relation between a self and its ends, in Sandel's view, leads to an impoverished understanding of political community. Communal goods are then only one contender among many; community is a possible aim but not an ingredient of our human identity. In Rawls's liberal paradigm, citizens think of themselves "as participants in a scheme of mutual cooperation, deriving advantages they could not have gained by their own efforts, but not tied to their fellow citizens by bonds whose severance or alteration would change their identity as persons."[16] This conception of the person is highly implausible and it relegates our sense of identity to nonpolitical social relations. Rawls limits our notions of the good to the attachments nurtured in families, religious communities, and ethnicity. Liberalism is thereby metaphysically myopic. The individualistic and asocial foundations of a liberal society preclude by definition those human experiences around which conceptions of the good and a range of human values are crystalized and can flourish.

Ignoring the importance of goods held in common, the political community is merely "a system of cooperation between mutually disinterested individuals" rather than a possible home of constitutive attachments.[17] In Sandel's view, this leads Rawls to "a particular picture of the process by which an individual chooses her ends or conception of the good—one in which choices are seen as arbitrary expressions of preference, and which seems to imply that moral judgments in general are entirely subjective."[18] Citizen decision making is thus understood as instrumental rationality—determining the various goods and options available and their consequences in terms of one's own wants and desires.

But if our conceptions of the good are contingent upon personal preferences, they have no more validity than any others. The liberal conception of the self leads to moral skepticism and is at odds with its own definition of justice as fairness. "Rawls's commitment to equality presupposes the very possibility of constitutive communal attachments that his conception of the self prohibits."[19] And in presupposing our fundamental union as humans with the political community, Rawls confirms what Sandel considers obvious in its own right,

> namely, that our sense of identity is inseparable from our awareness of ourselves as members of a particular family or class or community or people or nation, as bearers of a specific history, as citizens of a particular republic; and that we look to participation in the political realm as a way in which we can develop and refine our sense of ourselves by developing and refining forms of community with which we can be proud to identify.[20]

Charles Taylor also emphasizes the possibility and importance of a constitutive bonding to goods. However, for Taylor, the human preoccupation with life's worth and meaning is best understood as situating ourselves in relation to moral goods in common rather than to political community per se. In his terms, our sense of the good is woven into our understanding of our lives as an unfolding story. An orientation toward the good and a concern for life's narrative unity are mutually implicating. "Because we have to determine our place in relation to the good, therefore we cannot be without an orientation to it, and hence must see our life in story."[21] "The life of a human being can only be understood in terms of its narrative form—the narrative of that individual's progress towards (or away from) the good."[22]

In another formulation of the communitarian perspective, political liberalism confuses an aggregate of individual rights with the common good. The good is mistakenly presumed to equal the desirable. Because persons appear to seek rights, this quest of particular persons is considered good, and a general doctrine of rights is goodness itself— as if to say, "This is good because I say it is or because most people identify it as such." But in a communitarian world view, claims to individual rights ought not exist independently of communally shared conceptions of the good. "The good is always primary to the right. . . . The good is what, in its articulation, gives the point of the rules which define the right."[23] Appealing to asocial and ahistorical rights tends to justify selfishness and buys the freedom to be ourselves at too dear a price.

Rights are a friendly companion but vapid and unhelpful in complicated matters. They serve as a bodyguard against moral bullies but are inarticulate and boring.[24] Rights provide us no conceptual apparatus for coping with the intolerance that flourishes when settled roots dry up and traditions turn cold. When faced with the need for broadly shared values as societies fragment and break down, rights language is mute. When demands for individual rights prevail among jostling rights bearers, the winner takes all and losers must get out of town. The conversation is over.[25]

Commitments to human freedom and cultural pluralism make sense when the community is understood to be axiologically and ontologically prior to persons. Human identity is constituted through the social realm. In the communitarian perspective, our selfhood is not fashioned out of thin air. We are born into a sociocultural universe where values, moral commitments, and existential meanings are either presumed or negotiated. Social systems precede their occupants and endure after them. Therefore, morally appropriate action intends community. Unless our freedom is used to help others flourish, our own well-being is negated. Fulfillment is never achieved in isolation but only through human bonding at the epicenter of social formation. Contrary to the Lockean dualism between individuals and society, we know ourselves primarily as whole beings in relation. Rather than paying lip service to the social nature of the self while presuming a dualism of two orders, the positive liberty of communitarianism is interlocked with communal well-being.

The common good is the axis around which communities and politics become a social organism. "More is lost through the eclipse of community than a sense of belonging and secure identity. Citizenship itself disappears from view."[26] For linking communal values with the political ideals of freedom and equality, only democratic models of community are appropriate.

Some forms of association are authoritarian, hierarchical, exclusionary, or gender biased. Professions and occupational groups often are not communities in the sense that one's self-identity is derived from the whole.

Thus Carole Pateman advocates participatory democracy as the normative core of community formation.[27] As Rousseau understood most clearly, only participatory or self-managing democracy leads us to the civic ideal. "A community is composed of a limited set of people who are bound together in networks of relationships, . . . share a set of beliefs and values, . . . and demonstrate solidarity with one another."[28] Therefore, community formation is public journalism's overriding mission. Civic associations in any meaningful sense are only possible through active participation in articulating the common good and mutuality in implementing it. As Craig Calhoun insists, we should build "the conditions of public life so that publics, always in the process of making themselves, might also make themselves good."[29] The communitarian model seeks the affirmation of ordinary experience—

the human dignity of production and reproduction in contrast to the elitism of philosophers, military heroes, and the aristocracy. Communitarianism is founded on the distributive principle of commonness, not merely on individual autonomy.

Promises

The common good entails obligations to one another. But the liberal democratic state confuses obedience with communal obligation. Pateman develops the argument this way: Liberal theory claims that a citizen's obligation to the government results from a voluntary contract with other citizens. The assumption is that political obligation is self-assumed, a commitment into which we enter freely. In the liberal heritage bequeathed by the contract theorists, political obligation is unproblematic. Through the voting process, individuals decide for themselves how to order their obligations and offer their consent. However, the crude equation of voting and consent is a problem. Liberal–democratic voting is largely ritual, and for those denied a vote or refusing to vote or losing to the majority vote, how can voting be called free and deliberate consent?[30]

Locke's tacit consent is another option, of course. Arguments in this tradition appeal to an individual's acceptance of benefits from the state as giving rise to obligations. Using schools or highways, it is said, obligates citizens to the government that builds and maintains them. But tacit consent does not constitute an argument. It looks suspiciously like an extended collection of conceptual truisms.[31] It is not clear that benefits entail political obligations; most people do not benefit equally and many benefit hardly at all.

Rawls, in fact, owns up to these dilemmas and argues that only better placed and active members in society have a political obligation; the rest of the population has merely a natural duty to obey.[32] Such an all-inclusive scheme reduces the concept of obligation to meaninglessness or at best to obedience. However, liberal–democratic theorists refuse to argue in terms of obedience instead of consenting obligation; this would strip the democratic state of its ideological mantle. "To admit that some individuals may have a lesser obligation than others, or that some have only a 'natural duty' of obedience, is to shake liberal–democratic theory to its foundations."[33]

Therefore, Pateman insists on starting over philosophically in communitarian terms. We assume an obligation by making a promise. When individuals promise, they carry an obligation to act accordingly. Making promises is one of the basic ways in which consenting individuals "freely create their own social relationships."[34] But promises are made not primarily to the state but to fellow citizens.[35] If obligations are rooted in promises, obligations are owed to fellow members of institutions and participants in social practices. Only under conditions of participatory democracy is there self-assumed political obligation.

Pateman understands the nature of moral agency. We know ourselves primarily in relation to action and derivatively as thinkers withdrawn from it. Only by overcoming the traditional dualisms between thinker and agent, mind and body, reason and will, can we conceive of being as "the mutuality of personal relationship."[36] Thought arises out of action and returns to action for its incarnation and verification. Buber calls the human relation a primal notion in his famous lines, "in the beginning is the relation" and "the relation is the cradle of life."[37] Social relationships, not individuals, have primacy. "The one primary word is the combination I–thou."[38] This irreducible phenomenon—the relational reality, the in-between, the reciprocal bond, the interpersonal—cannot be decomposed into simpler elements without destroying it.

All meaningful action is for the sake of community building; the bonding of persons is the epicenter of social formation. Given the primacy of relationships, unless I use my freedom to help others flourish, I deny my own well-being. "Since the relation of persons constitutes their existence as persons, . . . morally right action is [one] which intends community."[39] Pateman cuts personal being into the very heart of the social universe. The common good is accessible to us only in personal form; it has its ground and inspiration in personality. "Ontology must be rescued from submersion in things by being thought out entirely from the viewpoint of person and thus of Being. . . . Ontology is truly itself only when it is personal."[40]

Though he did not read Pateman, Sandel, and Taylor, Edward R. Murrow intuitively understood our obligations to one another when he produced the classic documentary of migrant farm workers, *Harvest of Shame*. Tears flowed in the screening room after the first exhibition. The sorrowful song at the end tore into every conscience in the room. But Murrow did not seek pity; he wanted responsible action, civic transformation. So he reworked the final scenes consistent with a documentary format: "Is it possible we think too much in terms of Christmas baskets and not in terms of eliminating poverty? . . . The people you have seen do not have the strength to influence legislation. Maybe we do. Good night and good luck."[41] Murrow knew that great television news does not end with pity or fear but is actionable toward community building. He realized that holding up injustice as a spectacle is to trivialize it. The statistical calculations that public journalism increases voter turnout or otherwise enhances the political process could only be a patina under which citizens are mobilized into the state apparatus but not obligated meaningfully to one another. Murrow sought to empower his viewers toward the mutual dependence that makes commerce and politics possible.

In 1993, the *Akron* (Ohio) *Beacon-Journal* published a five-part series, "A Question of Race," dealing with racial issues in terms of education, housing, crime, and economic opportunity. From the beginning, this project in public journalism involved the community. Facilitators hired by the paper conducted focus groups, businesses and churches committed themselves, until a network of 160 organizations and 15,000 people were involved—even needing a newsletter to communicate among themselves. The last of the series ended with cut-out coupons pledging to fight racism, and when more than 22,000 readers sent theirs in, the *Beacon-Journal* printed the names in a special section. The newspaper's editor, Dale Allen, felt qualified to serve as catalyst:

> Government is distrusted by minorities. Civil rights organizations have lost their luster. Churches who rightfully take moral leadership are so splintered they are unable to do anything. When we looked around at the other public agencies we concluded we were probably more compatible than anyone in the community to do something about it.[42]

Promise making to one another was nurtured through this web of human relationships and open participation. To help rejuvenate public life, journalists moved beyond telling the news to become what Merritt calls "the fair-minded participant."[43] The success of this effort in "community connectedness" was rooted in pledges made to one another, and appropriately the *Beacon-Journal* was awarded the Pulitzer Prize for public service in April 1994.

Communities as Moral Entities

Liberal theory argues for language as the marrow of community. Persons are displayed, made accessible, nurtured, and integrated into social units through symbol, myth, and metaphor. Words are concrete forms of life, whose meaning derives from an interpretive context that humans themselves supply. Our indispensable relations as human beings are linguistic. In libertarian liberalism, unfettered information must be guaranteed by the First Amendment. In egalitarian democracy, we enter the ongoing conversation which constitutes public life and negotiate the human order through language.

The Canadian philosopher Charles Taylor argues strenuously that social entities are moral orders and not merely lingual structures. His *Sources of the Self* is a sandwich book—75 pages of philosophical reflection on either end, but 400 pages of relentless history in between to document that moral commitment constitutes the "self in relation." Our identity is defined by what we consider good or worth opposing. As a result, for public journalism the moral task cannot be reduced to professional ethics. The focus ought to be not on professional practice but on the general morality. How the moral order works itself out in community formation is the issue, not first of all what practitioners consider virtuous. The challenge for journalists is not to limit their moral perspective to their own codes of ethics but to understand ethics and values in terms of everyday citizenship.

As Robert Adams argues, the survival of societies is ensured in the socialization of their children. Morality becomes a social reality as entering generations are schooled in belongingness. Children learn moral agreements and disagreements in the process of learning technical skills for human survival. The biological and moral grow up together. Children ascertain that in general, "certain things belong to certain people" and as such they are "learning a partly moral fact . . . important to the structure of society."[44] They learn tolerance—at least that physical assault is forbidden, though perhaps not sophisticated versions of tolerating various opinions. Disapproval of lying emerges too at some basic level; certain kinds are punished at school and others are legally penalized (lying to a police officer), but, in addition, a predisposition against lying generally (our shared disapproval of it) takes hold as a social threat.[45]

Such moral learning sticks when "children find (as they normally do) that a central core of the moral 'facts' they learned" from their progenitors and siblings are also viewed in fundamentally similar ways by the wider community to which they belong. This common core—theft, murder, and lying as contrary to social life—is not driven by ethical theory or authoritarian command but in Rawls's terms represents "an overlapping consensus."[46] Without broad acceptance of such a core, or what appears to be a natural affinity for its values, a liberal social order is impossible and a police state inevitable. Without a framework broadly owned and roughly understood, resolution of practical issues and constructive theorizing on particular matters is impossible.

As Adams concludes, "Every society must, and therefore will, have a shared morality; but . . . a shared ethical theory is not required for a common morality. . . . No comprehensive ethical theory . . . is likely to meet with general agreement in any modem society that permits free inquiry."[47] The killing of and violent assault on human beings may be generally condemned, while disagreements rage at the same time over capital punishment, euthanasia, and justified warfare. All things being equal, societies are predisposed against lying while debating exceptions and theorizing the nature and parameters of deception. The status of property is a complicated problem in political theory and redefined in environmental ethics of the land, while our ordinary moral obligations about other people's property are undisputed in everyday affairs.

Moral duty is nurtured by the demands of social linkage and not produced by theory. However, though the core of a society's common morality is pretheoretical agreement, ethical theory is not useless or marginal in shaping the common good. Societies speak with divided voices and often in error. "What counts as common morality, indeed, is not only imprecise but variable . . . and a difficult practical problem."[48] Ethical theory is primarily an effort to articulate moral obligation within the fallible and irresolute voices of everyday life. Among disagreements and uncertainty, we look for criteria and wisdom in settling disputes and clarifying confusions. Although metaethics has been largely abstract and fragmented, normative theories of an interactive sort invigorate our common moral discourse. However, generally accepted theories are not necessary for common goods to prosper. The common good is not "the complete morality of every participant . . . but a set of agreements among people who typically hold other, less widely shared ethical beliefs."[49]

Alasdair MacIntyre may be correct in thinking that societies ought to share some moral goods—such as a conception of justice—that are developed theoretically enough to enable us to resolve conflicts through reasoned agreement rather than brute force.[50] But justice is a distributive principle and seeking the common good is a collective one.[51] Instead of expecting more theoretical coherence than history warrants, Reinhold Niebuhr inspires us with a rationale for constitutional democracy in which we work through inevitable social conflicts while maintaining "an untheoretical jumble of agreements" called here the common good.[52] Through a common morality we can approximate consensus on issues and settle disputes within democratic institutions.

Communitarians challenge public journalism to participate in a community's ongoing process of moral evaluation. The possibility exists in principle. Taylor, for example, emphasizes that moral judgments are capable of rational elucidation. Our widely shared moral intuitions—respect for the dignity of others, for instance—are developed through discourse within evaluative frameworks shared by or derived from the community. On the one hand, our moral intuitions seem fundamental and purely instinctual, like reactions of nausea to certain tastes; on the other, agents manifesting them are often capable of explaining just what it is about human beings that merits or deserves the reaction, in other words, we articulate our intuitions by developing a particular ontology of the human.[53]

Agreements and disputes about the good life can be articulated and sifted. Our accounts specify the character or identity of our moral intuitions.

As public journalism deals with the moral dimension in news, features, debates over social issues, and so forth, it is not in alien territory. According to Taylor, we cannot make sense of human agency without it.

Developing, maintaining and articulating [our moral intuitions and reactions] is not something humans could easily or even conceivably dispense with. ... We can no more imagine a human life that fails to address the matter of its bearings in moral space than we can imagine one in which developing a sense of up and down, right and left is regarded as an optional human task. ... Moral orientation is inescapable because the questions to which the framework provides answers are themselves inescapable.[54]

Moreover, the communal character of our moral interpretations enables public journalism to come to grips with the common good. Our references to moral matters involve the community. A self exists only within "webs of interlocution," and all self-interpretation implicitly or explicitly "acknowledges the necessarily social origin of any and all of their conceptions of the good and so of themselves." Moral frameworks are as fundamental for orienting us in social space as the need to "establish our bearings in physical space."[55] In this regard, investigative reporting has been deficient and public journalism can rectify it:

The hard-hitting stories, the investigative stories, lack a morally sensitive vocabulary. They don't talk about moral issues in moral terms. They go to great lengths to do what, in a more technical language, might be called "objectifying morality"—by taking moral claims and making them appear to be empirical claims.[56]

One illustration of casting issues in terms of the general morality is the death of Cardinal Joseph Bernardin. Cardinal Bernardin, Archbishop of Chicago, died in November 1996 from pancreatic cancer. Born of Italian immigrants in South Carolina, his mother was a seamstress and his father a stonecutter. At 38 he became the youngest bishop in the United States, and 30 years later upon his death the best known and most influential Roman Catholic leader in North America.

Joseph Bernardin often made the news as chair of the National Council of Catholic Bishops—its far-reaching reports on social issues frequently controversial within the hierarchy. Given his church's enormous size and power in Chicago, he became a household word in the midwestern media also. But in the last three years of his life the press was challenged to another order of magnitude. Reporting on religion often provides occasions for making the moral dimension public, but not necessarily so. In Joseph Bernardin's case, the press had extraordinary opportunities for engaging the Chicago community in moral discourse and took advantage of them. It didn't simply publish an obituary of a famous clergyman.

On November 10, 1993, a rumor began circulating that Bernardin, while he was Archbishop of Cincinnati 18 years earlier, had sexually abused a seminarian. A lawsuit was filed against Bernardin the next morning and the newsrooms across the country claimed to have pictures to prove the charge. CNN began airing promotional pieces every hour for its evening special, "Fall from Grace," about priests guilty of sex crimes. At the Pastoral Center that day in Chicago, 70 reporters jammed the pressroom for a news conference called by the Cardinal himself. From his perspective, "How do you say anything about a charge you have not seen from persons you do not know about something you did not do?"[57] But he accepted the press's adversary role and believed the truth would set him free, even through the waning moments of the news conference, when a young reporter asked him, "Are you sexually active?" "I paused only a moment," he replied, "feeling briefly the enormous gulf between the reporters' world and my own. 'I have always led,' I said simply, 'a chaste and celibate life.' "[58] One hundred days later Steven Jones retracted the charges of abuse, and when he died of AIDS on September 22, 1995, he had reconciled with the church.

In June 1995, Cardinal Bernardin was operated on for pancreatic cancer at Loyola Medical Center, and chemotherapy held the cancer in remission. But 15 months later, on August 30, he announced at a news conference that the MRIs had confirmed inoperable tumors, and no cure was possible. "My prayer is that I will use whatever time is left in a positive way to benefit the priests and people I have been called to serve." He promised "for the people of the Archdiocese—and everyone of good will"—to help them prepare for death by having them "share in that awesome experience."[59] On November 14, 1996, he died. Fourteen days earlier, finishing a book on his last three years, the *Gift of Peace,* he invited those reading it "to walk with me the final miles of my life's journey . . . so you too can enjoy the deep inner peace that I now embrace as I stand at the threshold of eternal life."[60]

The news coverage of his death and funeral was overwhelming in the Chicago media and other cities, with echoes around the world. A churchman spoke not merely to his parish but resonated with moral values deep in the human spirit. Civic-minded journalism had to engage him and represent his voice in moral dialogue over the most frightening struggles of all—with false accusation, illness, and death. He showed

> he was in favor of life by living directly, being honest, not dissembling, not sparing himself any of these experiences. He is, in fact, in himself, far more than any lawsuits or court material, the counter-cultural figure to Dr. Kevorkian. . . . He really spoke about the details of his suffering, not in the macho ethic of pretending there were no emotions when life and death are in the scale. . . . His convictions for the value of human life, in a time of great pain and suffering, prove life's value for himself and all others.[61]

What happened here illustrates the way public life can be phrased in moral terms. The media appealed on a primal level to readers and listeners about ordinary human values. The moral commitments of Joseph Bernardin activated their conscience, whether they were Roman Catholics or not. There are epiphanal moments in our social life that provide us with a vision of who we are and inspire us morally. Thinking is presuppositional, so our social vision and political action will always be value driven. Demanding neutral discourse in public life, in the hope of achieving a nondescript consensus, is phony. Since Antonio Gramsci, we have realized that our politics manifest our deepest social values.[62] The only salient issue is whether our value commitments are life affirming or not. Among contending values, some meet the community test and others do not. When the Cardinal spoke publicly in everyday language about accusations destroying his reputation, life-threatening surgery, and death itself, the public sphere was invigorated. Those who included his struggles in their everyday dialogue were empowered not only to greater self-consciousness but to a common citizenship that takes the moral dimension seriously.

Conclusion

When we contextualize individual rights within communal goods, when we insist on promise keeping rather than contract, when we go beyond the lingual order to communities as moral entities, then the common good comes into its own conceptually. Through these three motifs, we identify and define the first principle for public journalism.

Critics insist that the common good cannot constitute an effective criterion in debates over public life. "We can understand the need of food and clothing and housing for everyone," but the common good as a moral and political principle seems indeterminate.[63] However, although it is impossible to agree on the one and only solution narrowly understood, the common good as a matter of fact constitutes a rationale for decision making and an ideal "in light of which rights, procedures, and policy should be assessed. . . . A political society that is not concerned to promote the common good is apt to become slavish to its own system of rights and take the protection of these rights as its sole business."[64]

In his famous book *Totem and Taboo,* Sigmund Freud argued that every society has taboo boundaries that distinguish it from others. But Freud claimed that every society also raises up totems, ideals, a vision of what makes life worth living. And these totems are not fashioned out of thin air. They come into being when communities agree on some kind of common commitment.[65]

Regrettably, raising up totems, recovering the common good, is nearly impossible these days. It seems to be more like chasing fool's gold than anything else. Historically the foundations of the common good have been theism, pure reason and metaphysics, or humanism. To specify the common good, we have appealed to God, to reason or to humanity. All of them are obviously problematic now in a secular age with enlightenment reason on the ropes. And the humanist project is usually cut short by war and evil.

In fact, in pursuing a common good, we may unleash a spate of tribalism. If we're not careful, we will wrongly conclude that the common good refers to whatever an ethnic, religious, or linguistic subculture values. However, if the common good is elusive or inconceivable, public journalism doesn't have much of a future. It is fatalism not to try. And public journalism gives us a reasonable chance. When community formation is paramount, we at least have the appropriate arena, day and night, day after day, to give the common good the attention it deserves.

Notes

1. An earlier essay on the common good connected it to universal human goods (Clifford Christians, "The Common Good and Universal Values," pp. 18–33 in *Mixed News,* ed. Jay Black [Mahwah, NJ: Erlbaum, 1997]). This chapter works the other end of the conceptual spectrum delineating the constituent features of the common good.

2. Davis Merritt, *Public Journalism and Public Life: Why Telling the News Is Not Enough* (Hillsdale, NJ: Erlbaum, 1995), p. 114.

3. Davis Merritt, "Missing the Point," *American Journalism Review* (July–August 1996): 29–31. Cf. C. R. Dykers for a summary of public journalism's roots in 300 years of Western intellectual history; "A Critical Review: Reconceptualizing the Relation of Democracy to News," paper presented at the annual convention of the Association for Education in Journalism and Mass Communication, Washington, DC, August 1995.

4. Bernard J. Diggs, "The Common Good as Reason for Political Action," *Ethics*, 83,4 (1973):283–284. This paragraph parallels his summary.

5. Aristotle, *Politics: A Treatise on Government*, W. Ellis, trans. (London: George Routledge, 1888), Bk. III, Chs. 6–7, pp. 90–93.

6. M. Tullii Ciceronis, *De Re Publica* (Rome: Typis S. Consilii Prop. Fidei, 1846), Ch. 1, Art. 25, pp. 44–45.

7. Thomas Aquinas, *Summa Theologiae*, T. Gilby, trans. (New York: McGraw Hill, 1964), Vol. 28, Quest. 92, Art. 1, pp. 41–45.

8. John Locke, *Second Treatise of Government*, T. Peardon, ed. (New York: Liberal Press, 1954), Ch. 9, Para. 131, p. 73; Ch. 13, Para. 158, p. 91.

9. Jean Jacques Rousseau, *The Social Contract and Other Political Writings*, V. Gourevitch, ed. (Cambridge, UK: Cambridge University Press, 1997), Bk. II, Ch. 1, p. 57.

10. Jürgen Habermas, *Justification and Application: Remarks on Discourse Ethics*, C. Cronin, trans. (Cambridge, MA: MIT Press, 1993), p. 66; cf. also Habermas, *Moral Consciousness and Communicative Action*, C. Lenhart and S. W. Nicholson, trans. (Cambridge, MA: MIT Press, 1990).

11. Diggs, "The Common Good," p. 284. The "public interest" literature is generally understood as covering the same terrain as the common good; for a classic review, see V. Held, *The Public Interest and Individual Interest* (New York: Basic Books, 1970). However, this tradition tends to push the notion of public interest away from ethics and argue it in terms of positivistic political science. The arguments then typically revolve around whether a common interest can be found or calibrated in an explicit or meaningful fashion.

Critics within this framework have argued that whenever someone appeals to the public interest, it is either meaningless or a cover for his/her own special interests. However, as Bernard Diggs makes clear, there is an obvious difference between a person's interest and the thing in which he or she is interested. Parents' special interest may be the common interest of their children.

> We shall be in hopeless difficulty if we do not take seriously the distinction between a person's talk and what the talk is about. . . . If a person has a special interest in the common interest, let us have the good grace to acknowledge it. . . . Unselfishness, impartiality, and being unprejudiced are human virtues. They are not to be reduced to drivel by speaking of the impartial person as being partial toward impartiality and the unprejudiced as being prejudiced in favor of a lack of prejudice. (Diggs, "The Common Good," p. 285)

In a similar vein, when political philosophers identify the common interest as an ethical concern in social life and statecraft, they are not identifying the interests all citizens have or what all citizens are interested in. When legislation is passed in the public interest, it does not mean all citizens are interested in it or that the legislation will benefit every person in the same way. Interstate highways or graduated income taxes or referenda do not benefit everyone or everyone equally. However, it is rational to support such cooperative enterprises instead of living in Hobbes' state of war. We prefer on balance to be reasoned with rather than commanded or forced; therefore, if the common good appears to be a reasonable solution, we consider it to be in our interest.

Rewards and benefits are not merely instrumental. Total victory or getting an advantage over another is not entailed by either the common good or one's special interest. Joint projects necessitate a fair distribution of benefits, either short term or long term, but not all the benefits for oneself. As Diggs argues in clarifying the common good as a moral concept, we enter into shared arrangements in competitive situations by following elementary moral notions of fairness. Our assessment of social arrangements is guided by what we are reasonably entitled to expect and by complex understandings of mutual acceptance (Diggs, "The Common Good," pp. 287–288). In fact, only within a sensitivity to the common good can we recognize the deep chasms of exclusion and powerlessness as morally outrageous.

12. "Communitarian" as a common label for these academic theorists (plus Michael Walzer and Alasdair MacIntyre) obscures their particular differences. Although useful as a label, it also disguises their fundamental difference collectively from the political movement and parties by that name on both sides of the Atlantic. As Mulhall and Swift put it,

> Amitai Etzioni, whose book *The Spirit of Community* contains a communitarian platform to which individuals are invited to subscribe, occasionally draws upon the ideas of . . . the philosophical communitarians, but it is difficult to find anything more than vague and general connections to the kind of programme he has in mind. . . . So far as we are aware, none of [the] communitarian theorists has signed up to Etzioni's programme. (Stephen Mulhall and Adam Swift, *Liberals and Communitarians*, 2nd ed. [Oxford, UK: Blackwell, 1996], p. xiv)

13. John Rawls, *A Theory of Justice* (Cambridge, MA: Harvard University Press, 1971), p. 302.
14. Mulhall and Swift, *Liberals and Communitarians*, pp. 52 and 49; cf. Michael Sandel, *Liberalism and the Limits of Justice* (Cambridge, UK: Cambridge University Press, 1982), pp. 59–65.
15. Mulhall and Swift, *Liberals and Communitarians*, p. 10.
16. Mulhall and Swift, *Liberals and Communitarians*, p. 54; cf. Sandel, *Liberalism and Limits*, pp. 15–23.
17. Mulhall and Swift, *Liberals and Communitarians*, p. 56; cf. pp. 54–55.

18. Mulhall and Swift, *Liberals and Communitarians,* p. 56; cf. Sandel, *Liberalism and Limits.*

19. Mulhall and Swift, *Liberals and Communitarians,* p. 68.

20. Mulhall and Swift, *Liberals and Communitarians,* p. 67.

21. Charles Taylor, *Sources of the Self, The Making of the Modern Identity* (Cambridge, MA: Harvard University Press, 1989), pp. 51–52.

22. Mulhall and Swift, *Liberals and Communitarians,* p. 16.

23. Taylor, *Sources of the Self,* p. 89.

24. Daniel Callahan, "Autonomy: A Moral Good, Not a Moral Obsession," *The Hastings Center Report* (October 1984): 42.

25. Cf. Clifford Christians, John Ferré, and P. Mark Fackler, *Good News: Social Ethics and the Press* (New York: Oxford University Press, 1993), p. 46.

26. Sara M. Evans and Harry C. Boyte, *Free Spaces: The Sources of Democratic Change in America* (Chicago: University of Chicago Press, 1992), p. 185.

27. Carole Pateman, *The Disorder of Women: Democracy, Feminism and Political Theory* (Stanford, CA: Stanford University Press, 1989), p. 62.

28. Markate Daly, ed., *Communitarianism: A New Public Ethics* (Belmont, CA: Wadsworth, 1994), p. xv.

29. Craig Calhoun, "The Public Good as a Social and Cultural Product," keynote address to Lilly Foundation Conference, Indianapolis, IN, November 1993, p. 6.

30. Carole Pateman, *The Problem of Political Obligation: A Critique of Liberal Theory* (Cambridge, UK: Polity Press, 1985), pp. 17–18.

31. Pateman, *The Disorder of Women,* pp. 63, 66.

32. Rawls, *A Theory of Justice,* pp. 14, 116, 344.

33. Pateman, *The Disorder of Women,* p. 62.

34. Pateman, *The Disorder of Women,* p. 61; cf. Pateman, *The Problem of Political Obligation,* pp. 26–29.

35. Cf. Michael Walzer, *Obligations: Essays on Disobedience, War, and Citizenship* (Cambridge, MA: Harvard University Press, 1970), pp. 190–225.

36. John Macmurray, *The Form of the Personal: The Self as Agent,* Vol. I (London: Faber & Faber, 1961), p. 38.

37. Martin Buber, *I and Thou,* 2nd ed., R. G. Smith, trans. (New York: Charles Scribner's Sons, 1958), pp. 69, 60.

38. Buber, *I and Thou,* p. 3.

39. John Macmurray, *The Form of the Personal: Persons in Relation,* Vol. 2 (London: Faber & Faber, 1961), p. 119.

40. J. B. Lotz, "Person and Ontology," *Philosophy Today,* 7 (Winter 1963): 294, 297.

41. Cited in Michael Moss, "The Poverty Story," *Columbia Journalism Review,* 26,2 (July/August 1987): 43.

42. For this quotation and further description, see Lynn Waddell, "Adding Color to Public Journalism," pp. 160–161 in *Mixed News,* ed. Jay Black (Mahwah, NJ: Erlbaum, 1997).

43. Davis Merritt, "Public Journalism: What It Means, How It Looks," in *Public Journalism: Theory and Practice,* eds. J. Rosen and D. Merrit (New York: Kettering Foundation, 1994), p. 23; cf. Jay Rosen, *Community Connectedness:*

Passwords for Public Journalism (St. Petersburg, FL: Poynter Institute, 1994), p. 26.

44. Robert Merrihew Adams, "Religious Ethics in a Pluralistic Society," in *Prospects for a Common Morality*, eds. Gene Outka and John P. Reeder Jr. (Princeton, NJ: Princeton University Press, 1993), p. 93.

45. Cf. Sissela Bok, *Common Values* (Columbia and London: University of Missouri Press, 1995). Bok argues constructively for minimalist values, a limited set of fundamental moral commitments that are necessary for collective survival. Minimalist moral values provide a basis for political dialogue and negotiation but do not call for agreement as to their source or exceptionless character (pp. 18–19, 53–59). The minimalist values "most easily recognized across societal boundaries" are "the positive duties of care and reciprocity; constraints on violence, deceit, and betrayal; and norms for procedures and standards of justice" (p. 41).

46. Adams, "Religious Ethics," p. 94.

47. Adams, "Religious Ethics," p. 93.

48. Adams, "Religious Ethics," p. 96.

49. Adams, "Religious Ethics," p. 99.

50. Adams, "Religious Ethics," p. 103.

51. Brian Barry, "Justice and the Common Good," in *Political Philosophy*, ed. Anthony Quinton (Oxford, UK: Oxford University Press, 1967), pp. 190–191; see also Gerald F. Gaus, "The Commitment to the Common Good," pp. 26–64 in *On Political Obligation*, ed. Paul Harris (New York: Routledge, 1990).

52. Adams, "Religious Ethics," p. 103.

53. Mulhall and Swift, *Liberals and Communitarians*, p. 103.

54. Mulhall and Swift, *Liberals and Communitarians*, pp. 106, 108, 107; cf. Taylor, *Sources of the Self*, pp. 27, 29.

55. Mulhall and Swift, *Liberals and Communitarians*, pp. 112–113; cf. Taylor *Sources of the Self*, p. 36.

56. Theodore L. Glasser, "Squaring with the Reader: A Seminar on Journalism," *Kettering Review* (Winter 1992): 44.

57. Joseph Cardinal Bernardin, *The Gift of Peace* (Chicago: Loyola Press, 1997), p. 22.

58. Bernardin, *The Gift of Peace*, p. 23.

59. Bernardin, *The Gift of Peace*, pp. 134, 136.

60. Bernardin, *The Gift of Peace*, pp. x, 11.

61. "Catholic Cardinal Bernardin Dies," Online News Hour, November 19, 1996.

62. Chantal Mouffe, "Hegemony and Ideology in Gramsci," in *Gramsci and Marxist Theory*, ed. Chantal Mouffe (London: Routledge & Kegan Paul, 1979), pp. 181–186, 191–192.

63. Diggs, "The Common Good," p. 292.

64. Diggs, "The Common Good," p. 292.

65. Sigmund Freud, *Totem and Taboo*, James Strachey, trans. (New York: Norton, 1952).

Chapter 5

Making Readers into Citizens— The Old-Fashioned Way

Thomas C. Leonard

University of California, Berkeley

Public journalism—whatever else it stands for—wants citizens to be conscious of themselves, informed on the issues, and ready to act on their conclusions. The press cannot be neutral on these core values. It must care and work actively to make connections. Readers must be linked to one another, to the real issues, and finally to public officials. This approach may be wise or unwise (depending on the circumstances, it can be either, I believe). But critics cannot appeal to tradition to scorn public journalism. These core values have long inspired the American press.

In developing public journalism, reporters and editors have drawn on the experience of a lifetime. But it is rare to see reflection that goes back further than that. The faded clips of journalism early in this century, even the musty subscription records of this era, reveal surefire ways to engage the public on civic matters. Whether these methods suit the conscience of public journalism today is an open question. But because the war stories of today's press corps have probably passed the point of diminishing returns for public journalism, a visit to the archive will do no harm.[1]

A century ago, newspapers were much more likely to be part of the life of an American household than they are today. Legions of working-class Americans, including the large component of immigrants, were won over to the habit of following news about public affairs. The polyglot cities, with many newcomers who had not relied on papers in their homeland, were conquered by English-language publishers. Joseph Pulitzer and William Randolph Hearst led the way, sure that a popular paper needed civics lessons to prosper. Jürgen Habermas, in his influential history of the public sphere, credits this American approach but argues that the new marketing of news lessened "its political character."[2] There is much evidence to the contrary. Hearst worked through the Democratic Party and also built clubs and leagues to advance his ideas. His papers attempted to sweep readers into these organizations. Hearst wanted votes much more than he wanted elevated political discourse, but he had a habit of furnishing minds with fresh ideas before he asked for these votes. A variety of socialists, for example, reached a large audience through his papers. For all his eccentricities, many publishers shared Hearst's insight that a journalism of civic ideas was a good commercial formula. At the turn of the century, magazines for the middle class discovered that political reform could be as compelling as the world of entertainment. A consumer society and a better society seemed compatible, and advertisers paid the way for some searching exposés of powerful people and institutions. This was the time that *Cosmopolitan* (then, as now, owned by Hearst) was more likely to put corruption rather than a pretty face on its cover. A century ago, eligible voters paid far more attention to elections than they do today. Some states had an 80 or even 90 percent turnout before 1900 and voting remained strong, by today's standards, in the next 20 years.

There is no point in romanticizing this defunct political culture, which was riddled with injustices more serious than the ones we take into the year 2000. The press of the early 20th century may even have contributed to early forms of apathy and cynicism in the public sphere. But as public journalism seeks to connect citizens through news, there are lessons in the bold methods that won a democratic readership in the first place.

Mobilizing Readers

Publishers who learned their business in the 19th century knew that they must bring citizens together and make them conscious of one another. This was the bedrock of much daily journalism in an age of great partisan feeling. Unapologetically, many dailies put out campaign editions in their state or region to mobilize voters. "A Tribune Campaign Club is needed in every neighborhood in the West, to supply the people with reliable facts and correct political information," the *Chicago Tribune* insisted when elections rolled around. The aim was to turn out Republican voters, of course, but the process was second nature in all the parties and pressure groups. The fierce voice in reporting encouraged readers to believe that they were children of light, set against the children of darkness. Here, for instance, is how the *Tribune* saw two demonstrations over the key economic question in the 1896 campaign, "free silver" versus a currency backed only by gold. These stories ran next to each other, after a single day of frenzied political activity[3]:

The Pitiable "Free Silver" Parade

In straggling column they stumbled through the streets . . . marching in weariness for fancied glory, but in reality hastening their own doom; tottering under banners which proclaimed an era of rotten money, lower wages, less work; proclaiming devotion to a cause which will bring destitution and want to their friends, will fill the public charities with their wives and children, will cut off their labor, will reduce them to pauperism; and bringing to this pitiful sacrificial function the blazing eyes of fanatics, the zealous shouts perverted from honest causes, the hoarse cheers of ignorant dupes.

The Sound Money Demonstration

. . . Unprecedented in the history of the country as a civic pageant and political display. . . . It was a polyglot gathering. All the diverse nationalities of this cosmopolitan city came together in this pageant, moved by a common impulse and inspired by a common purpose. They represented the trades, industries, and commerce, the factories, mills, shops, and stores, the railroads and other transportation interests, the great corporations and the small dealers—in a word, the enterprise, ambition, intelligence, integrity and conscience of Chicago.

Now this is one way to call citizens to their responsibilities. The *Tribune* had helped to stage this civic gathering and promoted participation. "Gala Day at Hand," "All the Omens Are Good" were the headlines, summoning readers to the parades and rallies. Here was a journalism about the issues that stressed inclusion. But in this precursor of public journalism, the partisan press demonized some ideas and some citizens. It is hard to find journalists who write like this today because balance is the watchword and not many of us believe that we can read minds and tell the future. But the passion for debate and campaigns in such papers a century ago does not deserve contempt. Public journalism has found no better rhetorical strategy to get large groups to take issues seriously, to pressure government officials, and to vote on election day.

The mobilization of readers was important to publishers even when an election was not under way. Sales were not left to the reader's own impulse (magazine publishers had so little faith in this in the 19th century that most of them did not even change their covers from issue to issue). Magazines, and some newspapers, depended on "club" subscription arrangements where friends and neighbors were thrown into each others' arms to earn discounts and prizes. Nineteenth-century readers talked about their subscriptions in a wide circle of acquaintances, a process of disclosing tastes and new interests that contributed to citizenship. Promotions to gather readers were amalgams of neighborliness and prurience. Public journalism has been most vigorous outside the largest cities, and it is interesting to note that, a century ago, some of the boldest plans to connect readers with papers unfolded in rural America. In Iowa, for example, a paper held contests to find the most popular young woman. To have a ballot, you needed to get your hands on a newspaper or sign up new readers. Candidates and their supporters were given weeks of training on how to canvass. Then, for a month, the canvassers swept through the townships. The running vote totals for popular girls were such big news that daily extras were issued. The editor recalled that the excitement eclipsed that of the presidential runs of William Jennings Bryan and Theodore Roosevelt.[4]

City folk, too, were lured to journalism with contests that often pushed acquaintances, even strangers, to cooperate in the pursuit of prizes. *The Boston Globe*, for example, printed coupons that entitled readers to vote on the most popular war veteran, saleswoman, fireman, and so forth. Eager, prepared citizens took to carrying scissors. The *Globe* reported five million entries in one contest.[5]

In 1892, the *Globe* showed that a game of chance using community ties could draw attention to the presidential race. Every weekday, for four months, the paper ran a coupon inviting New Englanders to guess the vote total on election day. The best guesser would win $5 each week for life. The official entry form and news about the contestants was the largest feature on the sports page. The names, the home towns, and the exact guesses were printed, along with the political sentiments of the contestants—many of these in verse. The *Globe* pointed out how neighbors could cooperate to enter and used community involvement to help police the contest. The entry form has lines for witnesses to the bet. If you signed this line, showing that you listened to your neighbor's political forecast, and this was the best guess, the paper would send you "a crisp $50 bill." Whipping up interest in an election did not seem to embarrass anyone at this paper a century ago.

The manufacturing of a sense of community through marketing stunts was, of course, a mainstay of the "Yellow Press." (No one called the *Chicago Tribune* or *The Boston Globe* "yellow." They were thoroughly respectable.) Joseph Pulitzer got children to save their pennies (and extract them from softhearted readers) for the greatest civic monument of this era: the pedestal for the Statue of Liberty in New York Harbor. Liberty was a mythical hero, but in Pulitzer's papers, as well as in the press of his arch rival Hearst, there was often a contest going on that gave ordinary citizens the glory. E. W. Scripps lectured his editors never to depend on advertisers but to build their success by winning the trust of the plain folks. From his baronial ranch overlooking the Pacific in southern California, Scripps told his editors across the country to cling to the worker's point of view, especially about politics. The Scripps papers featured the cartoon characters "Mr. and Mrs. Common People" doing battle with injustice.

Making readers count in the discussion of public questions is the watchword of public journalism today. A century ago, publishers found ways to do this. Ordinary citizens were more likely to find their names and comments in the Yellow Press than in the more respectable papers that lost the circulation contests. The "People's Editorials" and "People's Forum" were creeping into the regular flow of news. And there were great displays of the common touch. In 1889, the Scripps League of Newspapers covered industrial shows in Europe by sending 40 working men from the Midwest on an expedition across the Atlantic. These skilled workers were untrained writers, but with the help of journalists, they filed stories interesting enough to be picked up by many American papers beyond the Scripps chain.[6]

Clearly, there was personal ambition in the popular press of a century ago that public journalism would not welcome in the year 2000. Hearst dreamed of the White House, for instance, and that distorted his coverage of politics. Frequently, his publications made all public questions revolve around his own thoughts and ambitions. There is much evidence, however, that readers of the Yellow Press looked beyond the narcissism of publishers and did value this journalism as it created a new forum for political discussion.

Hearst's flagship paper, New York's *Evening Journal*, is a case in point. By the end of his first decade in the crowded field of dailies, Hearst had risen to the top and boasted of 850,000 circulation. Early in the presidential year of 1904, the paper asked its readers to write letters explaining the appeal of the paper. As this was a Hearst operation, there was hoopla and cash prizes for the best letters. Here was a carnival of self-promotion for the paper, certainly not the sort of thing that the Pew Charitable Trusts would encourage today. But to a modern reader, much of the communication between these journalists and their readers sounds like public journalism. The appeal for letters was kicked off with a confession that the paper "is at present used only feebly and spasmodically for the public welfare." This would change, for "the *Evening Journal* is to labor especially in the line of education, and in the line of methodically advocating reforms, as well as methodically stimulating discussion and thought." Readers could now share their ideas with millions of other citizens and become "partners and creators of the power which the paper represents." Even though Hearst's editors managed to get the publisher's name into nearly every political story across the nation, the letter writers did not celebrate the man. Indeed, Hearst was rarely named. The readers spoke more broadly of how the paper had "become an indispensable element in the civic life of the people" and was "the people's open court." The paper was not credited with defeating any political faction, but it was the enemy of the "indifferent." One reader echoed the idea of many that the *Evening Journal* was now "a public institution."[7]

There is some independent confirmation that Hearst's circus of a newspaper was taken by many as a civics lesson. In 1907, a careful observer on Manhattan's Lower East Side noted that the editorials on "the big social issues of the age" had created a bond with readers. These were largely newcomers to America who did not know who wrote these columns. At a rally, "this man was introduced simply as, 'The man who writes the *Journal* editorials.' And in the instant outburst of applause, rising higher and higher, in the sudden hush, then the thousand of faces, tense and eager, pressing forward to listen—it was clear enough that the tenement masses are eager for just such discussion."[8]

It *was* easier to believe that a common voter mattered in the first years of this century than it is today. In the political parties at that time, there was a sifting in the local community to find that ordinary person who commanded a bit of respect, enough to sway a few votes. These people were to be nurtured by politicians. The press, in giving a small platform for citizens and conjuring up local heroes, was joining this effort to make individuals count.[9]

The high road of finding citizens who were sages or heroes was certainly not the only direction for the press at the beginning of the 20th century. As the columns from the *Chicago Tribune* showed, editors then, far more than today, offered their readers villains. Self-consciously, to gain working-class readers, editors such as Hearst, Pulitzer, and Scripps looked for plutocrats to ridicule. In the muckraking magazines of the first decade of the 20th century, industrialists, financiers, and the politicians who were their friends were exposed as (in one happy phrase) "enemies of the republic." Public journalism may be passive–aggressive (in leaving blanks on the page when a candidate does not speak to an issue, for instance) but stories to restore our civic life are nearly always polite and respectful. If popular journalism of a century ago was to become our model, we would see reporting that is far more ill-mannered and aggressive.[10]

Consider how this century began with coverage of the oil king John D. Rockefeller Sr. The industrialist turned philanthropist lost all his hair suddenly as he passed his 63rd birthday, and the popular press made a joke of his illness. Cartoonists settled into work on the old man with wig askew, or dollar signs in his last strands, or gallons of hair restorer that would do him no good. Reporters who had been covering the man for years explained that the industrialist now symbolized "a withered and fruitless life." The celebrated Ida Tarbell shadowed him in his church to note his "curiously unhealthy pallor" and "unclean flesh." Reporting like this filled columns in the best publications of the new century. The newsstand favorite *Cosmopolitan*, then mixing progressive politics with notes on imperfect flesh, reported that "the Rockefeller eyes are small and glittering, like the eyes of a rat. By the same token, the contour of the Rockefeller mouth is suggestive of the cutting, gnawing rodent teeth." These were far from the cruelest cuts. Tarbell, otherwise a superb reporter, speculated on the intimate lives of Rockefeller's long dead relatives. Pulitzer topped her by putting a reporter on the trail of Rockefeller's aged and mysterious father. The publisher spent more than $100,000 in 1999 dollars to nail down an article that the father was a bigamist. "The Rockefeller family will get their first knowledge of the revelation from this article," Pulitzer's papers chirped.[11]

Today, coverage this rough is imaginable only if Ted Turner were to profile Rupert Murdoch, or vice versa. The mainstream press has pretty much lost that streak of cruelty. This appears to be a good thing for all who want a rational discussion of public questions. But it is sobering to note that along with marketing gimmicks, our heritage of robust political debate is an admixture of the ad hominem and the melodramatic. When the Supreme Court outfitted journalists with sturdy protection from public officials in *New York Times v. Sullivan* (1964) it was correct in noting "a profound national commitment to the principle that debate on public issues should be uninhibited, robust, and wide-open, and that it may well include vehement, caustic, and sometimes unpleasantly sharp attacks on government and public officials." No one knows whether journalism can engage citizens without occasional use of unbridled passion. Public journalism with the gloves off is one way of describing what the press was up to at a high point of citizen participation. The press then had an anger and an edge that we ignore at our peril.

Coupon Democracy

For attention-getting marketing tricks, anyway, I believe that this legacy of American journalism *can* be compatible with the improvement of public discourse. The historical record does not justify the distaste that serious political commentators have for marketing gimmicks.

The journalist Alan Ehrenhalt has recently reminded us of how the passion to gather readers can sustain a shadow government. I don't mean the time-honored tradition of giving a column or seat on an editorial board to a politician who has left office—that has been going on since the days of Teddy Roosevelt. I mean the creation of local heroes with an honorary role in governing. In the first half of this century, this was done in Chicago out of the mixed motives of community pride and lust for subscribers. In *The Lost City*, Ehrenhalt explains how the black newspaper, the *Chicago Defender*, published ballots that allowed readers to vote for their own mayor, deputy mayor, and a fire commissioner on the Southside. Every two years, dozens of the black bourgeoisie campaigned for these honors, to the shared delight of the community and the *Defender's* circulation manager.[12]

Does any of this suggest quality journalism? I invoked Pulitzer's name as a reminder that it is often not possible to draw a clear line between circulation stunts and the use of the press to enlighten. Ehrenhalt makes the argument that the *Defender* "was the best newspaper in the city," and by this he means "the most honest in dealing with . . . the community it served." It is not hard to find other examples of community-building features in the minority press of the first half of the 20th century. The *Forward*, a daily Yiddish newspaper that held out the promise of socialism, created space for immigrants to tell their stories of hardships in the new country. Beginning in 1906, the greenhorns found their voices in the paper and competed for the honor of this recognition. In this precursor of public journalism, readers were allowed to identify their problems and speak their minds before the editor offered advice.[13]

One of the tricks dreamed up a century ago by publishers has become a mainstay of political involvement and persuasion. The great contribution to public journalism was the coupon. It was in the mid-1890s that the coupon came into our press, with the dotted line and invitation: "Cut Out—Mail Today!" The idea of slicing into a newspaper or magazine was hard to get used to when many copies were passed on to friends and wound up in handsome bound volumes for the parlor. Even advertising trade journals condemned the extraction of coupons as an "injury" and a "mutilation."

By the early years of the new century, however, the press was filled with rectangles and triangles and surgery was wildly popular in political campaigns. Hearst mobilized readers to express themselves on pending legislation with forms that readers were to clip from his papers. In 1913, the million readers of the weekly *Menace* were given a coupon with the "rules" set by Catholics to control daily papers. These guidelines required that news of lascivious, gun-toting priests be suppressed while every blemish on Protestant America was put on the front page. "Cut this out," the *Menace* directed, "send it to the daily newspaper you subscribe for, and ask them why this rule is followed." Many readers did just that. The *Chicago Tribune* received so many that it drafted a standard letter of reply.[14]

Coupons have loomed large indeed in some of the most successful social movements of the late 20th century. Civil rights workers were sustained by the coupon as well as by the march and the sit-in. "Heed Their Rising Voices," the full-page ad that appeared in *The New York Times* on March 29, 1960, contained language that won protection in the famous *Sullivan* decision by the Supreme Court four years later. But the words that counted most to the movement in the days after the ad appeared were "Please mail this coupon TODAY!"

The Committee to Defend Martin Luther King was testing conscience and marketing at the same time. Similarly, conservationists have reaped the benefits of coupons. This began in the 1960s with the Sierra Club's campaign to stop a dam at the Grand Canyon ("Should we also flood the Sistine Chapel so tourists can get nearer the ceiling?").

I don't mean to suggest that coupons have simply given voices to voiceless citizens across the political spectrum. Coupons conditioned Americans to live in the bureaucratic state and increased their vulnerabilities as consumers. There was significance in the timing of their invention. Advertising and other marketing techniques took hold of the American household in the first decades of this century. Coupons gave businesses their first clues about how to segment markets. There was an explosion of government forms—for the military draft and income tax, driver's licenses, and social security programs. Coupons in commercial media accustomed Americans to putting information in the right space and to sending the paper on to the correct office. The reader was getting used to a more bureaucratized society in which unseen agencies would gather information. But another way of putting this is that a format for information and advertising in the press was teaching readers how to behave as citizens. Making readers has a way of making citizens, and in insisting that this be done self-consciously, public journalism is asking the press to think through the implications of its inherent power.

Coupons have done something to enlarge the possibilities of citizenship. They need not be badges of captivity to either government or industry. It is a rare week when *The New York Times*, for instance, does not offer its readers several issues that may be advanced if the reader will only reach for the scissors. Both general circulation and specialized periodicals continue to call citizens to speak to Congress through the coupons they provide. "Cut here" may not be an utterance the press wishes to celebrate, but with these words journalism changed our relationship to the printed word and invented a new form of persuasion. Experiments in public journalism can profitably build on this old form of gimmickry. Indeed, this has already happened in several states. In Ohio, for instance, the *Akron Beacon-Journal* relied on coupons to get suggestions from readers on how to address racial issues that the paper had brought into view.[5]

I do not suggest that public journalism should rummage through the press archives and then copy things that worked many years ago. That is a misuse of history. But it makes no sense to ignore a popular press that has been taking risks to catch the attention of readers since the 19th century. Publishers such as Pulitzer, Scripps, and Hearst did not have voice mail, the fax, or the Internet to link their readers with the issues of their day. But the more we study their entrepreneurial strategies, the more we are tempted to call the spirit behind the high-tech tools old-fashioned. Inventing new forms of participation and deliberation is what the press has been about for a long time. Public journalism asks that more risks be taken so that the public engagement will grow. The defenders of reporting and editing who show no concern about participation have the burden of explaining why experimentation (or gimmicks) should stop. Public journalism has a usable past: With an eye on self-interest and civic responsibility, we must do whatever it takes to make more people care.

Notes

1. See, for example, Davis Merritt, *Public Journalism and Public Life: Why Telling the News Is Not Enough* (Hillsdale, NJ: Erlbaum, 1995).
2. Jürgen Habermas, *The Structural Transformation of the Public Sphere: An Inquiry into a Category of Bourgeois Society* (Cambridge, MA: MIT Press, 1989), pp. 168–169.
3. *Chicago Tribune*, July 8, 1876, p. 1; and July 24, 1876, p. 1, as well as this time of the year in later presidential campaigns. *Chicago Tribune*, October 11, 1896, p. 28; and front page, October 9, 1896. Taking all news reporting

into account over this weekend, the Silver factions did not fare much better in the pages of the *Tribune* than in these Sunday columns.

4. Ira A. Nichols, *Forty Years of Rural Journalism in Iowa* (Fort Dodge, IA: Messenger Press, 1938), pp. 80–83; *Circulation Manager* 1 (February 1903): 14. Thomas C. Leonard, *News for All: America's Coming-of-Age with the Press* (New York: Oxford University Press, 1995), gives a comprehensive account of gathering readers.

5. Louis M. Lyons, *Newspaper Story: One Hundred Years of the Boston Globe* (Cambridge, MA: Harvard University Press, 1971), pp. 101–102. *Circulation Manager*, 1 (February 1903): 14; (March 1903): 7; and (May 1903): 26. *Newspaper Maker*, 4 (November 26, 1896): 3; 5 (April 29, 1897): 8; and 5 (August 5, 1897): 4.

6. Milton A. McRae, *Forty Years in Newspaperdom* (New York: Brentano's, 1924), pp. 88–90. Gerald J. Baldasty, *E. W. Scripps and the Business of Newspapers* (Urbana, IL: University of Illinois Press, 1999).

7. *Evening Journal*, February 25, 1904, p. 12; February 29, 1904, p. 2; March 10, 1904, p. 3; April 6, 1904, p. 6; and April 7, 1904, p. 10.

8. Ernest Poole, "New Readers of the News," *American Magazine*, 65 (1907–1908): 45.

9. The classic statement of how an ordinary citizen could "get a followin'" in the urban machines of this era is William L. Riordon, *Plunkitt of Tammany Hall* (1905). In the modern edition of this work, James S. Olson calls Tammany a "shadow government." See *Honest Graft: The World of George Washington Plunkitt* (St. James, NY: 1993), pp. 6, 60.

10. The phrase was used by Lincoln Steffens in articles such as "Enemies of the Republic, The Political Leaders Who Are Selling Out the State of Missouri, and the Leading Business Men Who Are Buying It—Business as Treason—Corruption as Revolution," *McClure's*, 22 (1904): 587–599. Thomas C. Leonard, *The Power of the Press: The Birth of American Political Reporting* (New York: Oxford University Press, 1986), puts the regional exposés and the national muckraking in context.

11. Charles Russell, "Rockefeller—An Estimate of the Man," *Human Life* (January 1908), in JDR Scrapbooks, microfilm reel 2, no. 11 from Rockefeller Archive Center, North Tarrytown, New York; Ida M. Tarbell, "John D. Rockefeller: A Character Study, Part II," *McClure's*, 25 (1905): 386–387. See also Thomas W. Lawson, *Frenzied Finance* (New York: Ridgway-Thayer, 1905), p. 291; Alfred Henry Lewis, "Owners of America: John D. Rockefeller," *Cosmopolitan* 45 (November 1908): 618–619. "The Rockefeller Mystery Solved . . . " St. Louis *Post-Dispatch*, February 2, 1908, sec. III, p. 1.

12. Alan Ehrenhalt, *The Lost City: Discovering the Forgotten Virtues of Community in the Chicago of the 1950s* (New York: Basic Books, 1995), pp. 150–151.

13. Ehrenhalt, *The Lost City*, p. 150. Isaac Metzker, *A Bintel Brief: Sixty Years of Letters from the Lower East Side to the Jewish Daily Forward* (New York: Schocken Books, 1971).

14. See, for example, *Evening Journal*, April 28, 1904, p. 5; James Kelley Papers, Chicago Historical Society, Folder 2; David Paul Nord, "Reading

the Newspaper: Strategies and Politics of Reader Response, Chicago, 1912–1917," *Journal of Communication*, 45 (1995): 66–93.

15. For example, *Good Housekeeping*, 222 (June 1996): 88; and Center for Science in the Public Interest, *Nutrition Action Healthletter*, 22,3 (April 1995): 4. Merritt, *Public Journalism and Public Life*, p. 101. Arthur Charity, *Doing Public Journalism* (New York: Guilford Press, 1995), pp. 25, 34, 138–141.

Part II

The Challenge
for Public Journalism

Chapter 6

Public Journalism
and Democratic Theory
Four Challenges
John Durham Peters
University of Iowa

It is hard to argue against the idea of public journalism. Who could object to more responsive and responsible public information? To vigorous debate and discussion among citizens? The ideals of public journalism are so noble that they can sometimes make even a friendly critic feel like an ingrate. Even so, doctrines and movements that seem to hold a monopoly on high-mindedness and goodwill can often benefit most from searching criticism. This chapter argues that the vision of democracy—democracy as conversation—that informs the key theoretical texts in the public journalism movement fails to grapple sufficiently with the obstacles to its realization. Public journalism envisions democracy as the participation of citizens in public dialogue and the press as an instigator of such dialogue. Unobjectionable as it may appear, this vision of democracy is, in fact, only one competitor among many. The idea of democracy represented by the public journalism movement misjudges, I argue, the best forms of communication for contemporary conditions and thereby misses some of the troubling, even tragic, sides of the dream of participatory democracy.

The Four Obstacles

In broad strokes, the story of democratic theory is the story of overcoming successive obstacles to democracy's realization. I want to review some well-known facts from the intellectual history of democratic theory to specify four specific challenges public journalism must face. My point is not to attack public journalism on theoretical grounds alone, for public journalism is more than a philosophy of public life; it is an experiment in news making and dissemination not confined to its programmatic statements. Problems in the architecture of theories do not necessarily bode the failure of a movement in practice. Still, theory can pinpoint the critical assumptions on which it rests and the critical challenges it faces. An adventure in social experimentation deserves the guidance of ideas just as ideas deserve the test of practice, as no less an authority than John Dewey would insist.

From its birth in ancient Athens to the 18th century, there were two classic obstacles to democracy: scale and human nature. The Athenian democracy rested on a population of citizens able to appear on a day's notice from a restricted geography.[1] Its most distinguished theorists, in fact, found Athens too large for a true democracy. Plato declared 5,040 to be the ideal number of citizens, well below the number of participating citizens in ancient Athens, a sum he derived on mathematical grounds.[2] Aristotle thought the limits on democracy were given by the number of people whose characters one could come to know closely. In any case, democracy was conceived of as a relatively small city–state ruled by the assembled will of the citizens. Essential to its conduct was the participation of citizens and the opportunity for public debate. Even so, despite the principle that each citizen deserves an opportunity to speak (*isegoria*),[3] public debate was rule governed and largely an auditory affair for most citizens; Athens certainly never had anything quite approaching to a dialogical polity. Knowing something more of Athenian democracy's complex history might cure us of our Athens envy.

Julius Caesar long symbolized the factors that spell the corruption of democracy: empire, military adventure abroad, suspension of liberties at home. In the 18th century Montesquieu had declared, much in line with ancient ideas, that geographically large polities could only be empires held together by military might. He restricted the more delicate bonds of democracy to small states, much to the consternation of some delegates to the Constitutional Convention of the United States.[4] Montesquieu's compatriot Rousseau nicely expressed the classic commitment to the principle of proper proportions:

> Just as nature has set bounds to the stature of a well-formed man, outside which he is either a giant or a dwarf, so, in what concerns the best constitution for a state, there are limits to the size it can have it if is to be neither too large to be well-governed nor too small to maintain itself.[5]

For most of its life, then, democracy has been thought to work best in polities small enough that citizens can gather and listen, if not speak, to each other. Assembly was historically democracy's only medium of mass communication. Until the 18th century, no political thinker dreamed of a democratic polity on an extended scale.

The second classic obstacle to democracy is human nature. I do not wish to offer a particular view, either about what human nature is or whether such a thing exists at all, only to suggest that one's vision of the rational and deliberative capacities of people in general will importantly color one's view of the viability of a regime based on the *logos*, the word. This much is well-known: Theoretical democrats must posit some sort of wisdom in the hearts of ordinary folks. The challenge to faith in the cognitive powers of the people is coeval with the idea of democracy itself. One event symbolizes the people's potential for folly. The death of Socrates haunts democratic theory like a guilty conscience. Leaving aside the much-debated reasons for this "sin against philosophy," as Aristotle called it, the fact remains that a jury of Socrates' peers found him worthy of death for teaching *philosophia*, a strange doctrine said to corrupt the youth of the city. Whether the verdict owes to stupidity, intransigence, fear, or some other sort of failure of public wisdom, democracy will forever be marred by the fact that the people of Athens, duly constituted as a democratic jury, chose to put to death the man since hailed as Athens's wisest citizen and the source of much of subsequent European civilization.[6] For many political theorists since, beginning with Socrates' disciple Plato, the Achilles' heel of democracy was precisely the free reign it gave the more dangerous parts of human nature, both individually and collectively.

Concluding his thorough study of democratic governments, ancient and modern, James Madison, in the famed number 10 of *The Federalist Papers* (1787–1788), did not paint a pretty picture. "Democracies," he wrote, "have ever been spectacles of turbulence and contention; have ever been found incompatible with personal security, or the rights of property; and have in general been as short in their lives, as they have been violent in their deaths."[7] He concluded that "faction"— the mobilization of a majority or minority around a common interest or passion that went counter to the common good—was the "mortal disease" of democracy.[8] The mode of communication in democracy—the direct assembly of the people—only increased democracy's combustibility, offering no checks to the flow of popular passion. The culprit was clear: "The latent causes of faction are sown in the nature of man."[9]

Madison's genius was to offer, with his concept of representation, an answer to the two classic obstacles to democracy. The election of representatives allowed extension of popular government to an unprecedented scale. Where the entire people in a vast polity could never assemble, their representatives could. Madison argued that large scale did not destroy democracy; it offered checks on its inherent vices. Specifically, an extended republic increased the number of factions competing with each other, thus preventing any single faction from gaining the upper hand. Second, the reliance on representatives not only checked the potential flammability of the people gathered in assembly but allowed a kind of filtering of popular opinions "by passing them through the medium of a chosen body of citizens."[10] It is not unfair to find in the word "chosen" overtones not only of *elected* but of *elect*; in contrast to Jefferson, Madison believed the wisdom of the few would surpass that of the many. Madison, like George Washington and many others of the generation of founders, had a frankly skeptical view of the wisdom of the people. His studies suggested the need for checking the internal obstacles to democratic life, a concern that some recent democratic theorists, more concerned with external obstacles such as political economy and exclusionary social structures, often ignore.

Once checks to human irrationality and devices for extending geography were instituted to some extent in the United States, new obstacles became clear. An implicit part of Madison's analysis was the "circumstances of civil society," including property relations.[11] The ordering of social structures, I argue, becomes a third chief obstacle to democracy in the past two centuries. Scale turns out in retrospect only to have been the most obvious barrier to popular participation. From the early 19th century, a series of social movements has argued that what impedes democracy is neither the blindness of the people nor the insuperability of scale but structures of exclusion, violence, and oppression based on class, race, and gender. Struggles to open the circumstances of civil society to the equal protection of all citizens have included abolition, the civil rights movement, and the women's movements. It is hard for anyone of goodwill not to see in these developments a salutary democratization. Since the 1960s, the arguments about exclusionary structures have moved from legal, economic, and social barriers to more refined and subtle modes of exclusion—cultural, psychological, or linguistic.

Finally, the most elusive obstacle facing democracy today is the question whether the democratic dream of popular wisdom and participation still compels credence. To what extent do democratic ideals and projects still have grip on the imagination and energy of the mainstream of society? In some parts of the globe, "democracy" is still clearly a prize to be sought after. Free elections, a government responsive to popular demands, and due process are major achievements in any society. But guarantees of civil rights and legal order—exceedingly precious, by any standard—are not necessarily the same as the vision of democracy as participatory government of, by, and for the people engaged in conversation. The 20th century has seen a series of stunning critiques of the practicality and wisdom of direct popular rule. Walter Lippmann argued in a series of books in the 1920s that social complexity, speed, global warfare, overstimulation, censorship, elite propaganda, mass inattention and stereotypes, the irrational character of human psychology, and an overworked and ill-disciplined news media all spelled the demise of popular sovereignty, or at least of its founding fiction of a well-informed public. At best, news was an occasional flare sent up to attract the public's fleeting attention, and politics was an elite job of decision making best left to expert administrators. Modernity, in short, made democracy's confidence in a wise collective knower and knowable world incredible.

Lippmann is only one of many thinkers suspicious of democracy in this century; from Freud to some postmodernists, many have argued the impossibility of an intelligent and engaged citizenry and the folly of ideals of human emancipation and historical progress. Key events of the 20th century (the rise of the national security state, an unprecedented persuasion industry, the uneven globalization of capitalism, or the apparent impossibility of healing racial and ethnic wounds at home and abroad) have not done much to help the democratic faith either. To what degree does democracy still compel devotion? The question of faith in democracy is a central subtle drama in the public journalism movement as well as in politics more generally at the end of the millennium.

Scale, human nature, social structure, credibility—these four are the obstacles that any theory of democracy has to confront today. The idea of public journalism implicitly takes a position on each issue.

Public Journalism and the Four Obstacles

1. Dialogue and Scale

Most initiatives in public journalism have a salutary emphasis on the local as the chief site for political engagement, which well fits the historic site-specific character of journalism. The problem, in my view, however, is that the chief political concerns facing people today, even more than in Madison's time, are a curious mix of the local, the national, and the global. The management of this link is a task whose complexity is often skipped over in communitarian literature generally. Dewey's *The Public and Its Problems*,[12] for instance, a foundational book for public journalism, is motivated by an acute sense of the crisis of scale in early-20th-century America. Dewey's diagnosis was not that far from Walter Lippmann's: popular disaffection owed to the mass production of entertainment, the multiplicity of 20th-century life, and the dizzying growth of political scale. "Athenians," Dewey noted, "did not buy Sunday newspapers, make investments in stocks and bonds, and want motor cars."[13] American political culture, however, looked to the past for its guiding ideals: "We have inherited, in short, local town-meeting practices and ideas. But we live and act and have our being in a continental nation-state."[14] Dewey's solution—a patchwork of interlocking face-to-face settings that somehow added up to a national conversation, thus reconciling town-meeting practices with continental scope—is noble in its insistence on local sites of engagement but unconvincing in its treatment of scale. Dewey is absolutely right that (1) the face-to-face setting is where most crucial experience happens, (2) face-to-face relations can benefit from the democratic attitude (e.g., in school, family, worship, and relations between the sexes), but wrong that (3) face-to-face talk ought to be the primary site for the business of governing. Dewey never grappled systematically with the profound disproportion between the necessarily dispersed sites of conversation in an extended republic and the need for concentrated points of decision making.

The dream of democratic dialogue, compelling as it is, is remarkably undertheorized in current democratic thinking, public journalism included. First, dialogue is a form of communication whose form is organically connected to scale. Dialogue can only be dialogue if strict rules are imposed on the number of participants. If the number of participants in government gets too large, Madison warned, we will reap only "the confusion of a multitude"; if too small, we will suffer the "cabals of the few."[15] The limiting fact of democratic theory, perhaps even its tragic flaw, is the human inability to listen to more than one voice at a time. The chatter of a party, the roar of a crowd, or the song of a choir may all blend many voices at once, but none provides the deliberation that Dewey and so many of his disciples, inside and outside the public journalism movement, call for. As Jay Rosen puts it, "Dialogue defines the relationship" that ought to prevail within the public and between the press and the public.[16] Again, it is hard to criticize such thoughts without a guilty conscience, but the political dream of democracy as a grand dialogue of all citizens or groups of citizens is, without radical restrictions on what dialogue means, flawed in compelling ways.

The pragmatic conditions of dialogue need careful scrutiny. Other challenges loom besides the aforementioned distortion of conversational dynamics with a large number of participants: the political economy of media ownership and control, the image-based character of contemporary politics, and the pull of a consumer society away from public debate to private pleasure. Perhaps equally important, dialogue, as a whole series of 20th-century playwrights, filmmakers, and existential philosophers have shown, is not necessarily the homeland of mutuality and understanding. Dialogue is haunted by gaps[17] just as important as those that inform mass communication. A little reflection suggests that our most intimate relationships are rarely governed only by dialogue; as Michael Schudson has pointed out, the need for dialogue often declines the more intimately acquainted people are. Even in small groups, opportunities for consensus arise, but also for cronyism, filibustering, exclusion, or voluntary withdrawal. Why would we expect the polity to work any differently?

More important, there is a deeper moral flaw to the dream of conversational democracy: the limitations of human energy. The life of political engagement can be exhilarating, as the ancient Greeks knew. But we often forget that the Greeks knew equally well the danger, trouble, and instability of a life given to practical–political affairs.[18] There can be rational reasons for wanting to check out, for a season, from politics. The cultivation of disaffection among select portions of the electorate, a strategy apparently pursued by some political consultants in recent years, is plainly despicable, but the choice to trust one's representatives to manage the commonwealth and one's neighbors to guard against major abuses is a moral stance more complex than a simple abdication of responsibility. The "freedom from politics, which was unknown to Rome or Athens," writes Hannah Arendt, "is politically perhaps the most relevant part of our Christian heritage."[19] Care for the household and the lifeworld can be a jealous master, as can political engagement. Human finitude keeps us from all being participatory democrats. It is a dangerous romanticism to expect all citizens to have the desire, time, or skills for active engagement in political life; it is also dangerous to forget the degree to which politics is full of hassle and conflict. Whoever calls for participatory democracy should be ready to spend lots of time in meetings. The problem with socialism, as Oscar Wilde supposedly quipped, is that it takes too many evenings. It's no accident that The Port Huron Statement (1962), the great document of participatory democracy in postwar America,[20] was written by a group of single young men. The choice to devote one's energies to ordinary life at the expense of active political engagement cannot be dismissed as a failure on the part of a fellow citizen. The world-making work of everyday nonpublic action ought to have its place in democratic theory as well.

Public journalism is right to call for better sources of information and fresher forums of debate. But, beyond this unexceptional call, it has failed to probe the larger flaws in a vision of democracy as the conversational engagement of everybody. The insistence on dialogue undervalues those modes of public action that defy and interrupt conversation. St. Francis and Martin Luther King bore witness; they did not engage in conversation. Any account of democracy has to make room for moral stuntsmanship, for outrageous acts of attention getting employed by an Ezekiel or Gandhi, greens, antinuke activists, or even right-to-lifers. (If such acts involve violence to people or property they are, in my view, beyond the pale of democratic theory—but not of political theory.) Just as there is a dignity in dialogue, there can be a dignity in refusing to engage in dialogue as well.

Genuine dialogue not only means participation but, even more often, refraining from participation. One weak link in conversational democracy is loudmouths, bores, and fanatics. The temptation to strut for one's cause is almost overwhelming in a public forum. Dialogue cannot be dialogue unless everybody but the speaker bites his/her tongue. Silence is a crucial part of dialogue. The suspension of participation is just as crucial a part of democracy as is an open forum for all. The neurophysiological fact that we can only pay attention to one voice at a time is, again, the eternal limit to dialogical democracy. It is crucial to be clear: I am not defending the censors or those who call for martial law. The point is the contradictions of the democratic ideal of conversation. To have a dialogue, some silencing mechanisms must be in place, whether the moral force of self-regulation or the punitive force of policing. Some sort of access regulation, however nervous it makes our democratic hearts, is essential for successful public dialogue, as any teacher knows. One might allow for a lot of repetition in public discussion on the grounds of personal fulfillment it gives to each speaker (and belongingness is a crucial dimension of public spirit), but at some point discussion needs to stop. Allowing the loudest to gain the floor excludes voices, but elaborate procedures of inclusion can be just as exclusionary of those who are in a hurry or who have a burning truth to proclaim.

James Carey writes that "a democratic life is a life of conversation."[21] But as Michael Schudson argues, there is an aristocratic model of conversation as well, and the political valences of conversation as a communication style are ambiguous.[22] A democratic life is also a life of caring for those who cannot or will not take part in the conversation—the foreigner, the aged, the child, the dissident, and the unlettered. Something below conversation (solidarity) and something above it (witnessing) are necessary for a just polity. The discussion democrats might say, "of course," as if these things could be taken for granted in a vision of democratic communication. The neglect of what lies before and beyond conversation is a weakness in most current thinking about discursive democracy. Journalism ought not to be only a forum for the literate mainstream but for the cries of strangers as well. Outrage, frivolity, show stopping—all these and more have to be theoretically allowable as modes of public life. With no civil conversation, there is no democracy; with only civil conversation, there is no democracy either. Dialogue is indispensable for democracy but also destructive of it. The urge to interact on every issue would lead to a vertiginous quest for inclusion and make closure impossible. It would also keep almost everyone from participating.

The notion of the press as an instigator of public dialogue distorts the vision of the press and overburdens its role in society. This notion contrasts starkly with the chief story that accompanied the rise of a free press in early modern England, namely, that of "publicity."[23] Opposed to the despotism of state censorship, the notion of publicity called for the utmost freedom of information in the press, a wide dissemination of news and views. Implicit in the notion is discussion at local sites such as coffeehouses,[24] but publicity is essentially a one-way affair. The unilateral character of publicity is not a defect. It is intensely democratic: the equal access to all of political knowledge. This notion—the press as dissemination rather than dialogue—has been a governing narrative of journalism whose trace is inscribed in many mastheads. Names such as the Planet, Star, Sun, Herald, Mercury, Chronicle, Globe, Times, World, and Post all imply universal dissemination, "news for all," as Thomas Leonard puts it.[25] They offer a democracy of knowing or access, not of interaction.

Dialogue, in short, is not the only mode of communication worthy of democracy; dissemination is equally worthy. Many thinkers have attacked one-way media as agents of alienation and apathy. Although they have a legitimate complaint about the inequalities of access of a commercial media system, it is not quite right to blast one-way forms of communication per se. Too often critics talk of passive listening or viewing, when listening may be one of the most active and difficult things we do. Likewise, it is a fundamental error to think of one-way communication as only stultifying or undemocratic; it is a moral ideal of some power.[26] When Rosen calls for journalism to act "publicly, in an open, deliberative manner,"[27] his prose mixes two conceptions of publicness. Openness is unidirectional; deliberation is interactive. Expecting the press to stir or even inform the public is a more modest and realistic ideal than expecting it to sponsor and create the forums in which citizens can engage in authentic public dialogue. The press should handle the openness; civil society, as I argue, should handle the deliberation (in which the press would, of course, be one important part). Deliberation, it is important to point out, is not restricted to the interpersonal setting or the mutuality of dialogue.[28] In sum, the advocates of public journalism risk overlooking Madison's lessons about scale and the inevitability of representation—representation in both the sense of entrusting delegates to an assembly and the necessity of public, noninteractive forms of culture and argument. The romance of dialogue is stirring, but it can become the bread and butter of political life today only by being scaled back radically. If dialogue means the attempt to listen to others, to have the right of reply, and to compel the government to respond to public demand, I have no objections. But I fear that the nobility of the dream has prevented sufficient grappling with the subtleties—practical, moral, and political—of conversational democracy in the fuller sense. Dialogue is a peculiar, precarious, and precious form of talk that perhaps ought not to be elevated to paradigmatic status. Many productive and just social arrangements are not achieved by the dialogue of the many, but by tacit consent, goodwill, stewardship, and delegation to trusted leaders. My point is not to give the rulers a brief for shutting the people out of the machinery of government but to respect the robust Madisonian tradition and rehabilitate publicity as a nondialogical political good.

2. Play and Human Nature

Public journalism banks on a rational public. If its vision of democracy is participatory, its style of public talk is deliberative. Of all the many forms and genres of news, public journalism privileges hard news and opinion. Its vision of proper political activity is relentlessly serious. Though public journalism starts from the assumption that political life is broken in this country and provides an incisive account of public disengagement, it never questions the ideal of a public whose primary relation to political life is one, essentially, of rationality. Public journalism often locates the pathology of the public in the sociology of the newsroom, the norms of journalists, and the manipulations of politicians. It does not consider the possibility of a more deep-seated nonrationality (for good or ill) within the public itself. As Lippmann put it, the vision of a fully informative press assumes "an appetite for uninteresting truths which is not discovered by any honest analysis of our own tastes."[29]

Lippmann saw the dark side of human nature, and theorized a shift of burden of democracy from the people to experts. Dewey, in contrast, called for more radical experimentation in the communicative modes of journalism itself. In a key but neglected moment in *The Public and Its Problems,* Dewey called humans "sportive animals," sug-

gesting that we do not live by reason alone. Furthermore, in his prog-
nostications for press reform, the foremost item on his agenda was a
radical transformation in presentation.[30] He thought that the news, as
thitherto practiced, relied on too narrow a band in the spectrum of culture. In a distant way, perhaps, he was the prophet of photojournalism
and the 1930s muralists. He wanted to make the news an aesthetic as
well as purely intellectual experience. Enticement was as important as
facts, forms as important as information. Despite his high standing in
the discourse of public journalism, Dewey's call for artistic experimentation in news has been largely ignored. Dewey wanted vehicles of public instruction fitting our status as sensuous, practical, and playful
beings. Unlike Lippmann, who took the evidence of modern psychology to refute quite fundamentally any prospect of a wise public, Dewey
thought the ideal of public rationality was itself too sober and restric-
tive of the full range of political and expressive activity.

Like his philosophical predecessor Friedrich Schiller, Dewey
believed in an "aesthetic education" of people and citizens. Schiller
argued that people are most free, and most human, when they are at
play. For him, play was not mere frivolity; it was a training of the faculty
of judgment and hence had important ramifications for how people
live together as citizens.[31] Something of this notion echoes in Dewey's
claims, both in *The Public and Its Problems* and other works of the 1920s
and 1930s, that all human experience has an element of aesthetic form
in it that can be either heightened or suppressed. It is not going too far
to say that for Dewey, democracy was in large part a matter of serious
play and participation in it a kind of collective art making. With his
shift in the terms of democracy from rational cognition to embodied
action, Dewey also saw the possibility of a journalism open to adven-
tures in form, style, and appeal.

In a curious way, much in public journalism is more closely aligned
with Lippmann than with Dewey on this point, with its focus on the
menu and sources of information instead of on the sensuous variety of
forms. The idea of public journalism is marred by the cursory attention
it pays to entertainment and art as media of public debate. First, tone
and style lie at the very heart of public life.[32] The ancients knew that
the decorum of public address was not merely decorative but the thing
itself. Perhaps the recent past helps clarify public journalism's resistance to the aesthetic. Public journalism emerges at a moment of high
cynicism about democracy and the press, the fall of the house of Nixon
and the theater–states of Ronald Reagan and Bill Clinton. It calls for
"heroes in a post-Woodstein age."[33] Its exponents eschew dark tonali-
ties: Irony, they argue, is the symptom of a defective public sphere in
which we cannot call things by their names, sensationalism is empty

information calories for a public that could just as well be nourished by debate and discussion, and sex and murder and cop shows are just cheap product that grabs the public by its lower organs.

Fair enough. But the abuse does not ruin the use. Sensuous appeal in public life is too important to leave to the advertisers and sleaze mongers. The preferred tonality of public journalism is earnest, not silly; straightforward, not baroque; elevated, not vulgar; dialectic, not declamatory; discursive, not spectacular. It neglects the centrality of a variety of communicative styles to democratic life: the *sermo humilis* of a Lincoln; the clipped eloquence of an FDR; the fire of a Jesse Jackson.[34] It neither sounds the depths of human passions nor explores the full range of democratic expression. It asks journalists and the public to speak all but exclusively in moderate and genteel tones.

The long history of yellow journalism gnaws at the conscience as soon as one argues that the play drive has a crucial part in democratic life or that something besides reasonableness should be granted central status in public information. My point is not to praise sensationalism but rather to learn from it. Public participation flourishes when people are moved. And people are moved by more than their minds or hearts. Crime, punishment, lust, love, rivalry, and children at risk are the stuff of Genesis, Shakespeare, and the evening news. Public journalism needs a deeper account of what moves the public—what Lippmann called "an honest analysis of our own tastes." The darker visions of the human soul offered by thinkers such as Augustine, Montaigne, or Freud ought to be required reading for public-minded journalists as much as cheerier thinkers such as Tocqueville, Mill, or Dewey. However little we might want to admit it, the former group sounds our will to distraction, our bloodlust, our status as sportive animals, our relentless attachment to the shows and circus, and our delight in personalities, to an uncommon depth. Whether they are right in every particular or not, they give a bracing challenge to the rather flat psychology of the citizen that tends to prevail in recent dreams of democratic community. This is not to require public journalism, an experimental movement still in its early stages, to answer one of the great questions of the ages (i.e., what is the nature of the human being); it is to ask that an honest account be given of people's interests and passions as key data for any project of democratic reclamation.

Public journalism might experiment more widely with form of news as well as its content. Intelligence, as Dewey long taught, can take a wide variety of forms. Entertainment in its many forms brings "tales of common life" as much as does news; more precisely, the very contrast of entertainment and information ought to be contested. I am not endorsing either the tendency in recent cultural studies to elevate small acts of consumption into grand gestures of political will or the increasingly exploitative tactics of tabloid television.[35] Still, people gain access to common life via the ruling genres of culture, whether sermons, cartoons, tall tales, rap, stand-up comedy, the blues, sports, advertising, fashion, or stray bits of conversation. Public journalism might think about the news in a less argument-heavy way. Clearly, argument and deliberation have much to offer as modes of public debate. The question is their relative privilege in the rhetorical panoply of democracy. The potential is to think about altering not only the wellsprings of public information but the styles themselves. The human thirst for drama ought not to be disparaged as a distraction but as a major source of public engagement. Political parties, in 19th-century America, were often aptly named, given their knack for festival.[36] The human capacity for enjoyment is a key political resource, for good and ill. Here we need both Dewey's endorsement of play and experimentation and Lippmann's unflinching inspection of human nature.

3. Civil Society and the Press

Lippmann put my point cogently, "The problem of the press is confused because the critics and the apologists expect the press to . . . make up for all that was not foreseen in the theory of democracy."[37] The press, essential as it is for democracy, is only one of many institutions and practices of public life. In its more messianic moments, public journalism holds up the press as the savior of democracy, an old progressive hope. No single institution, however, should have to bear the burden of furnishing democratic life. Indeed, such centralization would be profoundly antidemocratic. In terms of their centrality to democratic life, one would have to put families, schools, communities of faith, and forms of work life above the press. Civil society needs a variegated array of institutions—neighborhoods, public libraries, the rule of law, and a basic level of security and welfare. An informative and critical press is a necessary condition of democracy but not a sufficient one. Democracy is a structural problem that implicates the total organization of society. Its health depends not only on access to facts and forums of argument but on will, public spirit, and socioeconomic structure. As Dewey would insist, democracy can exist only as interwoven with the material conditions of life. It should not be addressed as a problem of epistemology, of better data, but of collective experience and action.

To be sure, public journalism is about the constitution of forums, not just the provision of news and views. The effort cannot but be lauded. Yet it is curious to find the newspaper as a vanguard agent—

calling town meetings, getting people talking, reflecting, and posting the public agenda. One danger I see is a potential conflict of interest. The creation of community spirit and of community at a distance has long been one of chief strategies of commercial media in this country. Feedback from audiences has been the key financial link in the history of broadcasting[38] and to a lesser extent in print media. In an age when focus-group results are both political weapons and proprietary goods, one ought to think twice about making institutions that have a commercial stake in community constitution into organs of civic rejuvenation. The market, in my view, needs a place in any viable theory of democracy today, but it alone is surely not enough to assure proper support for a rich political culture in civil society.[39] Democracy needs the market's funds, not its flaws; its subsidies, not its asymmetries. Though far from the intentions of its architects, it is not hard to imagine public journalism turning into market research by other means, one of many ways media agencies simulate interaction with a dispersed and distant audience.

Putting the issue another way, the question is the aptitude of commercial culture as a basis for political community. The long ideal of the informative press and informed public equates newspaper reading with public participation. It is a tribute to the imperviousness of dreams to fact that the ideal has persisted so long, considering American journalism's rather lurid talent at providing readers with crime, scandal, sex, and violence, along with news, sports, recipes, and, above all, advertising. I am suspicious of a campaign of press reform that lacks a sustained critique of the commercial nexus of news production. As Hanno Hardt argues, public journalism needs more of a critical examination of its ties to the changing technological, economic, legal, and professional context of journalism.[40]

In sum, if the chief democratic battles of the last two centuries have concerned the opening up of access and opportunity to those excluded on various grounds, public journalism chooses to focus less on the structures of civil society than on the practices of journalists. One cannot, of course, do everything; the production of news is a key site for intervention. But the movement has a greater chance of contributing to the revitalization of public life in proportion to which it advocates structural change, not only of the forums of discussion but of the whole sum and substance of civil society, including its political economy. This suggestion clearly does not do much to save exponents of public journalism from the common and irksome charge of being utopian, but there's nothing so practical as a good theory. If we are to hunker down for the long haul, as I believe democratic thinkers today of every stripe must, we need the most sober analysis we can get of the structural conditions and obstacles of democracy.

4. Tragedy and the Question of Faith

Many of the intellectual supports that once connected democracy, popular wisdom, and the press are in trouble in late-20th-century culture. News as we know it is a cultural form that emerged with a variety of other modes of realist representation in 18th-century England—the novel, social statistics, and the ideas of the public and of public opinion. Late-20th-century culture has witnessed the breakdown of realism as a mode of social representation at every turn.[41] Scientists no longer talk of mirroring nature but of fabricating conditions that allow knowledge to emerge. Objectivity is an increasingly troubled ideal for professionals of every stripe, including journalists; even as metaphors of mirroring reality persist in journalism,[42] the grander vision of objectivity as the royal road to a truth beyond dispute has certainly lessened. Further, the image (not the word) has become perhaps the chief vehicle of political discourse today. The waning of realism is just one of many background assumptions of democratic ideals that are in trouble today. What, in short, is the status of democracy as a faith and way of life in a time when its intellectual and political environment is undergoing a massive transformation?

The viability of democracy in radically changed conditions was of course a guiding question in the implied debate between Lippmann and Dewey in the 1920s, a debate from which much contemporary democratic reflection still takes its bearing. In one sense, their debate turns on our four questions of scale, human nature, structure, and faith. Lippmann thought modern scale an insuperable obstacle, human nature too irrational and social structures too chaotic for popular sovereignty, and democracy a tragically flawed project. Dewey, in contrast, dreamed of a public conversation that would somehow incorporate the nation's local communities in conversation, considered the human play drive an impetus, not an obstacle, to democracy, called for imaginative reinvention of the material conditions of collective life, and exhorted us to see past democracy's flaws for its rosy possibilities.

Many commentators, including myself a decade ago, have claimed that Dewey got the better of the debate, but I no longer think so. I side with Lippmann on the questions of scale and faith and with Dewey on the questions of human nature and social structure. That (1) dissemination, not dialogue, ought to be the governing form of political communication in a gigantic nation–state and (2) democracy always breaks blessedly down—in this much Lippmann was right. That (1) public life is at its best a festive experience that calls on the full expressive resources of our natures and (2) political–economic structures ought to be democratized—here Dewey is also right. Each saw key parts of the puzzle productively.

Despite its claim to be following in Dewey's footsteps, public journalism sides ultimately with Lippmann in its call for a more rational tone and its focus on the reform of news-giving institutions (as opposed to social reform generally) and with Dewey in its calls for dialogical democracy and faith in the great community. On each of these crucial issues, the idea of public journalism ends up, I believe, on the wrong side. Against dialogue, rationality, the press, and faith, I would advocate dissemination, play, civil society generally, and a tragic sense. To be sure, theorists of public journalism disagree. Whereas Rosen calls for faith, Carey (in a spirit ultimately more Jamesian than Deweyan) calls for a cheerful recognition of democracy's tragedy; where Rosen calls for more deliberative modes of speech, Carey frankly entertains the ritual, if not ludic, possibilities of collective life.

Jay Rosen ends a key essay with Dewey's call to keep faith and justify it with works.[43] Perhaps the central drama of public journalism is the question of the viability of the democratic faith today. Public journalism is a quest for the reasonable middle in an age of data bits and sound bites. In this sense public journalism is a profoundly Clintonist project in its quest to reclaim the center, specifically, from the right-wing loudmouths and left-wing stunt artists in public life as well as from the apolitical social scientists and the left-leaning identity politicians and postmodernists in academic life. Public journalism's preferred mode is sincerity, like Clinton. It eschews cynicism as a disease eating at democratic engagement.[44] Public journalism opposes cynicism to faith. Either you share the hopes, one is made to feel, or you're contributing to the erosion of a sense of common purpose and humble sharing.

I do not think these two stances exhaust the alternatives. The critic of democratic hopes is not just a spoilsport, who by undermining hope also undermines the fact of robust civic culture, but a check on the hubris of the one true faith. Rather than fighting the losing battle of keeping one's democratic heart pure and one's wits intact, it is better to take democracy as tragically flawed and yet still worthy of admiration. In fact, the flaws are what make democracy admirable; they are not things to be transcended (as the model of faith implies). Democracy, I argue, is a form of government and way of life whose peculiar strength lies in its ability to cope with the inevitable failure of our best laid plans. Democracy is the final and clearest refutation of all ideals and utopias. It wrecks every romantic ship. Its history is a catalog of error and grace, stupidity and fumbling genius. At its best, democracy reminds us not of the great wisdom of the people but of our great folly, and it teaches us to check ourselves. It suggests to us not that distance can be scaled but that local life is hard and in need of our labor. And it warns that the effort to knock down all barriers to participation is an infinitely receding horizon, for the causes of exclusion are sown in the nature of interaction. A heroic pursuit of the horizon is perhaps a less apt democratic attitude than a compassion for the struggles of our neighbors. Democracy needs not our faith but our tenderness, being a form of political life that insists on its own, and our own, incompleteness at every turn. It is the principle of imperfection in politics, something to embrace, not to be embarrassed by.

In a tragedy, self-knowledge is the only answer. An accounting of democracy's troubles need not damage our faith; it allows us to cope with its possibilities more productively. In the same way, a recognition of journalism's tragic flaws might save us from trying to keep the Jeffersonian ideal of an informed citizen and informative press alive in the face of so much contrary evidence. To sustain the ideal costs too much, as it forces us to ignore blatant facts, not only in the recent history of the United States but in the entire history of democratic thought and practice: the difficulty of distance, the twists of the human heart, and the spell that money and power casts on the shape and dissemination of knowledge and belief. A more robust vision of public journalism that faces the difficulty, and even productivity, of these obstacles is better equipped to contribute, in appropriately small ways, to the more equitable distribution of the chance to become a collaborator in the making of history, which is all that democracy can ultimately mean. The vastness of the world outside, the antics of human behavior, the stubborn structures of the market and the state, and the difficulty of knowing what to believe are more than challenges to the dream of public journalism; they provide, and always have provided, both the challenge to and the topic of journalism itself.

Notes

1. See Mogens Herman Hansen, *The Athenian Democracy in the Age of Demosthenes: Structure, Principles, and Ideology* (Cambridge, MA: Basil Blackwell, 1991).
2. See Robert A. Dahl and Edward R. Tufte, *Size and Democracy* (Stanford, CA: Stanford University Press, 1973).
3. Isegoria, or equal opportunity to speak, was a characteristic notion in Greek democracy. One of its classic descriptions is in Herodotos, *The History*, Bk. V, Section 78.

4. See James W. Carey, *Communication as Culture* (Boston: Unwin Hyman, 1989).
5. See Jean-Jacques Rousseau, *The Social Contract*, Maurice Cranston, trans. (London: Penguin, 1968), p. 90.
6. See I. F. Stone, *The Trial of Socrates* (Boston: Little Brown, 1988); Harvey Yunis, *Taming Democracy: Models of Political Rhetoric in Classical Athens* (Ithaca, NY: Cornell University Press, 1996); J. Peter Euben et al., *Athenian Political Thought and the Reconstruction of American Democracy* (Ithaca, NY: Cornell University Press, 1994).
7. See Alexander Hamilton, James Madison, and John Jay, *The Federalist Papers*, Garry Wills, ed. (New York: Bantam Books, 1982), p. 46.
8. *The Federalist Papers*, p. 42.
9. *The Federalist Papers*, p. 44.
10. *The Federalist Papers*, p. 46.
11. *The Federalist Papers*, p. 44.
12. John Dewey, *The Public and Its Problems* (1927) in *The Middle Works*, Vol. 3, ed. Jo Ann Boydston (Carbondale: Southern Illinois University Press, 1981).
13. Dewey, *The Public and Its Problems*, p. 300.
14. Dewey, *The Public and Its Problems*, p. 306.
15. *The Federalist Papers*, p. 47.
16. See Jay Rosen, "On Making Things More Public: The Political Responsibilities of the Media Intellectual," *Critical Studies Mass Communication*, 11 (1994): 379.
17. See John Durham Peters, *Speaking into the Air: A History of the Idea of Communication* (Chicago: University of Chicago Press, 1999).
18. See Hannah Arendt, *The Human Condition* (Chicago: University of Chicago Press, 1958).
19. See Hannah Arendt, *On Revolution* (New York: Viking Press, 1965), p. 284.
20. See Jim Miller, *Democracy Is in the Streets: From Port Huron to the Siege of Chicago* (New York: Simon & Schuster, 1987).
21. James W. Carey, quoted in Rosen, "On Making Things More Public," p. 382.
22. Michael Schudson, "Why Conversation Is Not the Soul of Democracy," *Critical Studies in Mass Communication*, 14,4 (December 1997): 297–309.
23. For two views on this notion, see Jürgen Habermas, *Structural Transformation of the Public Sphere*, Thomas Burger, trans. (Cambridge, MA: MIT Press, 1989); and John Keane, *The Media and Democracy* (Cambridge, MA: Basil Blackwell, 1991).
24. See Habermas, *The Structural Transformation of the Public Sphere*.
25. See Thomas C. Leonard, *News for All: America's Coming-of-Age with the Press* (New York: Oxford University Press, 1995).
26. See John Durham Peters, "Beyond Reciprocity: Public Communication as a Moral Ideal," pp. 41–50 in *Communication, Culture and Community: Liber Amicorum James Stappers*, eds. Ed Hollander, Coen van der Linden, and Paul Rutten (Houten, Netherlands: Bohn, Stafleu, van Loghum, 1995).
27. Rosen, "On Making Things More Public," p. 374.

28. See James Bohman, *Public Deliberation: Pluralism, Complexity, and Democracy* (Cambridge, MA: MIT Press, 1996).

29. Walter Lippmann, *Public Opinion* (New York: Macmillan, 1922), p. 362.

30. Dewey, pp. 349–350.

31. Friedrich Schiller, *On the Aesthetic Education of Man*, Reginald Snell, trans. (New Haven, CT: Yale University Press, 1954).

32. See Robert D. Hariman, *Political Style* (Chicago: University of Chicago Press, 1996).

33. See Arthur Charity, *Doing Public Journalism* (New York: Guilford Press, 1995).

34. See Kenneth Cmiel, *Democratic Eloquence: The Fight over Popular Speech in Nineteenth-Century America* (New York: William Morrow, 1990).

35. See John McManus, *Market-Driven Journalism: Let the Citizen Beware?* (Thousand Oaks, CA: Sage, 1994).

36. See Michael E. McGerr, *The Decline of Popular Politics* (New York: Oxford University Press, 1986).

37. Lippmann, *Public Opinion*, pp. 31–32.

38. See Eileen R. Meehan, "Conceptualizing Culture as Commodity: The Problem of Television," *Critical Studies in Mass Communication*, 3 (1986): 448–457.

39. See Keane, *The Media and Democracy*.

40. See his review in Appendix B in this volume.

41. See John Durham Peters, "Realism in Social Description and the Fate of the Public," in *Vox Populi, Vox Dei*, ed. Skavko Splichal (New York: Hampton Press, forthcoming).

42. See Theodore L. Glasser, "Journalism's Glassy Essence," *Journalism and Mass Communication Quarterly*, 73 (Winter 1996): 784–786.

43. Rosen, "On Making Things More Public," p. 383.

44. See Kenneth Cmiel, "On Cynicism, Evil, and the Discovery of Communication in the 1940s," *Journal of Communication*, 46 (1996): 88–107.

Chapter 7

What Public Journalism Knows about Journalism but Doesn't Know about "Public"[1]

Michael Schudson
University of California, San Diego

Public journalism claims to offer a significantly new model of how journalism can and should contribute to a democracy. Jay Rosen, the most eloquent advocate of the movement, argues that journalism can no longer aim simply to inform the public—because the public may not be out there.[2] For Rosen, "Traditional journalism assumes that democracy is what we have, and information is what we need. In public journalism, we think the reverse is often true: Information is what we have—we live in a sea of information—while democracy is what we need." The assumption of traditional journalism that the public already exists is "complacent." Journalism should be as much about "forming" as about "informing" a public.[3]

These ideas have stirred the most impressive critique of journalistic practice inside journalism in a generation. They have helped fuel the best organized social movement inside journalism in the history of the American press. These considerable achievements notwithstanding, the ideas of public journalism deserve critical scrutiny. I want to contribute to this examination by first placing public journalism in relation to other models of journalism's role in democracy. I argue that public journalism is a conservative reform movement, much in the tradition of American social reforms of the Progressive Era. As such, it speaks loudly of "the public" but addresses itself to a professional group without challenging that group's authority. Second, I want to suggest that public journalism's ideas share in the communitarian strand of contemporary political thought and, like other voices in the communitarian tradition, prove much better at identifying the limits of liberalism than at truly understanding either "community" or public life.

Models of Journalism in Democracy

To oversimplify dramatically, there have been three general models in American history of how journalism might serve democracy. These are the market model, in which journalists serve the public best by providing whatever the public demands; the advocacy model, in which journalism serves the public by being an agency for the transmission of political party perspectives; and the trustee model, in which professional journalists provide news they believe citizens should have to be informed participants in democracy. I discuss each of these models briefly and try to explain the challenge public journalism poses in urging a revised trustee model on the press.

In market model journalism, journalists should seek to please audiences or, at least, those audiences that advertisers find attractive. Whatever these advertiser-friendly audiences demand, they should receive. Consumer demand is the ultimate arbiter of the news product. Market model ideologists may speak of democracy or at least of consumer sovereignty, but they do not mean it: The consumer is sovereign only as long as the consumer is willing to choose among commercially viable choices, only as long as consumer preferences are to be evaluated in the short run, and only as long as consumers with more dollars have more say than consumers with less.

Market model journalism is anathema to journalists themselves. They may cite it in apology for what they do, to explain why their best efforts are often thwarted, but they never refer to it as an ideal or aspiration. It is the model of the business office, not the newsroom. This gives it enduring influence; for instance, it almost exclusively governs all local television news. But it is the model that any self-respecting journalist fears and loathes.

In advocacy model journalism, journalism should provide news from the perspective of a political party. The aim of news gathering is to advance the party. Here journalism is a secondary or subsidiary institution deferring to the party rather than a wholly autonomous business enterprise. Advocacy model journalism has most often been

party journalism, but advocacy journalists also represent social movements (like the abolitionist press did), churches, or other interests and
communities. There are ethnic and community newspapers, magazines
of opinion, and hundreds of newsletters that operate in an advocacy
mode. But this is rare today for the general circulation press. In the
past, however, the advocacy model dominated, from the establishment
of the Jeffersonian opposition press in the 1790s into the early 20th
century.[4] Despite the Founding Fathers' dedication to a political theory
that judged parties, factions, and politically oriented voluntary associations to be dangerous to republican government, protoparties developed in the 1790s with newspapers as central organs, promoting and
disseminating their different viewpoints. By the time the mass political
party emerged in the Jacksonian era, party newspapers were well established as the central agents of party organizing and party propaganda.
The "party press" dominated American journalism until the end of the
19th century, and of course vestiges of the party press persisted for a
long time thereafter. But today scarcely anyone urges a return to the
party press. The advocacy model, despite its long service to American
democracy, lies on the scrap heap of history as far as the general circulation mass media are concerned.

In trustee model journalism, journalists are to provide news
according to what they themselves as a professional group believe citizens should know. The professional journalist's quest for truth and fairness, exercising sound and critical judgment as measured by a jury of
peers, should dictate the shape of the news. Journalists ordinarily
accept the trustee model as the only alternative to market-driven journalism. Journalism is understood as a constant battle between the bad
guys upholding market model news (i.e., the business office, the deal
makers, and the Frank Munseys and Rupert Murdochs) and the good
guys upholding trustee model news, the dedicated, professional journalists who speak truth to power and follow the story wherever it may
lead, whomever it may embarrass, and however few readers it might
attract.

In this model, journalists imagine a public that is often too preoc-
cupied and too distracted to be sovereign of its own citizenship. Citizens then entrust a measure of sovereignty to journalists just as people
entrust a measure of control over their bodies to doctors. The journalists are professionals who hold our citizenship in trust for citizens and
whose expertise or political analysis citizens rely on when they want
information about the state of the country.

Trustee model journalism established its commitment to reporting
over commentary in the late 19th century and its commitment to an
ideology of objectivity, to professional codes of ethics, and to princi-

ples of disinterested public service by the 1920s. These views reached some kind of zenith in the 1950s and 1960s. They came to a curious climax with the reporting of Vietnam and Watergate. Journalism's achievements in Vietnam and Watergate were, in fact, part of an assault on the virtues of autonomous professionalism held up as the standard in the trustee model. The aggressiveness of *The Washington Post* in Watergate, for instance, was itself part of a reaction against the complacency of professional "objectivity." The premise that journalists were or ever could be neutral professionals serving as trustees for the public interest was badly undercut in the Vietnam era. Reporters in the field indeed spoke truth to power, but reporters in Washington too often accepted power as truth. Inside journalism, there was the New Journalism, the entrance of a personal voice in writing, alternative journals, investigative reporting teams, and other developments designed to free up a rigid pattern of reporting that trusted far too naively in the statements of government officials.

Outside journalism, academics began to pepper away at the notion of objectivity itself. Sociologists saw it as a "defensive strategic ritual" and political scientists saw news gathering as a set of rote bureaucratic routines rather than a set of heroic or virtuous professional practices.[5] The authority of professional knowledge—what might today be termed a professional "discourse"—was under attack. Journalism was only one of many professional groups whose authority was challenged in the 1960s and 1970s. Critics in and out of journalism agreed that journalists, like any professional group, could become a conspiracy against the public. The critique of conventional journalism changed journalism. News became more sophisticated, more analytical and—a mixed blessing—more disillusioned. Critics assaulted journalists again in the 1980s for falling under the spell of Ronald Reagan and, after the 1988 election, for submitting to the Bush campaign strategy of flag-waving and racial innuendo. At the same time, with the downward spiral of newspaper reading, especially among the young, the news business was full of self-doubt and a growing sense of crisis—its continued profitability and the celebrity of many of its leading practitioners notwithstanding.

Along comes public journalism. Public journalism is a variant of trustee journalism, that is, a version of the very same ideology that dominates the world of professional journalists today. Where is authority for the news to lie? In public journalism, as in trustee journalism generally, the answer is: with journalists themselves, not with the marketplace, not with a party. Public journalism advocates sometimes sound as if they mean to empower "the public" relative to journalists. Some elite journalists have responded hysterically to this notion, as if the public journalists were inviting the mobs into the newsroom, or at least the pollsters and the focus groups (as if they were not already there!). But public journalism does not remove control over the news from journalists themselves.

In this regard, public journalism as a reform movement is conservative. It does not propose new media accountability systems. It does not offer a citizen media review board or a national news council. It does not recommend publicly elected publishers or editors. It does not suggest that the press be formally or even informally answerable to a governmental or community body. It does not borrow from Sweden the proposition that government should subsidize news organizations that would enlarge the diversity of viewpoints available to the reading public.

Public journalism, in other words, stops short of offering a fourth model of journalism in democracy, one in which authority is vested not in the market, not in a party, and not in the journalist but in the public. Nothing in public journalism removes power from the journalists or the corporations they work for. There are ways to grant the public greater authority in journalism—there are ways, in a sense, to democratize the practice of journalism itself. For instance, the movement of minorities and women to promote diversity in the newsroom is a form of democratization and a serious way to empower disempowered elements of the public by representing them in person among journalists. This does not offer any direct accountability, however, of the news institution to the public. Other forms do: The ombudsperson owes loyalty as much to the public as to the news institution. Media critics and media reporters take on their own institutions—at least, they are supposed to—with professional dispassion. Local or national news councils, never very popular among journalists, afford legitimacy to community press critics. Publicly owned news institutions such as the Public Broadcasting Service and its affiliated stations are responsible to boards representing the public and are sensitive to public criticism in ways that corporately owned news institutions can never be.

These are all ways in which a true fourth model might arrive, but this is not what public journalism proposes. Public journalism begins inside the trustee model. It urges that journalists themselves reimagine their work not as informing the public but as opening up democratic deliberation and discussion. Communication scholar Daniel Hallin put it this way:

> Journalists need to move from conceiving their role in terms of mediating between political authorities and the mass public, to thinking of it also as a task of opening up political discussion in civil society . . . it might be time for journalists themselves to rejoin civil society, and to start talking

to their readers and viewers as one citizen to another, rather than as experts claiming to be above politics.[6]

Public journalism exhorts journalists to put citizens first, to bring new voices into the newspapers, even to share setting the news agenda with individuals and groups in the community—but always authority about what to write and whether to print stays with the professionals. Even so, conventional journalists have responded to public journalism as a dangerous threat. Public journalists have risked ridicule and scathing criticism inside their newsroom. Although an outsider may detect the conservatism of public journalism, many newspaper insiders experience it differently. Perhaps what seems to me the cautious reformism of public journalism can be more fully understood if compared to Progressive Era reforms to which I think it bears kinship.

Public Journalism as Conservative Reform

Public journalism, like reforms of the Progressive Era, advances an unresolved blend of empowering the people and entrusting elites and experts with public responsibility. The Progressives supported both the initiative and referendum, which gave power to the people, and city manager government, which shifted power to professionals. The Progressives praised both direct primaries, giving power to the people, and a merit-based civil service, giving power to the educationally qualified. What all these reforms, both populist and elitist, shared was antipathy to political parties and to conventional partisanship. They also shared something like public journalism's ethical emphasis on proceduralism: advocate democracy without advocating particular policy solutions.

Progressive Era reforms, like public journalism, were unified by an ideal of the rational, informed citizen. The idea of an informed citizenry, as Richard Brown has recently shown, goes back to the 18th century. But also, as Brown observes, it was an "inconsequential" idea in the American colonies and was a sometime thing even after; the "actual lesson" of the historical record, he concludes, "is that no precise meaning for an informed citizenry has ever been established."[7] Brown ends his story in 1870, but the big change came in the next half century. In the Progressive Era, the notion that voters should know the issues and choose among the candidates without undue allegiance to political party or personal preconception came into vogue, and it has not been abandoned since.

In this respect, public journalism is a perfect extension of Progressivism. Progressivism was dedicated to rational public participation in the democratic process. Its promotion of the secret ballot supported the idea of the informed, rational voter. Its promotion of the initiative, referendum, recall, presidential preference primary, direct election of senators, and nonpartisan city governments all were part of advancing scientific government and broad public participation over the meddling and distortion of political parties. Public journalism seems very much in line with these developments. And in line with Progressivism, it speaks of involving the public and stimulating public discussion but addresses a group of professionals in the effort to reach these ends. It appeals to an elite and to the public at once, just as Progressivism did.

In this lies public journalism's conservatism: It orients its appeal to the goodwill and democratic sensibilities of professionals rather than speaking over the heads of professionals to the public itself. Public journalism misapprehends itself if it thinks it is taking John Dewey's side in the famous exchange in the 1920s between Dewey and Walter Lippmann. There is a tendency in the public journalism movement both to misunderstand Lippmann and Dewey, which is forgivable, but at the same time to claim too much for its own originality, which may turn out to be a more damaging error. Advocates of public journalism have suggested that Lippmann urged that "well-trained experts" would "manage the country's journalism as well as its governmental affairs."[8] In fact, Lippmann held out no such hope for journalism; he believed that journalists could never reform themselves. They could only improve if other institutions of intelligence arose outside journalism to feed better data to the press. He hoped these agencies of intelligence would improve the quality of public information.

Dewey conceded Lippmann's argument in *Public Opinion* that modern society had undermined the kind of community life in which citizens had a chance to be cognitively competent in democratic governance. Lippmann and Dewey disagreed only over what might be done to save democracy from the devastation wrought by the increasingly urban, industrial, impersonal national society burgeoning around them. Lippmann insisted that the masses could not govern a mass society but that experts advising elected officials would have to be entrusted with most of the daily decisions of public life. Dewey, in contrast, while an untiring advocate of science, doubted that experts could be trusted any more than any other elite group, and he still hoped for a revitalization of community life (though he never provided any account of the grounds for this hope). Neither Lippmann nor Dewey said anything in their encounter that might encourage a view that journalists should be central agents of social transformation or community construction.[9]

Public journalism finds expertise very embarrassing. It vests all authority for the news in journalists and then turns around to deny that journalists can or should have any special access to understanding the needs of democracy. This is, at least, a sign of confusion in the theory of public journalism. Perhaps more, it may be a failure of intellectual seriousness. Expertise should not be something to hide. Expertise is not a violation of democracy but the only legitimate authority in democracy apart from the popular will itself. Not everyone can aspire to be of royal blood, but everyone can aspire, in a properly functioning democracy, to be doctors or lawyers or, poor souls, journalists. But wherein lies the authority of the journalist?

Conventional journalism is confused about its own authority. Journalists will in one instant assure you that they are neutral vessels passing on information, with no authority but their own integrity; in the next breath, they will make it clear that their hard-earned, commonsense craft knowledge of the world outshines the academic's book learning any day of the week. There's an understandable edginess here as journalists anticipate the crude snobbism of the academic who puts down "journalism" as an inferior breed of knowledge. But there is also a deep reluctance to think too hard about the basis on which journalists choose stories, set news policies, follow up some leads and not others, seek additional sources sometimes but not always. How journalists do all this is not a well-articulated matter, and among most people who teach journalism as well as most who practice it, it is "untheorized." That is, trying to understand what might constitute the journalist's expertise is not a topic that has been widely addressed. Part of what must irritate conventional journalists about public journalism is that public journalism needles journalists into rethinking standard practices and assumptions.

What particularly irks elite journalists about public journalism is that they see public journalism as pushing journalists beyond the realm in which they *do* have some sort of legitimate authority, whatever that authority may be founded on. Whatever authority journalists may have, it does not lie in the area of community organizing or conflict mediation. It probably does not even lie in community interconnections. True, journalists with "good sources" gain authority inside the profession and can come up with stories that speak with greater authority than journalists without "good sources." But a journalist's sources are not normally from all walks of life or from all parts of town. The reward structure in journalism frequently leads star journalists to leave one city for another and so to divest themselves from the strong interconnections that might have provided the grounds of "community organizing" expertise.

Insofar, then, as public journalism asks news institutions to take on the task of restoring community, conventional journalists properly ask: Who elected you?

The inadequacy of this response, however, should be clear: Who elected *them?* What process of democratic control or democratic deliberation led to a set of norms that emphasize conflict, or campaign reporting that concentrates on strategy and tactics, or led newspapers to follow local football teams with greater constancy and a richer sense of history than they follow local politics, or led local TV news to succumb lock, stock, and barrel to the market model? As for the leading lights of the House of Journalism who have been the loudest in their critique of public journalism, no one who knows the first thing about the production of a daily newspaper could doubt for a second that *The New York Times* and *The Washington Post* are astonishing achievements, day after day. But for their editors to attack public journalism from that height is like declaring reform efforts in higher education out of bounds because Harvard is doing pretty well. Moreover, even the Harvards of higher education or of journalism could stand some serious self-examination.

Public journalism replies: We're all elected when democracy is failing. We're all elected to be citizens. Journalists, who profess a vocation dedicated to making democracy work, should certainly be willing to reexamine their work rules and work habits and be open to readjusting them if they have become irrelevant to or even counter to the aim of making democracy work. Is this a sufficient response?

Public Journalism, Communities, and Public Life

Public journalism invokes John Dewey's faith that strong community life is essential to democracy. Unfortunately, it fails to go beyond Dewey in developing a vision of what community, in 1997, not 1927, might be. This is not an age that can be governed by New England town meetings—but there is nonetheless a lot of talk in the favored texts of public journalism about the importance of the town meeting tradition as a model for today. (In real 17th- and 18th-century New England town meetings, voter turnout was low, the meeting agenda was set by small elites who dominated the proceedings, genuine discussion was frowned upon, conflict found unseemly, and all this in communities where everyone shared ethnicity and religion.)[10] There is much quoting of Tocqueville about the virtues of the American art of association, but there is little notice that Tocqueville found political parties to have tutored citizens in these arts and no serious effort to distinguish what public journalism admires as rich associational life from what is typically regarded as its corrupted counterfeit—interest groups. "When interest groups arrive upon the scene," James Carey writes, "the public ceases to have a real existence."[11] George Washington would have agreed, in his determined opposition to any private associations organizing on a permanent basis to discuss politics (see his opposition to the Democratic–Republican societies during the Whiskey Rebellion, repeated again in his famous Farewell Address). But de Tocqueville, with some qualifications, rejected this view and saw people organizing associations to pursue their self-interest, rightly understood, as the strength of American democracy.

But what does any of this have to do with the present? How, for instance, has public journalism built its own community? It got started out of dissatisfaction with contemporary journalism. That dissatisfaction was not only in the ranks of journalists and journalism professors but in the foundations and in national conventions of national journalistic organizations. The institutional nexus that is public journalism today, that stimulates, instructs, and encourages local efforts in public journalism, is made possible by hotels, commercial airlines, convention planners, foundations, journalism schools, journalism support organizations such as the Poynter Institute, and others. Yet none of this enters into public journalism's theorizing of "community." "Community" seems only to conjure local, territory-based, grass-roots organizations.

I do not deny that community must be located on a face-to-face plane, but face-to-face community life today is as often encouraged from the top down as it is spontaneously generated from the bottom up. Impetus for community activity frequently begins outside of face-to-face communities. The women's movement in the 1960s and 1970s did not simply bubble up from the bottom but was stimulated—even "caused," if you will—by outside agitators, notably Betty Friedan's *The Feminine Mystique*. The federal Women's Bureau and state and local commissions on the status of women actively nurtured the American women's movement.[12] The National Organization of Women was organized out of anger that Title VII of the Civil Rights Act of 1964 was not vigorously enforced. It sought to take advantage of opportunities for litigation that the Civil Rights Act, however accidentally, brought to life.[13] This is a case of public life building communities rather than communities providing the necessary background for public life. Public journalism's acute analysis of the faults of conventional news reporting is not matched by a comparably sophisticated analysis of the character of contemporary community and public life.

Public journalism tends to invoke, as John Dewey did himself, what has been termed the "neighborhood of nostalgia," the stable, secure,

homey world located back somewhere in immigrant ethnic neighborhoods of the early 20th century or in the settled communities of 19th-
century cities.[14] But urban life is not like that today. Even lower-income
urbanites are likely to have relationships that "extend throughout the
city." Neighborhood territorial proximity provides relatively little social
solidarity in itself; one study of a Chicago neighborhood found 27 percent of residents belonged to voluntary organizations—but less than
half of these citizens belonged to organizations that met in the neighborhood.[15]

Public journalism, in the abstract, tends less to analyze community
than to presume it (or its absence or its weakening), so it is not an easy
matter to tease out just what its idea of community is. But I would suggest that its understanding of community shares to a significant degree
the following:

1. Neighborhood is community, community is territorial. Very
often the language of public journalism identifies community with "the
neighborhood" or "the neighborhoods."
2. The assumption that "government" is more nearly the opposite
of community than a part of community or a catalyst of community or
an expression of community or even a forum for the articulation of
community. There is a repeated innuendo in the public journalism literature that people have to take decisions into their own hands rather
than leaving it to government. Rosen, for instance, describes the "People Project" of *The Wichita Eagle* as aiming "to persuade Wichita that at
least some public problems could be dealt with, and not necessarily
through the government. Accordingly, the subtitle of the project was
'Solving It Ourselves.' "[16] Government, in this idiom, is not the voice of
the people but the organ of bureaucrats or elites, something or someone disconnected from community life.
3. Community and public life are consonant and continuous, not
conflicting, ideals.

If this is a fair representation of public journalism's unspoken
assumptions about "community," then public journalism has some serious rethinking to do. A strong argument can be made that neighborhood is not community, that community and government may be complementary rather than antithetical, and that community and "public"
are better understood as opposites than as twins. Let me quickly sketch
the argument.

First, that neighborhood is not community: People do not live in
neighborhoods any more. Bertrand Russell observed this as early as
1930. The idea that one should know their neighbors, he wrote, "has

died out in large centers of population" and has, in fact, become "a foolish idea, since there is no need to be dependent upon immediate neighbors for society."[17] Perhaps the "neighborhood" has been declining for a long time—certainly American historians are doubtful that stable neighborhoods were very common in 19th-century cities any more than in 20th-century cities.

Even so, there is evidence that in recent years, neighborhood stability and neighborhood commitment have been increasing, not decreasing—that geographic mobility is slightly lower than in the American past, that home ownership is higher, and that individuals' involvement in their neighborhoods is greater in this country than in Sweden or the United Kingdom.[18] Americans seem to be more "'rooted,' practically and sentimentally, to their communities than ever before."[19] But if this is so, it is in part because nonneighborhood organizations, including government, help make it so. Neighborhood itself may be maintained only through other organizational support. Community organizations are often fostered by outside agencies—city or state government, banks, or insurance companies—that need them as "channels of communication, sources of legitimation, vehicles of social control, and a means to organize and direct resources."[20]

This speaks to my second point: that government and community may be complementary rather than antithetical. Public journalism, I think, may unintentionally reinforce the very cynicism about government that it sees as a symptom of contemporary decline and disillusionment.

My third point is that supporting community and supporting public life are not the same thing. This is perhaps the most fundamental difficulty with much contemporary discussion of civil society and public life. James Carey writes that we must recognize the story of our lives is both "part of a narrative of a public community, a community of general citizenship rather than one restricted by class, race, gender, and so on" and at the same time find that "our lives are also embedded in communities of private identity—family, city, tribe, nation, party or cause." Here Carey states the problem exactly right. But then, almost immediately, he subordinates the community of general citizenship to the richer, warmer communities of private identity. For him, "the expansion of individual rights and the erosion of common identifications, the growth of entitlement and the erosion of common judgment, is not a recipe for social progress." Here I part company with Carey. The expansion of individual rights may not be a recipe for unsullied social progress, it may not be a recipe for social progress without costs, but it is as close to a recipe for social progress as this country has been able to invent. Remember, too, that the "common identifications" and "common judgments" of American tradition have regularly been exclusionary—Christian (Protestant), white, Anglo-Saxon, heterosexual, propertied. I would say "good riddance" to most of the common identifications and common judgments we have lost. Welcome to one person, one vote, and good riddance to the rural stranglehold on state legislatures; welcome to desegregation and good riddance to Jim Crow; welcome to *Griswold v. Connecticut* and the right to privacy and the woman's right to choose an abortion, and good riddance to the common judgments that brought community standards, backed by law, into American bedrooms.

Carey identifies here with communitarian thinkers and I detect a tendency for public journalism advocates generally to lean in this direction. But how can one be both communitarian (rather than liberal) and an advocate of the public good while knowing that, in practice, "good" is generally defined in parochial terms, that is, in the idiom of and in the image of particular religious, class, or ethnic groups? The very idea of urbanism and urbanity and the "civility" that goes with it (civility was never an ideal in the small community—only politeness in a context of deference, hierarchy, and order) have been strongly opposed to the communal boundaries of traditional social life.

This is worth underlining in the present intellectual climate. The city has been identified historically with cosmopolitanism, a mode of human experience in which a variety of diverse styles of life and types of individuals coexist.[21] The city, in this view, is "the set of social structures that encourage social individuality and innovation, and is thus the instrument of historical change."[22] In city life, as Georg Simmel famously described it, the person is "'free' in a spiritualized and refined sense, in contrast to the pettiness and prejudices which hem in the small-town man."[23] This cosmopolitan freedom, Simmel emphasizes, comes at an enormous cost. In cities, cultural experience is dominated by an "objective" spirit—institutional structures accumulate more power, the individual relative to them shrinks and becomes

> a mere cog in an enormous organization of things and powers. [In cities,] in buildings and educational institutions, in the wonders and comforts of space-conquering technology, in the formations of community life, and in the visible institutions of the state, is offered such an overwhelming fullness of crystallized and impersonalized spirit that the personality, so to speak, cannot maintain itself under its impact.[24]

What is it that public journalism is supposed to be advancing? Is it "community"? Or is it a healthy public discourse? Or is it a well-endowed public domain? What makes public journalists believe that these things are consistent rather than at war? Sweden, for instance, in comparison to the United States, has bountiful public provisions of welfare but low levels of attachment to neighborhoods and high levels of experienced loneliness.[25] Thomas Bender, in casting doubt on the common view that societies move from *Gemeinschaft* to *Gesellschaft*, from "community" to more impersonal "society," argues that community and society are two modes of human experience that coexist. They need not (and cannot) be the same: "Our public lives do not provide an experience of community. The mutuality and sentiment characteristic of community cannot and need not be achieved in public." Politics belongs to the public realm, not the communal. What is necessary in political life is "a sense of commonweal, rather than community."[26]

Admirers of liberal political rules, like myself, tend not to have answers about how to link people in their embedded communities to a sense of obligation that extends beyond the communities. Admirers of community, like the advocates of public journalism, tend not to dwell on what happens when community values collide or how far illiberal community values are to be tolerated by the public. (Is segregation okay when it has been traditional for generations? Or are antisodomy laws acceptable when they express dominant community values?) Carey may be right that liberalism by itself is not a recipe to social progress—but neither is community and neither is democratic participation in itself.

We have no recipes for achieving a sense of commonweal. What guidance we have, from our own past, I think, suggests that public life will be occasionally morally invigorating (especially in wartime) and often contentious, bickering, nasty, compromising, bargaining, draining, unsatisfying, and trivial. The warm, convivial, multistranded social interactions of love, friendship, and a variety of symbolic kinships are what people are more likely to experience in communities but not in public life. In public life, the whole point is to stretch across communities that govern by trust and by feel to work out problems among people with few shared values, little trust, and a feel of anxiety and enmity.

Communities are not publics. Publics are where strangers meet to consider and to build a common life under rules by which they are treated as moral equals. Public journalism can contribute to that public life. My criticism notwithstanding, it has already done so. I think it could do so better if its view of modern life appealed less to colonial New England with visions of a long-departed, hierarchical moral order rooted in a rigidly maintained homogeneity of values and lifestyles and more to constructing humane visions of community life and public life that one might truly want to realize in contemporary society.

Notes

1. I want to gratefully acknowledge the careful criticism of an earlier draft provided by Theodore Glasser and Jay Rosen, neither of whom necessarily share in the views expressed here.
2. Jay Rosen, *Community Connectedness: Passwords for Public Journalism* (St. Petersburg, FL: Poynter Institute for Media Studies, 1993), p. 5 or p. 7. See also Jay Rosen, *Getting the Connections Right* (New York: Twentieth Century Fund, 1996), p. 83.
3. Jay Rosen, "What Should We Be Doing?" *Investigative Reporters and Editors Journal* (November/December, 1996): 7.
4. The Founding Fathers did not really subscribe to any of the three models I have outlined. As best as I can tell, they expected newspapers to be gazettes that relayed to citizens information about government proceedings, providing the documents and debates in the government to the dispersed citizenry. But they did not necessarily expect the journals to comment on and criticize government. The Founders in 1789 were alert to the fragility of the new nation; they viewed factions or parties as grave dangers to unity. Even such radicals as Sam Adams, an inveterate organizer before the Revolution, held after the establishment of the new, republican government that committees and conventions of the people were dangerous. See Pauline Maier, *The Old Revolutionaries* (New York: Norton, 1980), p. 30.
5. See Gaye Tuchman, "Objectivity as Strategic Ritual: An Examination of Newsmen's Notions of Objectivity," *American Journal of Sociology*, 77 (1972): 660–679; Edward Jay Epstein, *News from Nowhere* (New York: Random House, 1973); Leon V. Sigal, *Reporters and Officials* (Lexington, MA: Heath, 1973); and Herbert Gans, *Deciding What's News* (New York: Pantheon, 1979).
6. Daniel C. Hallin, *We Keep America On Top of the World* (New York: Routledge, 1994), p. 176.
7. Richard L. Brown, *The Strength of a People: The Idea of an Informed Citizenry in America, 1650–1870* (Chapel Hill: University of North Carolina Press, 1996), pp. 49, 205.
8. James Fallows, *Breaking the News* (New York: Pantheon, 1996), p. 236.
9. The key texts in this exchange are Walter Lippmann, *Public Opinion* (New York: Macmillan, 1922), and John Dewey, *The Public and Its Problems* (New York: Holt, 1927). For a fuller discussion of Lippmann and Dewey, Progressive Era politics, and many other themes in this chapter, see Michael Schudson, *The Good Citizen: A History of American Civic Life* (New York: Free Press, 1998).
10. See David Mathews, *Politics for People* (Urbana: University of Illinois Press, 1994), pp. 99–117, for a particularly romanticized view of the New England town meeting that severely overestimates the egalitarian and participatory character of town meetings. A more realistic view is provided in one of the sources Mathews cites but did not seem to absorb, Michael Zuckerman, *Peaceable Kingdoms* (New York: Knopf, 1970), and Jane Mansbridge, *Beyond Adversary Democracy* (New York: Basic Books, 1973).

11. James W. Carey, "The Press, Public Opinion, and Public Discourse," in *Public Opinion and the Communication of Consent*, eds. Theodore L. Glasser and Charles T. Salmon (New York: Guilford Press, 1995), p. 388. For a typically pious invocation of de Tocqueville, see Mathews, *Politics for People*, p. 161.

12. Georgia Duerst-Lahti, "The Government's Role in Building the Women's Movement," *Political Science Quarterly* 104 (1989): 249–268.

13. Betty Friedan, *It Changed My Life* (New York: Random House, 1976).

14. See Kenneth A. Scherzer, *The Unbounded Community: Neighborhood Life and Social Structure in New York City, 1830–1875* (Durham: Duke University Press, 1992), p. 2.

15. Richard P. Taub, George P. Surgeon, Sara Lindholm, Phyllis Betts Otti, and Amy Bridges, "Urban Voluntary Associations, Locality Based and Externally Induced," *American Journal of Sociology*, 83 (1977): 429.

16. Rosen, *Getting the Connections Right*, p. 43.

17. Bertrand Russell, 1930, cited in Claude Fischer, *To Dwell Among Friends* (Chicago: University of Chicago Press, 1982), p. 103.

18. Claude S. Fischer, "Ambivalent Communities," in *America at Century's End*, ed. Alan Wolfe (Berkeley: University of California Press, 1991), p. 85.

19. Fischer, "Ambivalent Communities," p. 86.

20. Taub et al., "Urban Voluntary Associations," p. 426.

21. See Richard Sennett, "An Introduction," in *Classic Essays on the Culture of Cities*, ed. Richard Sennett (New York: Meredith Corporation, 1969), p. 6.

22. Sennett, "An Introduction," p. 6.

23. Georg Simmel, "The Metropolis and Mental Life," pp. 47–60, in Sennett, *Classic Essays*, p. 55.

24. Simmel, "The Metropolis and Mental Life," pp. 58–59.

25. David Popenoe, *Private Pleasure, Public Plight* (New Brunswick: Transaction Books, 1985), pp. 100, 136.

26. Thomas Bender, *Community and Social Change in America* (New Brunswick: Rutgers University Press, 1978), p. 148.

Chapter 8

Journalism and the Sociology of Public Life

John J. Pauly

Saint Louis University

Journalism desperately wants to understand itself as a democratic institution. How might it do so? That is the deceptively simple question
posed by proponents of public journalism. It is a question that defenders
of traditional journalism are not prepared to answer. The conventional
answer, of course, is that journalists write about the world out there in an
unobtrusive and neutral way in order to provide conscientious citizens
with the information they need to make rational decisions. This answer
no longer convinces many people, however. It says nothing about how
journalists might help forge the communal bonds needed to make
newsreading feel like a public rather than merely a private activity. By
reducing journalists' work to information processing, the conventional
answer denies both writers' and readers' deepest experience of news as a
form of storytelling. It says nothing about the newsroom routines and
professional values that guide journalists when they select and parse
reality. It assumes that readers will know their place and sit politely in
their seats, waiting to serve as an audience for the performances of professional journalists, and not try to climb up on the stage themselves.

Journalists frequently tell us that they serve public life, but they
narrowly interpret that calling, and they struggle to understand the
wider social implications of their work. A simple example illustrates the
problem. In the opening chapter of his book *Read All about It! The Corporate Takeover of America's Newspapers,* James Squires describes the

sense of purpose that drew him into journalism. For more than eight years Squires served as editor of the *Chicago Tribune,* one of the most powerful and prosperous metropolitan dailies in the United States. Looking back over nearly 30 years of newspaper work, he writes that, for him, the words of Walter Lippmann "best defined the mission of a free press." "There was something solid and sacred," Squires writes, in the idea of journalism being "the beam of a searchlight that moved restlessly about bringing one episode and then another out of the darkness into vision." Remembering his early days at *The* (Nashville) *Tennessean,* Squires says he and his fellow reporters "danced to the music of Lippmann's words, finding in them the anchor for our judgment that journalism was an oasis in the desert of capitalism, a business with a conscience and a higher purpose."[1]

Something is deeply wrong in this passage. It is not so much the harmlessly wistful tone of Squires's reminiscence, or his dubious assumption that daily newspapers are less capitalist if owned by families instead of corporations, or even the sheer improbability of him and other young reporters sitting around the newsroom talking about Walter Lippmann. It is simply his total misreading of Lippmann's words. The metaphor of journalism that appeals so powerfully to Squires—being a searchlight in the dark—was offered by Lippmann as a way to describe journalism's tragic failure. The searchlight moves restlessly, without rhyme or reason, arbitrarily illuminating one part of reality for a few seconds but plunging the world outside the beam into darkness. "Men cannot do the work of the world by this light alone," Lippmann writes in the very next line. "They cannot govern by episodes, incidents, and eruptions."[2] In this passage Squires, once one of the most prominent newspaper editors in the United States, proudly turns one of the most devastating criticisms of journalism ever penned into a manifesto for his profession.

What should we make of an occupation filled with so many disillusioned dreamers, who stoke their cynicism with romantic fancy? Squires, like many of his colleagues, believes that journalists simply survey the environment in order to report whatever they see. But of course they do much more. Journalists help make public life what it is (or isn't). News stories summon the everyday world into public imagination. They portray a system of social relations, styles of political interpretation, and modes of preferred conduct. This much public journalism understands with perfect clarity: Journalists act, and their stories frame our experience of public life. What public journalism understands less clearly is the sociology of that public life. From what sort of social relations might democracy be created? And what role should journalists play in fostering those relations?

How Journalism Describes Itself

Public journalism proposes, as a first step, to examine the language journalism uses to describe itself. This suggestion that journalists rename their work has nettled critics of public journalism. Their retort is predictable: "Public journalism is nothing new," the critics say. "We already know what good journalism is; just get X out of our way and let us do our work"—the X factor being greedy corporate owners, bean-counting market researchers, manipulative public relations hacks, weak-willed editors, or dull-witted readers. Public journalism responds, again with unusual candor, "But just what is it that we, as journalists, really do? And what ought we be doing to make democratic life possible?" That prominent editors like Davis Merritt and Cole Campbell are willing to ask such questions ought to impress us. In their search for clarity, they have had to battle their own deeply rooted professional instincts. For their trouble, they have found themselves criticized in surprisingly ignorant, petty, and mean-spirited ways (or, as they have noted, they have had journalism done to them). Yet, more than their critics, editors such as Merritt and Campbell understand that if journalists hope to play any role in public life they must be able to explain the meaning of their work to others.

Though journalists work in the public eye, they hesitate to expose their daily practices to public scrutiny, or to admit that outsiders might have something useful to say about their work. To be sure, journalists talk incessantly about their business. They regularly compare notes on how their papers covered or played a story. They reluctantly accept criticism, but only if it comes from other professionals who open the newsroom door to reveal behind-the-scenes decision making. By this logic, outsiders' opinions are often treated as irrelevant, for nonjournalists are in no position to understand what really happened. When asked to contemplate the social consequences of their profession, journalists too often play dumb. They prefer to explain their work as a natural activity. They treat the public's taste for news as a form of innate human curiosity. They describe the ideal news story as being written in a plain style, without affect or coloration. They assume that reporters simply ask the same questions that anyone would want answered. They imagine a world always already filled with events and think that reporters do little more than write stories about things that would have happened anyway. They believe that news organizations merely make stories available to anyone who chooses to read them.

Journalists also propose an ideal stance toward the world on which they report. Anderson, Dardenne, and Killenberg have described this stance as a version of what Peter Elbow once called the "doubting game."[3] Professional journalists, they say, consider themselves unrepentant skeptics who constantly look for error and take pride in picking apart others' talk and behavior. In a democracy there is a time and a place for the doubting game, as well as rules to be observed in playing it. But public journalism has asked that journalists also learn to play what Elbow called the "believing game." The believing game asks participants to suspend immediate disbelief in order to listen more carefully to what others mean. If journalists were more skillful at the believing game, they might be more inclined to probe criticisms of the press in order to understand what citizens mean when they say, "The news is biased," or "That story stereotypes people like me," or "The news media are too negative." Confronted with such criticisms, conventional journalism's impulse is to disparage the critic, disprove what the critic said, and dismiss the criticism as unimportant. How can an institution that does such a poor job of listening to its own critics possibly be entrusted with the work of creating the fair and lively dialogue that a multicultural society needs to survive?

What Journalism Values

Most journalists now acknowledge the low standing of their profession in others' eyes. Some even take a perverse pride in the public's dislike ("We must be doing our job well if everyone dislikes us"). Some honestly struggle to address the public's criticisms by reaffirming their professional values, hoping that their declaration of sincerity will help them recover the public's trust. Too often, however, these efforts amount to repeating, ever more loudly, what journalists already believe. Consider the session on journalistic values at the 1996 convention of the American Society of Newspaper Editors (ASNE), at which Richard Harwood reported on discussions he had held across the country with editors, reporters, and citizens.[4] The 30 editors interviewed for the project identified six "core values" of journalism: balance, accuracy, leadership, accessibility, credibility, and news judgment. Harwood said his results offered "a strong foundation upon which journalists—newspapers—can strengthen their credibility."

Though Americans commonly talk about values in this way, using such talk to analyze journalism or any other complex social practice proves surprisingly difficult. The core-values metaphor suggests that human actions can be most aptly explained as the rational application of an individual's deep, inner, consciously held, fully defined, and consistently applied beliefs. When the assumptions of a core-values metaphor are spelled out this way, its limits become clear. Humans do not just answer to an inner voice or internalized social norms; they adapt, improvise, and invent in relation to others. A motive, seen this way, is better understood as an explanation rather than a cause of action; we invoke motives to make our behavior intelligible to others. By trying to trace every human act back to its philosophical origins, the core-values metaphor neglects the contingent and rhetorical aspects of human behavior. It is not enough to know what a group says it believes; we need to understand how groups decide when to invoke a particular value as relevant and how they perform that value in particular situations.[5]

The advantages of a core-values metaphor are predominantly rhetorical. I declare my allegiance to core values, in part, as a way to convince others to affirm my preferred version of myself. By proclaiming my "core values," I portray myself as an inner-directed, serious, self-reflective, and responsible actor. My explanation of why I behaved as I did leaves less flattering reasons unspoken. Invoking my foundational values as though they were natural means I need not answer questions about the social circumstances that led me to value some ends rather than others. Others, for their part, may not be convinced by my performance. My declaration of "what I believe" may satisfy me, but my contention that core values guided my action will likely seem puzzling or contradictory to others. Even if they accept my appeal to core values, they might ask how I decide which rules to follow when different values collide? Or, how do I decide between divergent actions that can both be justified as being consistent with my core values?

These shortcomings of a core-values metaphor become apparent when journalists try to apply it to their own work. Why, for instance, would journalists choose to characterize their profession by these six values rather than by six others that they could have invoked with equal plausibility? Who decided that journalists should prefer balance to dialogue? Leadership to social justice? Accessibility to access? Credibility to truth? One suspects that some values can be more easily discovered as "core" precisely because they are already embedded in conventional practices, not because they stand outside convention as enduring principles. The core-values approach accepts an *auteur* theory of journalism; it imagines reporters and editors as autonomous moral actors, capable of applying their principles in each situation, rather than as newsworkers tangled in a web of bureaucratic routines over which no single person has control. It imagines the improvement of journalism as a task that individual practitioners can achieve, with little reference to the structural forces that constrain actual news organizations.

Nor will appeals to core values convince skeptics outside the profession. To critics, the ASNE committee's work, even if well-meant, looks like a solemn ceremony of self-justification. The convention session publicly displays the profession's sincerity and concern; the report makes journalism's core values available as an authoritative response to be used against critics. ("My behavior was consistent with the core values spelled out by a prominent national professional organization.") Most surprisingly perhaps, the ASNE project and convention session ignore the distinctly conservative tone that any discussion of core values takes in American political discourse. (Harwood called his 1995 project, even more revealingly, "timeless values.") Core values is the preferred language of religious and political conservatives who hope to call their fellow citizens back to solid, old-fashioned, foundational beliefs. This is not a language friendly to those who argue (as John Dewey did nearly a century ago) that appeals to the verities do not help us explain the new situations in which modern people find themselves. What then are we to make of the ASNE committee's choice of this idiom? Was it deliberate or incidental? Neither answer flatters journalists. If deliberate, then the appeal to core values seems ideological and partisan, not neutral and universal as proponents claim it to be. If incidental, then the appeal to core values displays a stunning tone-deafness that is all the more striking in a profession that aims to mediate everyone else's discourse.

When Journalism's Crisis Began

Even though public journalism has uncritically used research like Harwood's, it does hope to make the profession less smug about its self-descriptions. But public journalism has sometimes tailored its language to soften others' misgivings. This approach offers tactical advantages to such proponents as Jay Rosen and James Carey. Making public journalism sound reasonable has helped scholars and journalists forge new alliances and kept the focus on what journalists and their critics share rather than on what divides them. What is good for public journalism as a reform movement, however, may not always serve it well as an intellectual critique. Still missing is what I am calling a sociology of public life—a strong and historically specific account of the social practices by which Americans have sustained democracy and of the role journalism might play in promoting democratic practices, not merely newsreading. In particular, public journalism continues to work with a truncated account of the origins of journalism's crisis, a dubious sense of the daily newspaper's exceptional role in American public discourse, and an overly rationalized conception of the social relations that democracy requires.

Public journalism has invented a myth of its own origins. It is a useful myth, but one that journalism historians would qualify and amend. According to this tale, the crisis in journalism has developed before our very eyes, within the last decade. Most accounts trace dissatisfaction with journalism back to the 1988 and 1992 elections. The myth describes an unprecedented moment of ideological polarization, political turmoil, and moral declension. Apathy and cynicism peak, and the public comes to feel disconnected from all its institutions, including journalism. Without denying the poignancy and confusion of this historical moment, or the value of public journalism's fight against it, we should recognize that we have all been here before. At no moment in American history has the authority or performance of the daily newspaper gone unchallenged.[6] Since the 1830s, one group after another has criticized the commercial daily—for encouraging sensationalistic tastes; unduly influencing politics; promoting cheap literature; favoring the wealthy and powerful; or denigrating women, African Americans, farmers, radicals, immigrants, and workers. Until World War I, critics periodically proposed alternative structures of production and distribution; they suggested endowing newspapers in the same way that museums and symphonies had been endowed, or operating newspapers as municipal utilities, or publishing them under the auspices of groups with higher morals.[7] After the war, perhaps recognizing the commercial structure of the daily newspaper as a *fait accompli*, critics proposed to improve performance by professionalizing newspaper staffs, sponsoring educational programs to promote news reading by children, or marketing themselves to new audiences.[8]

Public journalism shares a faith with each of these reform proposals. Like each, it hopes to recover an ideal journalism that stands above the corruptions of commercial and political influence. Journalism historian Douglas Birkhead has argued that this was precisely the rhetorical appeal of professionalism. It let journalists have it both ways: They could work for organizations that used powerful new industrial technologies and business methods but imagine themselves acting in the name of traditional liberal ideals of freedom.[9] Today this ritual purification of news is being played out as an attempt to distance journalism from the apparatus through which it is actually produced, marketed, and distributed. In one version of this argument, shared by both conventional and public journalists and found in Squires's book, corporate control corrupts once proud and independent family newspapers. In another version, proclaimed in a famous 1995 speech by Robert MacNeil, "the media" devour a once-noble profession, reducing journalism to just one more conglomerate property.[10] This symbolic redemption of journalists' profession rehearses a larger cultural ritual by which Americans use media technologies, organizations, forms, products, and professions as models of social order. In discussions of public journalism, proponents and critics alike treat journalism as a totem of democracy and of citizens' habits of speech, writing, and interpretation.[11] Whatever is good for journalism, the argument goes, is good for democracy.

Public journalism shares another mythology with the profession it criticizes. It believes that the daily newspaper's ascendancy was inevitable (and hence its decline a terrible tragedy). Actually, the long dominance of the daily newspaper in the United States now looks much more like an accident. Happenstance first elevated the commercial daily. It achieved its place of honor in the 19th century because it was, at that moment, the new technology—a material emblem of the triumphs of steam power, the telegraph, and the common school. It basked in the grandeur of city life and was its most visible embodiment.

In other circumstances, Americans might not have hung so many hopes and fears on the daily newspaper. The commercial daily newspaper in the United States would have struggled more against traditional forms of class and religious authority had it been born into an older society, or if Patriot papers had not played such an important role in the Revolution. The slow, steady development from electrical to electronic media created a long historical moment in which the daily newspaper could remain relatively unchallenged as the dominant popular medium of its age, protected from challenges by the new media that proliferated in the 20th century. Had the United States developed a strong labor press or socialist movement, as the European democracies did, commercial dailies would have competed for popular support with more ideologically oriented papers. The special role accorded the American commercial daily now seems a matter of luck, and journalists ought not assume that readers will forever associate the commercial daily with public life.

Where Community Resides

Most damaging of all, public journalism works with a thin and unconvincing account of the communities it hopes to serve. Taking its cue from a variety of contemporary upper-middle-class reform groups and the language of such sponsoring foundations as Pew and Kettering, it uses terms such as "civic culture," "civil society," and "social capital" with a breezy self-confidence. These terms have had pragmatic value in current political discourse. Political philosophers and social critics have used them to identify a theoretical space in which citizens might build a social commons. But like the references to core values, these metaphors for connectedness contain their own politics. In the spirit of Robert Bellah and colleagues' books *Habits of the Heart* and *The Good Society*, this language often attributes democracy's woes to individualism run amok. One of the most frequently used, and revealing, examples of this argument is Robert Putnam's article "Bowling Alone: America's Declining Social Capital."[12] It has been widely read and discussed by public journalism proponents and put forward as an acute analysis of the decline of civic life.

Putnam argues that the common good depends on "social capital," which he defines as "features of social organization such as networks, norms, and social trust that facilitate coordination and cooperation for mutual benefit."[13] He attributes the term's first use to the urbanologist Jane Jacobs.[14] But Jacobs applied the term in a much narrower way to city planning, not to whole societies. She used it to remind readers that even working-class neighborhoods, which lack the private wealth of suburbs, could make themselves politically effective by cultivating habits of reciprocity.[15] Unlike Jacobs, who immersed herself in the life and politics of Greenwich Village, the Lower East Side, and Boston's North End, Putnam wants to generalize about societies across the world. He proposes reasons why civic engagement withers or prospers in *any* society. He bases many of his conclusions on aggregate data such as the General Social Survey and on his comparative studies of Italian regional politics. Jacobs praised the range of groups living together who make a cosmopolitan neighborhood convivial and self-sustaining. Though Putnam's broad definition of social capital seemingly invites that same range of sociability, his examples seem to prefer some organizations to others. He admires Parent–Teacher Associations, women's clubs, the Boy Scouts, the Red Cross, and fraternal organizations but finds association memberships, nonprofit agencies, and support groups inadequate substitutes. It is easy to get the impression that social capital can be accumulated in polite, middle-class society but not in advocacy groups.

Putnam's use of the term "capital" oddly disconnects social from economic markets in ways revealingly different from the French sociologist Pierre Bourdieu's use of a similar term, "cultural capital." For Putnam, the only forms of capital worthy of being described as social are those that accrue to the common good. Societies that maintain networks of reciprocity accumulate social capital; societies that neglect such networks lose it. Yet a sociologist (rather than a political scientist) might observe that societies do not become less social for being more individualist or greedy, only social in a different way. All capital is social, regardless of whether it is used for the common good, because it derives its value from being exchangeable for something else—products, services, status, power. This was Jacobs's point, of course—that even poorer groups could pool their resources and experience. This is also Bourdieu's point, in a sense. He wants to talk about cultural capital as the symbolic practices that link the system of social distinctions to the economy.[16] For Bourdieu, taste and style articulate the forms of economic and social hierarchy. Putnam, in effect, imagines social capital as being important to politics and the economy but operating somewhat apart from the markets that assign value, one way or another, to all human activities.

As Putnam notes in another essay, social capital is one way to account for externalities—the indirect consequences of economic activity not usually included as a cost of doing business.[17] He acknowledges that one problem with his approach is that not all networks are equally open to all participants, because "social inequalities may be embedded in social capital."[18] Nonetheless, he seems to argue that democracy depends much more on the accumulation of social capital than on the redistribution of wealth or political power. Putnam's argument that the economy and social capital are somehow connected but not hinged leads him to odd emphases. For example, he mourns the loss of the union hall as a form of social capital but leaves unremarked the decades-long war against working people that has led to unions' decline. Citizens not being able to meet at the union hall seems more important to him than corporations exporting manufacturing jobs overseas, major law firms hiring themselves out as union busters, government officials neglecting to enforce labor and safety law, the tax system redistributing income upward, or innovation rendering old skills (and the skill holders) irrelevant.

Putnam's tendency to soft-pedal whatever divides Americans is nowhere clearer than in his article's title, "Bowling Alone." Putnam admits that bowling is a whimsical example, though the title has attracted the attention of dozens of editorial writers and critics who have taken up his argument.[19] He notes that between 1980 and 1993, the total number of bowlers in the United States increased by 10 percent, while league bowling decreased by 40 percent.[20] For Putnam, not bowling on teams represents a refusal of commitment, an example of vanishing social capital. But is it? Membership in bowling leagues has declined for many reasons, but none of them necessarily signals a weakening of solidarity. There are far fewer factory leagues than previously because American manufacturing has been decimated. More women work and thus are not available to join the daytime women's leagues that were once so common. Saturday leagues for children now compete with a range of sports considered more appropriately upscale by their parents. A long-term campaign that began in earnest in the 1950s to make bowling palatable for the middle class—by eliminating quarrelsome pinboys in favor of automatic pinsetters, introducing air-conditioning, and installing clean, New Look plastic seating and decorations in the 1950s—inevitably peaked. Bowling now competes with an endless array of new recreations, including more winter sports. People who do bowl alone often do so for entirely social reasons. They practice for leagues, tournaments, and Saturday night dates; like the dancer in the mirror, they are imagining and perfecting a future social performance, not salving their loneliness. Like any commercial recreation, bowling has adapted to changing demography and social tastes. Young people do not want to sign up for 36-week leagues, wear sponsors' shirts, receive arm patches and trophies, and force their spouses (usually wives) to sit and watch them, but some of them are interested in rock 'n' bowl nights that feature mirror balls and colored lights hung from the ceiling, fluorescent bowling balls, and raucous music.

Katha Pollitt has suggested that Putnam's real concern is Americans' loss of trust in their institutions and in the elites who run them. Putnam admits that his own evidence shows that even now, for all his talk of decline, "Americans are more trusting and more engaged than people in most other countries of the world."[21] He interprets Americans' loss of trust as a problem, but a different interpreter might look at that same evidence and praise Americans for facing up to modernity and becoming less naive about the corruption of their economic, religious, and political institutions. Pollitt writes:

> The bigfoot journalists and academic superstars, opinion manufacturers and wise men of both parties are worried, and it isn't about bowling or Boy Scouts. It's about that loss of "trust," a continuum that begins with one's neighbor and ends with the two parties, government, authority. It makes sense for the opinion and political elites to feel this trust. For them the system works. It's made them rich and famous. But how much faith can a rational and disinterested person have in the setup that's produced our current crop of leaders?[22]

People's abandonment of some group affiliations, like their abandonment of some forms of bowling, may not signal a decline in civic engagement. It may only mean that those older forms of affiliation no longer compel members' imagination or seem politically useful or expressive of peoples' sense of who they are or want to be.

Who Makes Democracy?

To read the literature on public journalism, one would think that Americans always embrace democracy, that the press always supports the common good, and that all that remains is to revive a tradition of solidarity that has only recently disappeared. A closer reading of the history of democracy in the United States, however, suggests that it has been achieved only through struggle, often against the weight of common sense and custom by groups that were condemned as controversial and uncivil in their time. There is no way to tell the story of any progressive social reform in U.S. history—be it winning civil liberties for women and minorities, fighting for an eight-hour day and the right to organize, allowing distribution of contraceptive materials, limiting the state's power to intimidate and harass dissenters, or promoting clean air or water—without talking about such movements.

These movements have often considered the commercial dailies part of the establishment, a mouthpiece for the forces impeding popular democracy. In the movement press of populists, feminists, and African Americans, for example, one constantly finds columns on the theme of "what others are saying about us," compiled from the pages of mainstream papers. Linda Steiner has documented the presence of such columns in early feminist periodicals, as well as in *Ms.* magazine today.[23] Populist papers similarly railed against the ideological power of urban dailies, which often sided with the bankers and commodity traders who were transforming the rural economy.[24] W. E. B. DuBois, first editor of the NAACP paper *The Crisis,* regularly critiqued the stereotypes of African Americans disseminated by mainstream papers. Reporters for *The New York Times* and other mainstream papers, though they occasionally complained about the excesses of Joseph McCarthy, still regularly supported the interests of the national security state and ridiculed peace activists in the 1950s. The daily press has never fought consistently on the side of popular democracy on any issue of public importance. Because it places such a high premium on consensus and civility, public journalism has thus far made no space in its theory of society for social movements or the enduring group conflicts that gave rise to them. As Lewis Friedland commented at the Stanford conference, the successful public journalism experiments in cities such as Spokane, Madison, Akron, and Wichita probably owe something to those cities' long histories of labor or populist activism.

Finally, the practitioners and theorists of public journalism have too often succumbed to their own myths about social life. Here is a pastiche, slightly exaggerated for effect, of the social world that public journalism proponents and practitioners hope to serve. They extol the wisdom of that middle class of great good Americans who possess the common sense not to succumb to radical ideologies on either end of the political spectrum. In a political universe that revolves around a wise center, group conflicts appear as temporary rather than permanent, and it is only unreasoning, ideologically driven, or impolite people who would argue otherwise. Optimism is the preferred style of self-presentation and public talk, pessimism is the enemy of consensus, and cynicism—well, it is uncivil, for it divides rather than unites communities. The power to address social problems is thought to lie within the grasp of individuals who, with enough goodwill, can change their own and others' behavior. There are no historical, structural forces beyond individual control. Public journalism never hints that the commercial daily newspaper might be one of the least promising places to plant the seeds of democratic reform.

Added up, these objections to public journalism's conception of society seem formidable indeed. Contrary to the exceptionalist myth shared by both conventional and public journalists, the daily newspaper no longer holds any particular pride of place in American life. What place it did hold, for so long, was won in part by historical accident and sustained by self-promotion and the marginalization of groups such as social movements that challenged its domination of "the popular." The daily newspaper can no longer control the distribution of information or command a community's advertising base, as it was so long accustomed to doing. Nor can it claim to monopolize the talents of the best nonfiction writers in the United States, however many awards the business invents to bestow on itself. Nor can it any longer control the methods and curriculum of university education, no matter how assiduously Gannett and other chains now apply themselves to that task.

Why Democracy Needs Cultural Reporting

For me, none of these objections justifies abandoning the public journalism experiment, for similar objections could have been directed even more forcefully at conventional journalism. But none of us will be able to create democracy from suspect political theories that define the United States's most pressing problem as a lack of core values or social capital or civic culture. Nor should public journalism's goal be to improve "deliberation," that narrowly rational practice by which political philosophers now hope to squeeze conversation out of democracy, in order to replace it with professionally organized and monitored committee work. Public journalism should choose to stand on other, more native ground, and use journalists' stories to reweave the web of social relations. What public journalism needs, in short, is a culturally informed theory and practice of feature reporting. So far it has accepted conventional practice in treating political reporting as the profession's highest achievement (and ultimate career goal). A democratic society, however, needs feature reporting to encourage the social solidarity and empathy that make public life possible.

A recent example of the power of storytelling is available in the history of the New Journalism. Unlike public journalists, the New Journalists chose to focus on the story rather than information aspects of their work. Michael Schudson pointed to this information–story distinction many years ago in *Discovering the News*.[25] In the late 19th century, he argued, two forms of journalism emerged: an information tradition, personified by *The New York Times*, and a story tradition, personified by *The New York World* and decried by critics as sensationalistic and entertainment driven. Public journalism hails journalists as participants in the information tradition. To some extent, this has been a practical decision, capitalizing on the opportunity offered by public skepticism and the recent failures of campaign coverage. Information, after all, is the profession's preferred way of talking about its role as provider of the political knowledge citizens need to participate. Here as elsewhere, public journalism finds itself working within as well as against the dominant conventions of the profession. Yet treating the press as an information utility makes it hard for public journalism to talk about the stories and myths through which groups imagine their relations to one another.

To say that reporters tell stories, after all, makes journalism seem a less elevated calling than to say that they provide the information crucial to democracy, but storytelling is just what they do. News consists of more than names, dates, places, and events, or even themes, coded and counted. News is dramaturgy. It conjures modern society into public existence. News stories invoke the moral order in order to praise the heroes who uphold it and bludgeon the villains who defile it. News dreams a community's destiny; it chants the future and invents the past. It smites a society's enemies, mourns their triumphs, and dances on their graves when they die. Reading the literature on public journalism, one might not know that the power of news is its ability to make reality, or that a democratic society requires the right kind of drama to prosper (though I take this to be exactly the point that Jay Rosen and especially James Carey have been trying to make).

Consider again the relation of daily newspapers to the lives of working people. Apart from running stories on labor strikes or corporate downsizing, or conducting focus group discussions of a community's job prospects, the newspaper constantly talks about working people, in both its echoes and its silences. If we are alert, we can feel the presence of working people in Dagwood Bumstead's (or Dilbert's) run-ins with his boss, or in the obituaries of middle-aged men killed in industrial accidents. But we can also read between the lines, as workers do, whenever the newspaper's business pages praise a new captain of industry, or the Sunday supplement names a prominent banker "Man of the Year," or the real estate section runs four-color pictures of lush suburban gardens and million-dollar homes for sale, or the restaurant critic weaves byzantine descriptions of five-course three-figure meals at the newest cafe, or the gossip columnist fills his space with bold-face names of celebrities, or stock market analysts rejoice at the news of higher unemployment.

Remembered now mostly as a stylistic revolution, the New Journalism once proposed an alternative politics of representation, as I have discussed elsewhere.[26] Where public journalism starts with philosophical principles and reasons back to the forms of social life it thinks will be necessary to enact those principles, the New Journalism started with politics and culture as it found them. New Journalists argued, in effect, that culture is politics by other means, especially in a society so devoted to publicity, celebrity, fandom, and spectacle. To document the astonishing range of life worlds Americans began creating in the 1950s, New Journalists took up the tools of sociology, not political philosophy. Because New Journalists were so vilified by the journalistic establishment, they were forced to find venues other than newspapers for their work, so they never felt much loyalty to daily journalism's claim of a sacred role in politics. As far as they could tell, daily journalism was one more act in the three-ring circus that was American society.

By relying on the language of core values, social capital, and civic culture, public journalists have settled for a demure, middle-class conception of public life. Like the Progressive reformers of the early 20th century, they feel most comfortable with the wisdom of the middle and with commonsense notions of what counts as legitimate political action. (A quick test: Name the daily newspapers in the United States today that would propose or vigorously support public demonstrations, rallies, or a labor strike.) As Walter Lippmann was one of the first to note, history has created a terrible mismatch between our politics and our forms of economic and social organization.[27] Critics such as Lani Guinier and William Greider continue to press the point, noting how the staggering number of local political units, the system of geography-based voting, and the two-party duopoly encumber political life today.[28] Yet conventional journalism continues to mimic these vestigial forms, shaping its routines to match the existing political structure. Thus does public journalism affirm deeply mythic structures of American politics as common sense, whether it means to or not. And it is those structures of special interest—not citizens' lack of civility—that have immobilized American politics.

In this sense, the proposals of Anderson, Dardenne, and Killenberg for "conversational journalism" go beyond those of public journalism.[29] They favor dialogue rather than deliberation. The distinction is significant. Deliberation in civic culture projects encourages focused conversation designed to solve specific problems. Dialogue may lead anywhere, and it allows groups to discover together things that they could not know singly. Because it encourages steady attention to others' modes of being in the world, dialogue also allows for a fuller play of cultural difference. But to make their work more conversational, journalists would need to develop a sociology of public life that acknowledges how their own professional practices and organizations inhibit dialogue.

David Eason, our most acute commentator on the New Journalism, has argued that we should read that movement as a running commentary on how writers and readers make reality, at a moment when the grounds of social order are shifting beneath their feet.[30] Instead of mourning the loss of stability, or looking for a new foundation on which to build our dream of the past, public journalism might simply accept that we live in a seismic zone and that we must learn to be nimble if we hope to keep our feet (and our heads) whenever the earth begins to rumble. This was the advice that Eason took from the French literary critic (and sometime newspaper writer) Roland Barthes:

> The fact that we cannot manage to achieve more than an unstable grasp of reality doubtless gives the measure of our present alienation: we constantly drift between the object and its demystification, powerless to render its wholeness. For if we penetrate the object, we liberate it but we destroy it; and if we acknowledge its full weight, we respect it, but we restore it to a state which is still mystified. It would seem that we are condemned for some time yet always to speak excessively about reality.[31]

Translating Barthes for our own purposes, we might say that journalism is forever condemned to speak about the conditions in which groups make reality. Public journalism hopes to make democracy more rational and intelligible, but making democracy work may mean acknowledging social life as we find it, giving groups the means and access to tell their own stories, and forswearing some traditional privileges of professionalism in the name of solidarity and empathy. Modern societies will continue to struggle for meaning, with or without the help of journalists. That is a lesson that public journalism could learn from the New Journalism.

Notes

1. James D. Squires, *Read All about It! The Corporate Takeover of America's Newspapers* (New York: Times Books, 1993), pp. 3–4.
2. Walter Lippmann, *Public Opinion* (New York: Free Press, 1965), p. 229.
3. Rob Anderson, Robert Dardenne, and George M. Killenberg, *The Conversation of Journalism: Communication, Community, and News* (Westport, CT: Praeger, 1994), pp. 138–140.
4. "Journalism Values: Who Are We and What Are We Doing Here?," panel presented at the annual meeting of the American Society of Newspaper Editors, Washington, DC, April 17, 1996.
5. A graceful explanation of this style of sociological analysis can be found in Anselm L. Strauss, *Mirrors and Masks: The Search for Identity* (Mill Valley, CA: Sociology Press, 1969).
6. John Pauly, "Reflections on Writing a History of News as a Form of Mass Culture," Working Paper No. 6 (Milwaukee: Center for Twentieth Century Studies, Fall 1985).
7. John J. Pauly, "The Moral Purification of Journalism: The Search for the Ideal Newspaper," paper presented at the annual meeting of the American Studies Association, New York, November 1987. Also see Marion Tuttle Marzolf, *Civilizing Voices: American Press Criticism, 1880–1950* (New York: Longman, 1991), pp. 34–49.
8. On the newsreading movement, see John J. Pauly, "Interesting the Public: A Brief History of the Newsreading Movement," *Communication*, 12 (1991): 285–297.
9. Douglas Birkhead, "The Power in the Image: Professionalism and the Communications Revolution," *American Journalism*, 1 (1984): 1–14.
10. Robert MacNeil, "Regaining Dignity," *Media Studies Journal*, 9 (1995): 103–111. This article is adapted from a speech that MacNeil gave at the 10th anniversary of the Freedom Forum Media Studies Center at Columbia University. MacNeil concluded his speech, and the article, by noting that "Names are important. We are what we call ourselves. And for 40 years I have been proud to call myself a journalist. I think media stinks!"
11. For examples of symbolic talk about journalism, see John J. Pauly, "Rupert Murdoch and the Demonology of Professional Journalism," pp. 205–227, or David L. Eason, "On Journalistic Authority: The Janet Cooke Scandal," pp. 246–261, both in *Media, Myths, and Narratives: Television and Press*, ed. James W. Carey (Newbury Park, CA: Sage, 1988).
12. Robert D. Putnam, "Bowling Alone: America's Declining Social Capital," *Journal of Democracy*, 6 (1995): 65–78.
13. Putnam, "Bowling Alone," p. 67.
14. Putnam, "Bowling Alone," p. 78.

15. Jane Jacobs, *The Death and Life of Great American Cities* (New York: Vintage Books, 1961), p. 138.
16. Pierre Bourdieu, *Distinction: A Social Critique of the Judgment of Taste* (Cambridge, MA: Harvard University Press, 1984).
17. Robert D. Putnam, "The Prosperous Community: Social Capital and Public Life," *American Prospect*, 13 (1993): 35–42.
18. Putnam, "The Prosperous Community," p. 42.
19. A May 1997 Nexis/Lexis search of "Putnam" and "bowling alone" produced 291 matches, in everything from newspapers and magazines to congressional testimony and bowling industry marketing news releases. For so many intellectuals and journalists to comment on bowling, a topic they rarely discuss except to mock the working class, amounts to a grandiose affectation and faux populism.
20. Putnam, "Bowling Alone," p. 70.
21. Putnam, "Bowling Alone," p. 74.
22. Katha Pollitt, "For Whom the Ball Rolls," *Nation* 262 (April 15, 1996): 9.
23. On suffrage periodicals, see Linda Steiner, "Nineteenth-Century Suffrage Periodicals: Conceptions of Womanhood and the Press," in *Ruthless Criticism: New Perspectives in U.S. Communication History*, ed. William S. Solomon and Robert W. McChesney (Minneapolis: University of Minnesota Press, 1993). On *Ms.*, see Steiner, "Oppositional Decoding as an Act of Resistance," pp. 329–345 in *Critical Perspectives on Media and Society*, ed. Robert K. Avery and David Eason (New York: Guilford Press, 1991).
24. Jean Folkerts, "Functions of the Reform Press," in *Media Voices, an Historical Perspective*, ed. Jean Folkerts (New York: Macmillan, 1992).
25. Michael Schudson, *Discovering the News: A Social History of American Newspapers* (New York: Basic Books, 1978), pp. 88–120.
26. John J. Pauly, "The Politics of the New Journalism," pp. 183–190 in *Literary Journalism in the Twentieth Century*, ed. Norman Sims (New York: Oxford University Press, 1990).
27. Lippmann, *Public Opinion*, pp. 175–184.
28. Lani Guinier, *The Tyranny of the Majority: Fundamental Fairness in Representative Democracy* (New York: Free Press, 1994); William Greider, *Who Will Tell the People: The Betrayal of American Democracy* (New York: Simon & Schuster, 1992).
29. See Anderson et al., *The Conversation of Journalism*. But see also "The American Newspaper as the Public Conversational Commons," pp. 96–115 in *Mixed News: The Public/Civic/Communitarian Journalism Debate*, ed. Jay Black (Mahwah, NJ: Erlbaum, 1997); and Rob Anderson and Mike Killenberg, "Listening in Journalism: All the News We've Heard About That's Fit to Print," pp. 311–331 in *Listening in Everyday Life: A Personal and Professional Approach*, ed. Michael Purdy and Deborah Borisoff (Lanham, MD: University Press of America, 1997).
30. David Eason, "The New Journalism and the Image-World," in *Literary Journalism in the Twentieth Century*, pp. 191–205.
31. Eason, "New Journalism and the Image-World," p. 202.

Chapter 9

Making
the Neighborhood Work
The Improbabilities of Public Journalism

Barbie Zelizer

University of Pennsylvania

When a new neighbor moves into an established community, a period of collective evaluation often follows. Veteran residents of the neighborhood carefully appraise the impact of the neighbor's arrival, while the new inhabitant ascertains how best to fit in with the community. So it is with public journalism. This recently arrived resident of the long-standing community of U.S. journalists has placed both itself and veteran neighborhood members on a heightened level of awareness. As each side gauges the attributes that resemble and distinguish public journalism from the rest of the journalistic world, the fit between public journalism and the larger journalistic community is being negotiated.

This chapter examines the rhetoric surrounding public journalists' entry into the neighborhood of U.S. journalists. In considering public journalism's claims about itself, it ascertains the degree to which this new mode of journalistic practice is displaying good neighborly relations. Specifically, this chapter questions the frame by which public journalism is being set in place, suggesting that proponents of public journalism may have overstated their role of saving journalism from itself. It argues that its formulators may be moving too quickly for the good of the idea, and it proposes a time-out in which all involved can think more closely about the viability of the concepts being promoted.

Such a time-out would facilitate a natural jelling of the new journalistic neighborhood, helping veteran neighbors to adapt to new practices at the same time as public journalists are figuring out how better to accommodate the larger journalistic community.

The Context for Considering Public Journalism

Since the early 1990s, the topic of public journalism has taken over much of the dead space in public conversations about contemporary news in the United States. Alternately called "civic journalism," "community journalism," and "community-assisted reporting," public journalism surfaces in nearly every current discussion about the state of contemporary news making. No fewer than 15 books now address public journalism in one form or another, most published within the last five years and many issued by foundations devoted to spreading news about this kind of journalism.[1] Professional journals and trade reviews—such as *The Quill, Editor and Publisher, Communicator, Columbia Journalism Review,* and *American Journalism Review*—regularly ponder the negative and positive sides of public journalism, under such titles as "Climbing Down from the Ivory Tower," "The Gospel of Public Journalism," and "Give Me Old-Time Journalism."[2] The media routinely generate their own conversations in articles that tend to vilify the lamentable dimensions of public journalism over its virtues,[3] although certain reporters have offered confessionals of how the idea won them over. Funding institutes such as the Kettering Foundation, the Twentieth Century Fund, the Poynter Institute for Media Studies, the Knight Foundation, and the Pew Charitable Trusts have lauded public journalism, funneling substantial monies, institutional attention, and other resources toward its development.[4] Symposia and workshops on public journalism are now regularly conducted for working journalists, and bibliographies about how to engage in public journalism can be found readily in most libraries.[5] Finally, an inventory of practices associated with doing public journalism has accumulated, as individuals behind early experiments at *The Charlotte Observer* and *The Wichita Eagle* have begun to make those ideas available to others.[6] In fact, some estimates hold that as many as 200 U.S. newspapers now practice some form of public journalism.[7] Calling the movement "the media's new fix," the newsmagazine *U.S. News & World Report* recently observed that "not since the turn of the century . . . has there been such turmoil about the mission and ethics of journalists."[8] There is, then, no dearth of conversation about this new frame for doing journalism.

For many, this new fix is thought to embody the hope and future of U.S. journalism. According to key advocate Jay Rosen, director of New York University's Project on Public Life and the Press, it provides a way of making journalism public by rendering the public integral to good journalism rather than merely incidental. It metaphorically makes the public into a place that can be "more supportive of the realm of meaningful public discussion," where things of importance can be debated.[9] Conceived as an antidote to ongoing problems surrounding media ethics in the United States, public journalism comes at a point when the general population is said to be despairing over the news media's mission and credibility. This despair, chronicled by such scholars as James Carey and Michael Schudson,[10] undermines the media's ability to function as a cultural and institutional force mandated with providing a public life for its citizenry. This means that public journalism is capable of reactivating what Carey saw as the god-term of contemporary journalism—the public.[11] It is capable of giving journalism back its origin narrative, its impulse for existence, its raison d'être.

This is a weighty responsibility. Yet it is one that public journalism proponents predict they can master. In identifying a fundamental disconnect between contemporary journalism and its public, proponents contend that public journalism can reactivate the public by coaxing its members into a more active participation in public life. In Rosen's view, published over the last few years in four monographs and numerous articles,[12] public journalism stipulates both that people need to participate in political life and that the news media must make their participation viable. By generating journalists' involvement in the process of finding solutions to community problems instead of only reporting them, news organizations become either advocates or moderators for change, implemented by regularly asking readers for feedback on stories that either have been covered or could be covered. Democracy is presumed safer by facilitating such activities as town meetings, community voice pages, neighborhood roundtables, and panels of community leaders who give feedback on stories. The public becomes central, correcting a situation in which a full 71 percent of U.S. citizens contend that the "media stand in the way of America solving its problems."[13] In reorienting itself toward the public, public journalism salvages the very journalistic practices on which it is positioned.

For one who has spent much of her academic life critiquing the world of contemporary journalism, it is difficult not to appreciate public journalism for precisely these reasons. It is no accident that journalistic ethics, and the challenge of doing one's job with integrity, continue to plague the majority of U.S. journalists, to the extent that sessions, discussions, and meetings on media ethics today draw more journalists than discussions of any other aspect of journalistic practice.

Journalism is a land whose practitioners generally act with impunity, without the socially recognized paths of training, education, licensing, and criticism common to other professions. Learning to be part of the journalistic world thus results from a loose "combination of osmosis and fiat,"[14] whose inhabitants generally improvise when attempting to standardize practice.

This means that the professional existence of journalists is shaped largely through situationally determined cues, functioning somewhat like a religion without a minister.[15] In purporting to reconnect journalism with its public and reinvigorate contemporary journalism's mission, public journalism thus responds to the malaise that has resulted in the lack of such a minister. It is no surprise, then, that as an idea public journalism feels right. It renovates the somewhat antiquated notion of social responsibility and promises a newfound sensitivity for those toward whom journalism is supposed to be directed. Conversely, critiquing it resembles pulling the punch out of a celebration before it has hit its high.

Yet there are serious questions surrounding this new gospel of journalistic practice. For despite all the attention, celebration, and ongoing conversation, it is doubtful whether public journalism proponents have produced sufficient articulation, clarification, or even consensus about what public journalism is and should be. Rather, the opposite may be the case, with the proliferation of excessive discourse possibly prohibiting public journalism from growing to maturity. In much the same way as a story requiring excessive coverage has been said to be the one least worth covering, it may be here too that a journalism producing such a large amount of self-generated rhetoric faces problems when it translates that rhetoric into practice.

Journalists as Interpretive Communities

Central to the premise that public journalism may be producing more words than action is the notion that journalists function as an interpretive community, one united by its shared discourse and collective interpretations of the real world.[16] The discourse of interpretive communities helps community members articulate what is important or relevant and offers suggestions about what can help the community continue functioning.

Among reporters, the notion of an interpretive community offers a way to talk about a slew of practices related to journalism but not accounted for when examining the dominant frame of a profession. These include a reliance on constructed realities, informal networking, and centrality of narrative and storytelling practices, all of which suggest that the work of interpretation is central to shaping journalism. In particular, how journalists develop certain interpretations of events, practices, or, generally phrased, challenges to the status quo helps consolidate the journalistic community. Journalists create collective interpretations of challenges that they routinely and informally circulate to each other, though such channels as informal talks and discourse, professional and trade reviews, professional meetings, autobiographies and memoirs, interviews on talk shows, and media retrospectives.

A key part of journalists' discourse about themselves is the discussion of breaches, changes, or adaptations of standardized journalistic practice. In a way reminiscent of the imagined communities discussed by Benedict Anderson,[17] journalists particularly use their discourse to lend shape to challenges that are thought to upset the status quo of journalism. Much as a renewed emphasis on investigative reporting arose following Watergate or interpretive reporting became an active setting for journalists' practices following the poor journalistic coverage of the McCarthy era, interpretive communities function to stabilize consensus. Sometimes they do so excessively or around inappropriate focal points, as when journalistic conversations about the recent murder of child beauty queen JonBenet Ramsey prompted excessive journalistic navel gazing for lack of a news story.[18] Other times journalists use discourse to establish interpretations over time that reflect more positively on their reporting than evaluations at the time suggested.[19] But in all cases, their discourse establishes and maintains boundaries around the community, allowing its members to consider and ultimately negotiate alterations of practices in accordance with what they deem appropriate or manageable.

At present, the lack of a vigorous public sphere is prompting journalists to look anew at how a change in their practices might alter public involvement. Within the frame of journalists as an interpretive community, discourse about public journalism serves a vital function for those attempting both to uphold and to alter conventional notions of journalistic practice. Journalists' discourse thus becomes relevant not only for what it says but for the role it plays in the act of community formation and maintenance.

The Improbabilities of Public Journalism

The rhetorical posturing of public journalism's key proponents calls to mind a number of questions—or improbabilities—that persist about the shape of public journalism. Each involves what appears to be a certain level of midlevel messiness in the idea, that public journalism proponents may profit by contemplating. Such improbabilities require reflection, experimentation, and fermentation before any more claims are made about what public journalism *ought* to do.

To begin with, the definition itself of public journalism requires clarification. Is it a movement, a philosophy, or a model of journalism? Its lack of clear definition has had an impact on the idea's implementation, for as discussions have moved from the idea of public journalism—about which there has been considerable discussion—to *acting* on the idea—about which there has been less discussion—the mechanics of the transition have not been made sufficiently clear. Indeed, the rather vast terrain connecting the compelling rhetoric about public journalism with its various pockets of practice makes one wonder whether public journalism advocates have gotten so caught up in what sounds good that they are no longer taking the time to figure out *how* to do what they are preaching.

Not surprisingly, then, the prescriptive domain of public journalism is almost nonexistent. Despite the fact that there are numerous publications about public journalism, no manual or checklist stipulates how one is supposed to engage in it. According to key proponents, the lack of a manual is intentional, for the phenomenon operates in an improvisatory fashion, with journalists and news organizations acting in response to the circumstances they encounter. As advocate Jay Rosen has stated, public journalism involves "a difficult test of professional judgment, for it means entering a territory where there are no clear rules, only broad goals."[20] Public journalism proponents have provided numerous discussions of how public journalism is accomplished at one given newspaper or television station,[21] but their discussions are inevitably accompanied by comments to journalists about tailoring the practices to the needs of their own communities. On a fundamental level, this kind of situational context is familiar to journalists, whose community has long been defined by situational cues in ethics, sourcing, dilemmas of performance, and other domains of journalistic practice. Yet situational cues that differ according to circumstance also cater to what is most problematic about journalism—the lack of standards, even contradictory standards, by which journalists evaluate how they are doing as journalists. The consequent lack of prescriptions that arises from situational posturing thereby may be exacerbating the somewhat obscure character of public journalism and minimizing the ability to clarify it to the rest of the journalistic community.

Four fundamental improbabilities presently cloud the idea of public journalism. Each has to do with the neighborhood of public journalism and the viability of its links to the world around it. Each has to do with how public journalism joins forces with others—with other agents who are similarly implicated in making journalism public. This is because in the end, public journalism cannot function as a self-contained community in which the proponents preach to the converted. Rather, it needs to develop neighborly practices with all those in its surrounding environment.

The neighborhood of public journalism is composed of four main neighbors, each of whom bears closer consideration by public journalism proponents—history, the journalistic world, the public, and the political system. Each of these neighbors offers different reasons for the neighborhood not yet jelling. Although each is involved in the broader project of making journalism public, each suggests in different ways that despite many compelling ideas, the shape of their neighborly relations (or lack thereof) with public journalism has allowed it to work only *some* of the time. When it does not work, it begins to look suspiciously like that which it is being held responsible for correcting.

Improbability I: The Historical Neighbor

The most fundamental improbability of public journalism emanates from a historical myopism that many of its proponents display. Public journalism has been situated in a largely ahistorical space, whose proponents have either misread, miscast, or simply missed the historical contingencies that helped generate a point in space and time which is presently amenable to public journalism. Such ahistoricism extends to both the content and the form of journalism's history, rendering the new neighborhood into a community with little understanding or sensitivity of its earlier inhabitants.

In content, public journalism's historical myopism has to do with the degree to which it codifies itself as new and different from other forms of journalistic practice. In much of its self-generated rhetoric, public journalism has set itself as separate and antithetical to the classic mode of neutral, or gatekeeping, journalism.[22] Proponents argue that the journalist's role "has to be restated" because "informing the public is too limited, too narrow."[23] Seen as an antidote to the claims of objectivity behind which traditional journalists have long assumed to hide, public journalists argue that objectivity is the primary causal circumstance for the ills of the press today.

Yet the resonance of reporters as objective, neutral gatekeepers of events, as value-free conduits of information, is only one of numerous models of journalism. As far back as the 1970s, John Johnstone, Edward Slawski, and William Bowman published a groundbreaking study in which they found that working journalists displayed allegiance to two competing belief systems in journalism—neutral and participant. They argued that more journalists in effect endorsed participant over neutral journalism, even if functions pertaining to both roles were widely accepted.[24] Decades later, David Weaver and Cleveland Wilhoit upheld the simultaneous existence of different belief systems among journalists, arguing that practices associated with neutral reporting were in fact differentially displayed in broader mind-sets about adversarial, interpretive, and disseminator notions of press function.[25] The modern journalist thereby blends "the classical critical role of the journalist . . . with the technical requirements of disseminating great volumes of descriptive information."[26] These studies suggest that journalists are more pluralistic about journalism than the stance of public journalism proponents suggests, and that the invocation of objectivity and neutral journalism resembles a straw man argument. That is, in setting themselves up against the neutrality of traditional journalists, public journalists may be overstating the resonance of the practices of neutral or gatekeeping journalism within the community.

At the same time, however, they may be overstating the differences between their practices and that of a whole panoply of more communally committed journalistic forms—the muckrakers at the turn of the century, the advocacy journalists of the 1960s and 1970s, even the strident investigative journalism of the post-Watergate era. Each argued, in different ways, for a predetermined reportorial presence in the story, and for a reporter committed more to community than to professionally oriented aims. For instance, for as long as journalism has existed, journalistic crusades of one sort or another—the Teapot Dome scandal, battling slumlords and drug lords, Watergate—have sharpened U.S. journalism's collective identity. Although earlier forms of crusade journalists did not use the terminology by which public journalism is now being set in place—employing such terms as "values clarification," "connectivity," and "connectedness," which many traditional journalists dismiss as jargon—the final objective of public involvement and change resembles that of public journalists. Advocacy journalism, in particular, favored activism and community participation over passivity and professional detachment. Thus, even a cursory look back in time raises crucial questions about public journalism's positioning on the continuum of journalistic practices. Rosen argues that "there are limits to the stance of the observer in journalism," and that the press offers "no philosophy that takes over when those limits are reached."[27] It seems that the press has many such philosophies, only perhaps they are not collectively identified in a way that public journalists recognize.

In form, too, public journalism proponents have not paid substantial attention to the history of professional adaptation in journalism.

Regardless of the period examined, rhetoric that insists on a too rapid pace of accommodation, as does that of public journalism, is often accompanied by a more cautious mode of actual adaptation to change. In numerous cases throughout history, journalists have accommodated slowly and tentatively to alterations of their own practices, and the latter part of this century displays many such examples: Calls for more interpretive reporting that were heard as early as the 1930s only substantially gained ground among a large part of the U.S. journalistic population at the beginning of the 1950s, following the Korean War and other events.[28] Similarly, during the 1970s, a newfound journalistic reliance on anonymous sources, related to a post-Watergate fervor over investigative journalism, fell on deaf ears 25 years later when it helped produce scandals as wide-ranging as the Janet Cooke affair or Joe Klein's scripting of *Primary Colors*.[29] And even the practices of New Journalism, hailed by many during the 1960s, were kept marginalized and separate from mainstream journalism, until a broader recognition of news narrative in the late 1980s facilitated their more reputable reintroduction as literary journalism.[30] In failing to admit a tradition of slow change, the rhetoric of public journalism seems out of step with journalism's past, resembling an advanced placement course that is wrongly targeting a community of mediocre students.

To be fair, the critics of public journalism have been similarly myopic about history's lessons. In reducing public journalism to a promotional tactic designed to offset dwindling circulation figures and declining revenues from advertisements, critics have conveniently misread the similarly ignoble beginnings of other kinds of journalism—neutral journalism, New Journalism, and muckraking, to name a few—and their insistence on removing profit tracking from existing discussions of good journalistic practice results in an incomplete picture of journalism.[31] They also ignore the point that positive consequences can and do emerge often from the least promising beginnings.

Historical vignettes are instructive, for they suggest that the ability to accommodate change in any professional milieu is not a certain or easy matter, and this is particularly so with journalism. In adapting, proponents need to make a new practice or set of practices doubly accountable: On the one hand, the practice must be compelling enough that it can convince whole populations, communities, or professions to move in directions at odds with their previous experiences; on the other, it must be sufficiently safe that those same whole populations see linkages between the norm and the deviation. The eclipses of time between the interpretive reporting of the 1930s and the 1950s, between the valorized anonymous sources of the 1970s and the problematic uses of such sources in the 1980s and 1990s, and between the

New Journalism of the 1960s and the more reputable literary journalism of the 1980s are all cases in point, for a temporal lag may be necessary to engender the kind of double accountability in regard to the alterations being proposed. Perhaps that much time was necessary for the proposed innovation to settle into some kind of consensual setting—to be seen either as viable both for those who believed in it and as nonthreatening for those who did not or, alternatively, to be seen as problematic by both its supporters and its challengers.

And so a slew of questions remain about public journalism's historical neighbor, all of which suggest a slower mode of adaptation than is being proposed. There may be a need to respect the slow pace of professional adaptation that journalists have traditionally displayed while recognizing the more rapid pace insisted on by public journalism advocates. Attending to such questions is necessary because it constitutes the core of neighborly relations. For just as one checks out a neighborhood before moving into it, so too might public journalism profit by considering who and what preceded its own arrival.

Improbability 2: The Journalistic Neighbor

Improbability 2 involves the relationship of public journalism to its journalistic neighbors and the degree of viability in forging a connection between the two. Affixing the term "public" to "journalism" is a somewhat problematic linguistic ploy that activates an underlying tension in this neighborhood. Somewhat like talking about *nurturing* parents or *melodic* music, the term "public" journalism requires affixing an adjective that declares the subjunctive state of the activity equivalent to the activity itself. Adding "public" to journalism, then, shows that journalism has been repaired by locating its constitutive feature—the public—in only one of its operative forms.

But such a ploy is somewhat deceptive and not very neighborly. Nor is it reflective about all that journalism tries to be, for many alternatives continue to exist in varying relations around that same constitutive feature. Just like music with jarring notes is still considered music or parents with less nurturing styles seldom lose their parental rights, so too with journalism. Its continuum of alternatives—some better, some worse—assume varying relations with the public, even if they are less articulated than that suggested by the rhetoric surrounding public journalism. In making its own nominal claims to the public, then, public journalism has inadvertently set itself up as the neighborhood's rent lord. Is it any wonder, then, that old-guard loyalists like Michael Gartner have labeled public journalism "a menace"?[32] Inadvertently or not, public journalism appears to have set itself against its journalistic neighbors, propelling them into a defensive stance over what they see too as their territory.

Such a lack of neighborly friendliness—that in the extreme case constitutes unneighborly imperialism—stems from what seems to be a certain degree of ambiguity surrounding the idea of public journalism. Recently called "an adventure,"[33] public journalism presents itself like a liminal experience, one predicated on a certain degree of separation from the rest of the world. Yet what happens when the worlds meld is not yet clear. What *is* the relationship of public journalism to the rest of the journalistic world? Is it supposed to replace, substitute, merge, or merely complement alternative journalistic styles?

If the least expansive scenario—that of complementing other journalisms—is the preferred vision, then public journalism's claim to the public becomes somewhat bewildering and gives rise to a series of questions. Is it possible for public journalism to maintain a status as one alternative among many if at the same time its own nominal stance neutralizes the claims of its neighbors to their shared territory? What, for instance, is the rest of journalism supposed to be called—nonpublic journalism? Private journalism? What should we make of all those agents of news who do not fit as readily into public journalism's mold as does the press—television, radio, and the Internet?

If, on the other hand, the most expansive scenario—that of replacing other journalisms—is implied, more needs to be said about how it can be accomplished, and whether or not it *should* be accomplished. Are *all* journalists supposed to abandon their belief in professional disinterest and devise new standards of journalistic responsibility? And if not all, which ones are supposed to do so? How much of public journalism's lament is directed at journalism as a whole? Conversely, how much of it has been antagonized by the Washington press corps and inaccurately generalized to all of journalism? For as long as the limits of public journalism are not stated, the idea of expansion remains the unarticulated background behind the practices at hand.

In its present form, public journalism seems to work best in situations in which people know and can act on their public wants and needs, and to this end it is assumed to bring about practices of good citizenship. The best example here might be a political campaign. Campaigns appear to be well suited to discussions of public journalism because they wrap coverage in broader assumptions about our sense of civic self, drawing on subjunctive notions about attending to the news media as the practices of good citizenship. Not surprisingly, then, numerous examples of public journalism have focused on political campaigns, including *The Wichita Eagle*'s "People Project" and *The Charlotte Observer*'s "Citizen's Agenda."[34]

But surely there are other deeper and perhaps murkier sides to political identity and citizenship—less rational, less conscious dimensions for which public journalism does not account. Such practices might not be identified immediately as the material from which good citizenship is made, yet they figure nonetheless in its making. Popular culture, for example, certainly provides one example of an ongoing challenge to journalism's claim to be the primary designer of public life. If existing notions of citizenship are pared down to the kind of articulated, vocalized statement of community that seems necessary to get public journalism moving, then in effect a new kind of tyranny has been created. It is a tyranny that privileges the neighbors who play by certain rules over others who reside nearby but are less vocal and perhaps less conscious about what their proximity means. Such a tyranny threatens to make public journalism doubly complicit because it comes wrapped in the rhetoric of communal concern. This makes public journalism into a rent lord, and an overly self-interested one too.

In addition, other types of journalism are not at all identifiably interested in community, as it is defined by public journalism. What are we to make of the journalisms of gardening, fashion, or perhaps even business? Each type of news manages only an ill-fitting match with the goals of public journalism, yet nowhere in its rhetoric has their place been clarified. This is not to suggest that the newest neighbor need account for the remainder of the neighborhood. But when it comes armed with claims that appear to displace other neighbors—even if only due to inadvertent exclusions—it sets the rest of the neighborhood justifiably on edge.

Improbability 3: The Public Neighbor

Improbability 3 involves the relationship between public journalism and its nonjournalistic neighbors—the public. In a functioning democracy, it is generally assumed that the optimum operation of public journalism depends on its good links with the community. In other words, public journalism depends on a workable neighborhood and on the continued ability to generate and maintain momentum with portions of the public deemed relevant. The idea of a functioning linkage between journalism and its public is rooted in the work of John Dewey, who argued for the creation of conditions by which people could routinely participate in public life.[35]

Such is the shape of what Jay Rosen has called "proper attachment" or "getting the connections right,"[36] an idea that suggests journalists can help publics accomplish civic responsibility by facilitating the discussion and enactment of intelligent decisions about public

affairs. Aside from the fact that this presumes that journalists will know
to frame the right questions, and that their questions will affect the
answers they receive, numerous additional problems come to light
here. For it has not yet been made clear *how* public journalism is to
make things public at the same time that it attends to the public's
needs. How is "proper attachment" or "getting the connections right"
to be achieved and maintained?

To begin with, the connections between journalist and public may
be easier to talk about than accomplish. Though Rosen has argued that
it invites the participation of citizens who have genuine concerns about
their public life,[37] there has been no focused debate about how this is to
be determined. At some level the neighborhood is overgrown, and the
public is too large to accommodate public journalism in its declared
form. It is for this reason that public journalism remains largely a phenomenon of the periphery of U.S. cultural, social, and geographical
life, associated with small towns and cities like Wichita, Kansas; Charlotte, North Carolina; and Columbus, Georgia, rather than large metropolitan settings like Washington, DC; New York City; or Boston. This
suggests that ultimately, public journalism will *not* be able to include
everybody, even on questions that all would agree deserve wide-
ranging community attention. Yet there has not been sufficient attention to the contingencies that this necessitates.

Problems surrounding the broadening of public journalism introduce additional questions concerning the idea's implementation. How
is the neighborhood to be drawn? Who is to be the community? Which
citizens will participate? The public of public journalism could be the
people around the corner from the news bureau, those most vocal in
community organizations, or those with enough bureaucratic savvy to
make themselves visible to journalism. It remains unclear who will
choose among them. And will those traditionally marginalized by
the media—minority groups, consumer groups, even environmental
groups—receive a larger share of the neighborhood or a share equal to
that which they have drawn in the past?

Furthermore, how is one to judge concerns as genuine? Who is to
make that judgment? When and on what basis will distinctions be
made about the self-serving nature of some concerns and its ability to
harm the needs of others? At times, as Michael Hoyt of the *Columbia
Journalism Review* has observed, the efforts of public journalists are
wrongly presented as being in the public interest.[38] Unlike campaigns,
where audience interest can be easily turned into the material from
which coverage grows, public journalism seems not to have developed
contingency plans either for events that fail to draw in communities or
for neighbors who simply do not care about, are not interested in, or

are not aware of the so-called public good. What happens when members of the public do not want to be citizens? What does one do when, to paraphrase the ideas of James Carey, communities continue to say that "this has nothing to do with me" even *after* public journalism intervenes? Does that make them no longer neighbors?

Issues such as these—and their lack of answers thus far—suggest that in the project of making journalism public, the neighborhood houses many types of residents, only some of whom can be ultimately accounted for. If public journalism is to work, it will do so most effectively by setting in place decisions made by the few for the many. And thus elitism creeps right back in just like in the old days, as Michael Schudson has suggested[39] and John Pauly argues in this volume. The only difference here is that the new elitism is far more user-friendly—and hence potentially more dangerous—than before.

But the danger does not stop here. For an inverse case generates additional unneighborly practices between public journalism and its public. That danger has to do with breaking the neighborhood down—with fracturing the public even more than it has already been divided. On any given day, lamentations can be heard about the disappearance of the public in the contemporary age. The media are filled with claims that the contemporary age has become a world of hyphenated identities, of agendas that come into play differently in accordance with the roles played at the time of their consideration. Taking issue with items on the public agenda is thereby both unpredictable and idiosyncratic. One never really knows which dimension of the so-called public will motivate an issue, because as the issues in public discourse change, so does the public. And who is to protect against public journalism being used as a mouthpiece for special interests that desire greater media control?

For public journalism, this means that its sense of a neighborhood is unstable. It means that as journalists cater more to audiences in shaping the news, they may end up sliding while looking for a durable anchoring point from which to cover public life. Can a public give cues about what is important and relevant when it no longer agrees on the salience of an issue among its own members? This may leave public journalism groping, searching for ground and more secure footing at the same time it is supposed to be providing the neighborhood in which public discourse can take place.

Equally important, it may also leave journalists doing the opposite of what public journalism hopes to do: further differentiating their messages about public life, often to the point of their complete washout as an index of the public imagination. Indeed, contemporary news is filled with an array of practices that constitute journalism—C-SPAN, the

Weather Channel, even *Inside Edition*—that suggest that news may be better today at capturing the few than uniting the many. In seeking to fit the appropriate shape of today's public discourse, we may hear more talk of many neighborhoods, publics, and a marketplace of communities. Public journalism may thereby produce not a prototype for one optimum neighborhood but its breakdown—to borrow another metaphor, a shopping mall of messages about how public life ought to work.

The shopping mall mentality, however, does not always reflect the best side of a shared communal life. The best testament to its limitations are those nagging questions of morality, where journalism has done a poor job of generating either consensus or community. According to the rhetoric of public journalism, why should the public be necessarily interested in issues like distant atrocities, AIDS care, or unwed pregnancies if they involve only a fraction of the public? In dissipating the very essence of what has been potentially important to large numbers of people, then, public journalism may in effect make a bad situation worse. There is already evidence that suggests this is the case. Although not even half the electorate voted in the 1988 presidential campaign—a circumstance that, by Davis Merritt's view, propelled him to activate his Voter Project and the public journalism initiatives it involved[40]—the 1996 presidential campaign brought similar returns. The only difference is that public journalism had by then already arrived on the scene in many of the locations where residents reported an ongoing sense of disconnection. The real effect of public journalism on publics, then, is yet unclear.

Both situations—that of catering to only part of the public and that of breaking it down—suggest that in its links with the public, public journalism is *in* the neighborhood but not necessarily *of* the neighborhood. That distinction—as here too the name "public journalism" implies—is made less as discussion proliferates more about the ways in which public journalism distinguishes itself from other kinds of newsmaking.

Improbability 4: The Political Neighbor

Improbability 4 brings the discussion back to the broadest neighborhood of all—that of the linkage between journalism and the polity. The praises of public journalism have come to be routinely sung in a highly normative tone in this most general wave of discourse. Public journalism has in many conversations become the model neighborhood, the default case of journalism in democratic settings, the background against which all other journalistic practices are measured in terms of their responsibility to democracy.

The tone of these praises, as John Durham Peters suggests in this volume, has had predictable effect. We hear of journalism as a "makeable truth," a bastion against the death of journalism, a provider of the information and analysis that are the "building blocks of public life."[41] Such comments are touched with the magic of the superlative and the drive to achieve perfection. Yet at some level the subjunctive tone they embody facilitates a slippage of the qualities that in effect constitute public journalism.

In fact, the model state to which public journalism has been elevated has itself produced a certain slippage of terms. Two sets of problems arise here. The first involves a disjunction between what observers know public journalism to be—just by virtue of what has been set in place over the past few years—versus the form its proponents would like it to assume. Often the former is argued on the basis of the latter. Claims are made about what public journalism does on the basis of what it *could* do in a perfect world. Such claims not only make public journalism less sensitive than it could be to its own ideology but also render premature some of the claims that have circulated. They imply that public journalism, in providing what Jay Rosen has called a support system for public life, may in fact become a primary support beam on which democracy rests. If only because of the many questions that linger in the neighborhood of public journalism, this seems risky, reductionistic, and rather naive. By harnessing so much of one's confidence in the future of democracy to public journalism, we may be giving the polity itself the status of a question mark.

A second set of problems is far more fundamental. It raises the question of who the public really expects to watch over its neighborhood. It was said earlier that one's public life is too precious to be left only to journalism. This has particular resonance for the function of news in democracy. When taken to their logical extension, the claims of public journalism advocates imply that public journalism provides one of the backbones of democracy, a mainstay of the polity, a fundamental hope of the republic. This implies that public journalism must rescue democracy from its relentless wash downstream.

Yet the flip side of the question that Jay Rosen asked earlier in this volume—"What are journalists for?"—is not to assume that journalists are alone in their function. Can journalism be tendered the chief vehicle by which democracy survives? Can journalism be held so responsible for that which has gone wrong with political life? Though Walter Lippmann long ago had another solution in mind when he made the claim,[42] even he warned that the press had become the whipping boy of democracy. Is it not wrongheaded now—60 years later—to claim that journalism be made the primary watchdog of the polity? What of the legal system, the educational system, and even religion, each of which plays a strong role in securing the broadest boundaries of existing neighborhoods? If proponents of public journalism continue to claim journalism's obligation to uphold the integrity of the polity, when journalism may be ill-equipped to do so, it is possible that they will institute a corrective that is certain to fail—a corrective by which journalism will never be able to sustain expectations of it yet will always be the first to blame when something goes wrong with political life.

Making the Neighborhood Work

So what are we to make of the neighborhood into which public journalism has moved? Specifically, how are we to make the neighborhood work in a way that accepts public journalism as a bona fide resident? A personal anecdote comes to mind that illustrates the folly of not taking one's neighborhood seriously.

Not long ago, a new neighbor arrived in the community where I live, a leafy, green Philadelphia suburb whose houses are kept separate and private, often to a fault, by trees of every shape and size imaginable. The neighbors arrived in the midst of summer, when the foliage was overgrown and untamed and, without inquiring about how things looked at other times of the year, cut down scores of 30-foot-tall trees. When the seasons progressed, the untouched foliage thinned and turned barren. As the new neighbors realized that in their zeal to gain sun and air they had left their house (and those of their neighbors) without any natural privacy, they became increasingly crestfallen. The veteran neighbors too, recognizing the inability to repair the damage, became angrier and angrier. Yet on one point both sides agreed: Had the new residents only queried the old inhabitants before changing the landscape, they might have finished their first year in the neighborhood in a more amicable fashion.

To date, public journalism enthusiasts have acted in a manner similar to those neighbors who cut down the trees. Neglecting to query the veteran neighbors of the community, public journalists have forged ahead often without checking for more secure or reasonable footing. Their desire to promote something different and better may have generated the overstatement of a model that is trying too fervently to capture the public imagination without taking the time to figure out how best to do so. This makes me—a willing proponent of the *idea* of public journalism—into an unwilling skeptic about the *mechanics* of public journalism. For what kind of journalism can public journalists possibly offer without a shared neighborhood in which they and all of their neighbors—history, other journalists, the public, and the polity—can thrive?

How, then, is it possible to correct the unworkable nature of the new journalistic neighborhood in a way that can accommodate public journalism? Ultimately, the unresolved issues surrounding the idea call for more careful deliberation. The neighborhood needs to be left to grow naturally over space and time, with an emphasis more on doing, acting, and experimenting than on talking. The idea of public journalism needs to develop into the practice of public journalism, by settling gradually into its linkages with the history of journalism, other journalists, the public, and the polity. It is for all involved parties to figure out how public journalism will end up differently from the neighbors who cut down the trees—isolated, misunderstood, and conflicted about their own shortsightedness. But that kind of deliberation can result only if the neighborhood is allowed to flourish naturally.

Although the title of this volume suggests otherwise, public journalism is more than an idea already. But if it is to stay more than an idea, it needs to have time and space to ground itself in practice. And like other innovations in journalism, it needs to do so by recognizing the value of its long-term capacity to shape the future as much as its short-term ability to shake up the present. Not long ago, James Carey wrote that "public life refers to an illusion of the possible rather than to something with a given anterior existence."[43] If the visionary quality of this new type of journalism is not grounded more firmly in practice, the adventure of public journalism may end up its improbability. And the notion of community on which it is founded—that of journalists, publics, and journalists and publics together—may end up more imagined than not.

Notes

1. For example, see Arthur Charity, *Doing Public Journalism* (New York: Guilford Press, 1995); Clifford G. Christians, John P. Ferré, and P. Mark Fackler, *Good News: Social Ethics and the Press* (New York: Oxford, 1993); Davis Merritt, *Public Journalism and Public Life: Why Telling the News Is Not Enough* (Hillsdale, NJ: Erlbaum, 1995); Jay Rosen, *Community Connectedness: Passwords for Public Journalism* (St. Petersburg, FL: Poynter Institute for Media Studies, 1993); Jay Rosen, *Getting the Connections Right: Public Journalism and the Troubles in the Press* (New York: Twentieth Century Fund, 1996); Jay Rosen and Paul Taylor, eds., *The New News versus the Old News: The Press and Politics in the 1990s* (New York: Twentieth Century Fund, 1996).
2. Judith Sheppard, "Climbing Down from the Ivory Tower," *American Journalism Review* (May 1995): 18–25; Alicia C. Shepard, "The Gospel of Public

Journalism," *American Journalism Review* (September 1994): 28–35; Michael Gartner, "Give Me Old-Time Journalism," *Quill* (November/December 1995): 66–68.

3. Tony Case, "Public Journalism Denounced," *Editor and Publisher* (November 12, 1994): 14–15; Max Frankel, "Fix-It Journalism," *New York Times Magazine*, May 21, 1995, p. 28; David Remnick, "Scoop," *New Yorker* (January 29, 1996): 38–42.

4. Many of these activities are chronicled in Jay Rosen and Davis Merritt Jr. *Public Journalism: Theory and Practice* (Dayton, OH: Kettering Foundation, 1994).

5. Edmund Lambeth, "A Bibliographic Essay on Civic/Public Journalism," *National Civic Review*, 85,1 (Winter/Spring 1996): 18–21.

6. Edmund Lambeth and David Craig, "Civic Journalism as Research," *Newspaper Research Journal*, 7 (1995): 149–160; Edward D. Miller, *The Charlotte Project: Helping Citizens Take Back Democracy* (St. Petersburg, FL: Poynter Institute for Media Studies, 1994); Jan Schaffer and Edward Miller, eds., *Civic Journalism: Six Case Studies* (Washington, DC: Pew Center for Civic Journalism and Poynter Institute for Media Studies, July 1995); *The Public Journalism Journey of* The Virginian-Pilot (Norfolk, VA: *Virginian-Pilot*, August 1995).

7. Mike Tharp, "The Media's New Fix," *U.S. News & World Report* (March 18, 1996): 74.

8. Tharp, "The Media's New Fix," p. 72.

9. Jay Rosen, "Making Journalism More Public," *Communication*, 12,4 (1991): 267–284.

10. See, for instance, James W. Carey, "The Press and Public Discourse," *Center Magazine* (March/April 1987): 4–16; James W. Carey, "The Press, Public Opinion, and Public Discourse," in *Public Opinion and the Communication of Consent*, ed. Theodore L. Glasser and Charles T. Salmon (New York: Guilford Press, 1995), pp. 373–402; James W. Carey, "A Republic, If You Can Keep It: Liberty and Public Life in the Age of *Glasnost*," pp. 108–128 in *Crucible of Liberty: 2000 Years of the Bill of Rights*, ed. R. Arsenault (New York: Free Press, 1992); Michael Schudson, *Discovering the News* (New York: Basic, 1978); Michael Schudson, *The Power of News* (Cambridge, MA: Harvard, 1995).

11. Carey, "The Press and Public Discourse," p. 392.

12. Some of the most comprehensive include Rosen, "Making Journalism More Public"; Rosen, *Community Connectedness*; Rosen, *Getting the Connections Right*; Rosen and Merritt, *Public Journalism*; Rosen and Taylor, *The New News versus the Old News*.

13. A 1994 Times–Mirror survey reported this percentage.

14. Tom Goldstein, *The News at Any Cost* (New York: Simon & Schuster, 1985), p. 165.

15. The limitations of viewing journalists as a professional community are discussed in Barbie Zelizer, "Has Communication Explained Journalism?" *Journal of Communication*, 43 (Autumn 1993): 80–88.

16. This view is developed in Barbie Zelizer, *Covering the Body: The Kennedy*

Assassination, the Media, and the Shaping of Collective Memory (Chicago: University of Chicago Press, 1992); and Barbie Zelizer, "Journalists as Interpretive Communities," *Critical Studies in Mass Communication,* 10 (September 1993): 219–237.

17. Benedict Anderson, *Imagined Communities* (New York: Verso Books, 1983).

18. Barbie Zelizer, "Journalism in the Mirror," *The Nation* (February 17, 1997): 10.

19. Zelizer, "Journalists as Interpretive Communities," pp. 219–237. Also see Zelizer, *Covering the Body.*

20. Rosen, *Getting the Connections Right,* p. 13.

21. Merritt, *Public Journalism and Public Life*; Charity, *Doing Public Journalism.*

22. Morris Janowitz, "Professional Models in Journalism: The Gatekeeper and the Advocate," *Journalism Quarterly* (Winter 1975): 618–626, 662.

23. David Mathews, "Public Journalism and Public Deliberation," *National Civic Review* (Winter/Spring 1996): 39. Also see Deborah Potter, "Redefining the Elements of News," *National Civic Review* (Winter/Spring 1996): 35–38.

24. John W. C. Johnstone, Edward J. Slawski, and William W. Bowman, *The News People: A Sociological Portrait of American Journalists and Their Work* (Urbana: University of Illinois Press, 1976).

25. David H. Weaver and G. Clevelane Wilhoit, *The American Journalist: A Portrait of U.S. News People and Their Work* (Bloomington: Indiana University Press, 1991 [1986]), pp. 112–124.

26. Weaver and Wilhoit, *The American Journalist,* p. 144.

27. Rosen, *Getting the Connections Right,* p. 2.

28. The most widely cited trajectory of the rise of interpretive reporting can be found in Edwin Emery and Michael Emery, *The Press and America* (Englewood, NJ: Prentice-Hall, 1984), p. 435. But examples that challenge a unilateral adoption of interpretive reporting as late as the mid-1950s are found in C. H. Hamilton, "Call It Objective, Interpretive, or 3-D Reporting," *ASNE Bulletin* (September 1, 1954): 6–7; and F. Christopherson, "Are We Being Objective in Reporting the Cold War?" *ASNE Bulletin* (January 1, 1953): 1.

29. See, for instance, David Eason, "On Journalistic Authority: The Janet Cooke Scandal," *Critical Studies in Mass Communication* 3 (1986): 429–447; Elaine Dutka, "Reaping New Profits from a Pulitzer Hoax," *Philadelphia Inquirer,* June 4, 1996, p. D3; Chris Satullo, "Journalistic Ethics No Oxymoron," *Philadelphia Inquirer,* July 30, 1996, p. A7.

30. John J. Pauly, "The Politics of the New Journalism," pp. 100–129 in *Literary Journalism in the Twentieth Century,* ed. Norman Sims (New York: Oxford University Press, 1990).

31. For instance, Schudson, *Discovering the News,* argues that the commodity form of journalism at the time of the penny press had substantial positive effect on journalistic practices of the time.

32. Gartner, "Give Me Old-Time Journalism," p. 66.

33. Jay Rosen, "Public Journalism Is a Challenge to You (Yes, You)," *National Civic Review* (Winter/Spring 1996): 4.

34. Miller, *The Charlotte Project*; Charity, *Doing Public Journalism.*
35. John Dewey, *The Public and Its Problems* (New York: Holt, 1927).
36. Rosen, *Getting the Connections Right,* p. 81.
37. Rosen, *Getting the Connections Right,* p. 1.
38. Michael Hoyt, "Are You, or Will You Ever Be, a Civic Journalist?" *Columbia Journalism Review* (September/October 1995): 27–33.
39. Schudson, *The Power of News.*
40. Merritt, *Public Journalism and Public Life.*
41. Jay Rosen, "Making Things More Public: On the Political Responsibility of the Media Intellectual," *Critical Studies in Mass Communication*, 11 (1994): 372; Rosen, "Public Journalism Is a Challenge," p. 3; Edward M. Fouhy, "A Sense of Community," *Communicator* (August 1995): 15.
42. Walter Lippmann, *Public Opinion* (New York: MacMillan, 1922).
43. Carey, "The Press, Public Opinion, and Public Discourse," p. 373.

Appendices

On Evaluating Public Journalism

Steven H. Chaffee
Stanford University

Michael McDevitt
University of New Mexico

Public journalism grows out of evaluation of a sort, a frustration with the limits of conventional journalism as practiced in the United States. The movement is conceived in values and in the belief that news media can improve conditions for democratic participation. In our role as evaluators we begin with a pragmatic question: Can we find evidence that public journalism activities make a difference in the civic life of a community? The answer turns out to be "in some ways, yes" but also that some goals of public journalism compete—and even conflict—with others. Hence the exercise of evaluation leads us full circle, back to a confrontation between values.

The hopeful quality of public journalism creates a vulnerability that is attractive to critics and worrisome for those committed to reform. But a self-conscious articulation of values is the very point of public journalism, and this chapter seeks to establish a rationale for realistic evaluation of whether public journalism projects reach their goals.

As newspapers and other media join with community institutions in local projects, various parties seek a wide variety of outcomes. Conventional empirical evaluation cannot, at least in the short run, capture more than a fraction of these effects. But some of them can be, in some measure at least, assessed by methods of social science. Not only do some goals compete with others, but journalistic professionals and scholars do not always agree that they are unarguably desirable. We share with public journalism's critics some skepticism as to whether lasting results can be achieved at all, and we worry as they do that some unintended effects of public journalism might be socially dysfunctional.

Internal and External Perspectives

The controversial nature of public journalism calls for evaluation from both internal and external viewpoints. By internal we mean assessments by those who are parties to the public journalism project itself; this includes not only journalists and media organizations but also their target audiences. What do these people think of the project, as distinct from the issue of how were they affected by it? The external perspective is more difficult to pinpoint; ideally, one would take into account not only affected institutions such as community organizations but also abstractions such as "democracy" and "the public sphere." These entities do not speak for themselves. The external evaluator's role is to examine public journalism (itself an abstraction) on their behalf.

Philosophical questions of whether these goals are desirable, or whether the cost to journalism is too great, are not directly addressable by empirical study. But an evaluation that examines what can and cannot be accomplished might lead both advocates and opponents of public journalism to recast their beliefs within a pragmatic context. One common objection to any public journalism proposal is that it is not needed, or that its goals are too lofty to be realized. If careful study finds evidence of intended effects, both these arguments would seem to be in error. On the other hand, a project might produce such limited impact as to seem not worth the effort expended. Such summary opinions are rarely formed by evidence alone, but they are often *in*formed by it. Statements about what the press *should* do should begin with an appraisal of what the press *can* do.

The task of evaluation cannot be divorced from the many judgments that all parties to public journalism inevitably make. A continuing, if amorphous, dialectic between evaluation and program practices is inescapable. So too it is with theory. Whereas a typical evaluation study flows directly from the theory that inspired the intervention, with public journalism there is no single conception of the process and no single image of what one should hope to find. Evaluation must be designed to serve many points of view, so that each theory's adherents can judge for themselves whether the results seem gratifying or disappointing. There is no single client to whom an evaluator delivers a final report. Even when a specific agency funds a project, or its evaluation, one's responsibility includes addressing various theoretical perspectives on journalism and on civic processes, and on the ways public journalism connects the two.

What theories underlying public journalism lack in coherence on goals, they also lack in clarity about each goal. A central problem for the evaluator is to identify within a sprawling discourse of exhortation and criticism, both of the press and of the public, ideas that can be represented in concrete evidence. In no realm is the linking task of explication,[1] tying normative goals to pragmatic indicators, more essential than in public journalism. This chapter describes some of the concepts and research procedures we have found useful in our evaluations of several projects.

Public Journalism and Civic Journalism

Even the administrative labels given to projects lead to somewhat different approaches to evaluation. Consider the term "public journalism" alongside the companion term "civic journalism." The two ideas clearly share many features, and the phrases are often used interchangeably. But we have encountered differences between the two in their implied criteria for evaluation. Civic journalism, the program backed by the Pew Charitable Trusts, stresses the contribution local media can make to the community. The press is urged (and often subsidized) to play an active role in fostering civic deliberation on locally identified problems. Evaluation, from this perspective, should be partly external in nature, looking for changes in the community that can be traced to an innovative media program.

The term "public" may be read as either a noun or an adjective. In its adjectival usage, "public journalism" expresses an urging by some press critics that the news media openly display their inner workings, to expose possible faults of the news business. A devotee of public journalism, then, would evaluate a project partly by the extent to which the media expose themselves to criticism and more generally would look for changes in the ways journalism is conducted. This internal approach would in the usual "civic journalism" exercise be considered at most a side effect, or a means to some more communal end. In other words, whereas advocates of both public and civic journalism share an ultimate interest in the implications of news for political deliberation, one immediate focus of public journalism is the news-production process itself. Press content, which in an external evaluation might be analyzed descriptively, could from an internal perspective be the main feature that is evaluated. Public journalism's goal is to improve the quality of news, for example, by opening journalistic forums to a greater diversity of voices. Benefits of this media self-exposure for a community's civic life are often assumed; the public journalism evaluator should begin with a careful examination of media content and process.

Public journalism, then, is concerned with reforming the press, making it a more responsible, accountable, and democratic institution. Civic journalism is directed instead toward the recovery of civic life. The civic journalism orientation looks outward toward the community, while the public journalism perspective looks inward at the profession. The one wants to reform the public through journalism whereas the other would reform journalism by making it more public.

We should not make too much of the public–civic distinction, which makes little or no difference to most practitioners. It serves, though, to remind us of the complexity one finds within this general movement. For simplicity, in this chapter, we use the term "public journalism" even when the projects we describe were conducted under the "civic journalism" rubric.

Evaluating the News: A Shift from Content to Consequence

An enduring assumption of journalism in the United States is that news media should concentrate on the transmission of accurate and balanced information. Citizens in turn bear responsibility to pay attention, to process information, to appreciate connections between issues, and to use information to vote or to engage one another in rational dialogue. Public journalism is not the first challenge to this straightforwardly informative role of the press under traditional libertarian theory. Half a century ago, the report of the Hutchins Commission marked a shift toward thinking about the responsibility of the press, based on some serious doubts about the capacity of citizens for civic engagement.[2] Social responsibility theory, as enthusiasts called it,[3] assumed that people are more lethargic than the active citizenry envisioned in libertarian theory. According to the Commission on Freedom of the Press, the media should do more than "provide a truthful, comprehensive, and intelligent account of the day's events"; they should provide a forum for exchange of criticism and comment; project a representative picture of constituent groups; clarify societal values; and provide "full access to the day's intelligence."[4] These putative responsibilities extend no further, though, than press content; none of them suggests a purposeful goal of stimulating civic participation. The Hutchins Commission adhered to a bounded, journalism-centered perspective in its exposition of press responsibility, focusing on the fidelity of news rather than its consequences for civic processes. To go beyond the role of information supplier would have undermined editorial impartiality; many professionals feel that such a demand undercuts journalistic autonomy as well.[5]

Journalists' traditional understanding of their civic role is ultimately a matter of faith that citizens will actively *use* the news as a basis for reasoned debate and participation. This belief stems from the hazier assumption that truth will win out in the marketplace of ideas[6] as citizens make rational choices based on diverse sources of accurate information.[7] Journalists often point out that they are not in the business of managing how the information they provide is used. Public journalism asks for more, inviting us to evaluate the influence of the news in the facilitation of public participation. It does not take for granted that merely by virtue of news being reported, the public will respond in ways deemed appropriate under normative conceptions of democracy.

To put the argument a slightly different way, public journalism asserts that democracy is not adequately served by a mass-media model of news communication. A unidirectional flow of information *from* news organizations *to* the public relegates citizens to a passive role in their relationship with media and makes the press at most an indirect contributor to public processes. Deliberative democracy requires that citizens *do something* with information supplied by media.[8] Public journalism evaluations, then, should conceptualize news as a resource for interpersonal communication, among other aspects of active citizenship. Evaluators are concerned with the ways people respond to news, and how their responses play out as civic behavior. Press content, news exposure, and knowledge acquisition are just the first steps in the process that concerns evaluators of public journalism.

Public Journalism as Bottom-Line Journalism

Public journalism is in many eyes equated with "bottom-line journalism," the practice of selecting news items to maximize audience. Bottom-line journalism aims at maintaining advertising revenues and thus net profits and the solvency of the firm; these goals are often scorned by press critics and professional journalists alike. Suspicions arise when public journalism is urged on a newspaper from above (e.g., by chain management) as a way to build readership. Potential readers are to be consulted, and ways devised to stimulate their involvement in the community; hence, they will come to need the newspaper. A public journalism project may be touted as a device for capturing reader interest by focusing news coverage on local problems that concern people. Thus the newspaper can do well by doing good.

This same bottom-line journalism is, however, one of the standard management practices that presumably should be exposed to readers under the doctrine of public journalism. Tailoring the news to polls, and emphasizing what will sell to the local audience, is both a major point of self-criticism within the journalism field and frequently decried by academics and other external critics. To return briefly to our distinction between "public" and "civic" journalism, a public journalism approach to a civic journalism project might entail the media's airing of their own commercial motives in what would otherwise appear to be a purely altruistic undertaking.

Having undertaken a public journalism project in the hope of increasing circulation, a newspaper might understandably approach its own internal evaluation by immediately checking circulation figures. If subscriptions go up in a way that can be linked to the project, the firm is likely to try it again. Public journalism advocates, however, would want a lot more than that before they would adjudge the effort a success. They might ask, for example, for evidence of substantial effects on the level of debate in community organizations. Those whose values center on diversity might examine whether social groups that had been outside the community's elite circle got involved in the effort stimulated by the media. Reform-minded public journalism advocates would be concerned with increased diversity within the newsroom itself.

Public Empowerment and the Public Sphere

Philosophers who prize conversation as an ideal will question whether the intervention stimulated people to talk about the problem it emphasized in the news. Champions of an enlightened electorate might ask about voting turnout, or evidence of enhanced understanding of the issues behind voters' decisions. Those concerned with citizen attachment to the political community will want to know whether attitudes such as cynicism, efficacy, or community identification have been affected. In all, the community is viewed as an instrument for achieving its own political and social goals, with the media as its engine and steering mechanism.

An important background theme running throughout these approaches to evaluation is Habermas's concern for "the public sphere" in modern life. Public journalism asks the press to improve social communication by including the public in deliberative political processes. The press is expected to promote as well as enhance community deliberation.

Given these divergent purposes, evaluation must be approached with the understanding that no one goal will be fully agreed upon, and that priorities among goals will not easily be set. No body of measures, no matter how extensive and varied, will satisfy all parties and all critics. Whereas in most evaluation research an agreed-upon "contract" is often reached in advance between the evaluator and those conducting the project, it would be rare to get questions about goals or measures fully settled in advance. Nonetheless, an evaluator must try to find both the concepts that could satisfy skeptics and those that might give adherents reason for pause, and plow ahead.

Designing a Public Journalism Evaluation

Public journalism, like democracy itself, is a messy social experiment. From a formal evaluation perspective it is unavoidably problematic in that there can almost never be a "control group" to compare with the community in which the intervention takes place. The ideal design would contrast the same community to itself during the same period, with and without the public journalism experience. This is patently impossible, as it is with all human and social experimentation. In the case of public journalism, though, the possible "make-do" alternative designs fall far short of providing the evaluator with evidence to counter skepticism regarding positive results.[9] For example, in evaluating effects of certain kinds of messages on individuals (e.g., pornography or advertisements), it is usual to assign people randomly to one message condition or another. As long as they have not sought the message in question, conclusions about cause and effect can be drawn with confidence. But it is the essence of public journalism that the community itself seeks the intervention; topics are often elicited from focus groups composed of local residents or leaders. In the best event, no single community is comparable enough to another to serve as a "control" in the usual sense. And one could not sensibly assign large numbers of communities randomly to a public journalism condition versus a control condition even if such fabulous power existed. Each intervention is designed in and for a specific local community and may mean rather little elsewhere.

Public journalism projects are particularly subject to certain problems that beset all field evaluations of social interventions. There is no need here to repeat general methodological principles that govern evaluation designs in general, but we should point out some ways in which public journalism programs differ from the usual case.

One quasi-experimental design popular with evaluators is the before–after study without a control group.[10] As individuals we often use this method, for example, when we watch a new television series to see how we like it, or when we try out the latest remedy for hay fever. If the individual is otherwise relatively stable, this is not a poor research design; it is indeed the most likely design for evaluating public journalism projects. It requires, though, that the same measures be gathered, in the same way, before and after the intervention. It also presumes that the "after" measures are affected by the intervention itself and not by historical processes in the larger society that were happening anyway. For example, it may be hard to isolate the impact of a voter education series in local media from effects of the concurrent election campaign; even candidates' advertisements can be informative to voters.[11]

When before–after comparisons are planned, unobtrusive measurement procedures are advisable. For example, it is helpful to use data that are collected apart from the evaluation itself, such as records of community organizations that might experience a rise in membership. If survey research on individuals is used (and it often is), there is a trade-off to consider between remeasuring the same people before and after the intervention versus selecting successive random samples composed of different individuals. The panel design, where one remeasures the same individuals, enables us to see what kinds of persons are most affected by the intervention. It runs the risk, though, of sensitizing respondents to the intervention by the "before" questioning, so that the results of the evaluation study are not representative of the larger population that was not questioned before the intervention.

Units of analysis for study are less straightforward in evaluating public journalism than in most areas of communication research. The individual is the kind of unit most often interviewed, or otherwise observed, in surveys to evaluate media effects. But individual behaviors, attitudes, and knowledge are among the weaker indicators of the kinds of goals practitioners and sponsors set for public journalism. The public sphere, wherever it may exist, is an interpersonal place. It is often an organizational and mediated one as well, when public journalism projects are envisioned. Conversations are much harder to sample than are individuals. One person can be interviewed about a recent discussion, but is incapable of seeing it from the viewpoints of others who were involved. It is at best difficult to capture the spirit of a conversation that is later recalled by a participant, compared to what an observer might be able to note if present during the encounter in question.

Organizational activity, a major locus of public journalism's hoped-for effects, is even harder to observe than is interpersonal discussion. A major sign of success of a civic intervention on a topic such as juvenile crime might be the formation of one or more neighborhood associations devoted to this problem. But creation of such an organization is a rare event, involving very few people at first. Even when it does occur it is unlikely to surface in a community sample survey of the general citizenry. Special methods need to be devised to locate novel outcomes of public journalism in civic life.

Whereas creation of new civic organizations may be a hoped-for goal, evaluators should also consider possible changes in existing primary groups and social networks. For example, although families and peer groups do not constitute forums for formal political participation, they do provide settings in which political dialogue is likely to occur.[12] By devising dyadic or group-level interviewing strategies, evaluators can increase their ability to trace social influence processes that are set in motion by the news.

In all, influences of public journalism can be evaluated at many levels, including effects on primary groups, formal civic organizations, community values, the news media, and policymakers. Table A.1 suggests some common public journalism goals at each level.

Competing Goals

Success of a public journalism project is never self-evident. Evaluators might, for example, presume that the more participation the better. But much depends on the quality of that participation, the distribution of active citizenship within the social structure, and the consequences of participation for the community decision-making process. A public journalism project represents the work of many participants, and it might aim at mutually incompatible goals. Judgments about "success" in one area, then, might mask dysfunctional effects in another dimension. It is important not only to make goals explicit but to consider them in relation to one another. A few examples may help to anticipate this kind of conflict.

Serving Different Groups

A journalistic intervention that increases knowledge and participation on the average might nevertheless exacerbate disparities between citizens of high and low social status.[13] In turn, inequality in public journalism effects would imply inequality in citizenship. An evaluator might be pleased to

TABLE A.1. Goals of Public Journalism at Different Levels of Analysis

Level of analysis	Public journalism effect
Individual	Knowledge gain; change in attitudes such as efficacy and tolerance; voting turnout
Primary groups	Political discussion at work, schools, or within families
Civic organizations	Members = attendance; formal efforts to influence public policy
Community	Informed public opinion; creation of social capital
News media	Media agenda setting; adoption of public journalism techniques in regular news coverage; *public journalism goals such as self-criticism*
Policy makers	Policy initiatives in response to intensive media coverage

find that a project resulted in an aggregate improvement in a community, but this does not suggest an increase in the diffusion of information or the social distribution of participation and effective citizenship. If those groups that were already knowledgeable become more so while the "have-nots" remain unaffected, the quality of community dialogue may very well have suffered due to the intervention. One goal of public journalism is to reduce the informational gaps between socioeconomic strata, and an evaluation should provide a method of ascertaining whether this was achieved.

Fostering Different Cognitive Processes

Public journalism sets out to increase awareness of public issues, but news stories do not activate the same cognitive processes for all people all the time. Although critics decry media emphasis on personality over substance,[14] there is evidence that personalized features attract the attention of people who would otherwise remain uninterested in politics. (The same is true of "horse race" journalism.) News that mobilizes public attentiveness is not necessarily the same news that activates higher levels of intellectual processing. Sophisticated information designed to stimulate discussion among those already familiar with a community problem might fail to engage many other people in the dialogue. People are more likely to talk about personalities than about technical issues, at least early in a public journalism effort, however much social critics might wring their hands over this human tendency.

Serving Different Community Goals

Public journalism tends to be communitarian in prizing loyalty and consensus above other considerations.[15] When the press works to coordinate and stimulate community institutions a danger arises of simply reinforcing dominant values.[16] Evidence that a community has reached consensus on a divisive issue might represent an achievement of public journalism, but the particular consensus reached is open to a separate evaluation: Has this choice been "good" for the community? Simply bringing local constituencies into line with prevalent sentiment is not necessarily what one hopes for in undertaking public journalism. A process that clarifies the diversity of opinion within the community might be evaluated quite positively from some perspectives.

Serving Public Opinion versus Public Policy

Protess and his colleagues have shown that investigative journalism can directly influence policy without any attendant change in public opinion as measured at the individual level.[17] Many public journalism projects are solution-oriented, but journalism that prompts policymakers and community leaders to act will not necessarily entail a demonstrable public response except in those elite circles. Whether institutional action in the absence of public deliberative processes is desirable is at least arguable. By the same token, an intervention that arouses public response at the microsocial level but has no macroscopic consequences should not be judged a complete success either.

Quality versus Inclusiveness

There can also be conflicting goals within public journalism. For example, the desire to infuse news content with as many diverse voices as possible is at cross purposes with a responsible press's news filtering function; the media actively exclude more than they include. Alexander Meiklejohn commented, "What is essential is not that everyone shall speak but that everything worth saying shall be said." Although free speech advocates criticize Meiklejohn on this point, journalism is inherently exclusionary to some degree.[18] This conflict lies at the heart of some of the fiercest objections to public journalism; reporters and editors naturally resist relinquishing their precious column inches for use as a printed version of talk radio.

When online forums are linked to standard news formats, the constraints of the traditional "news hole" are in a way relaxed. That is, new media can provide a two-tiered journalism, adhering to standards of quality in the main text but making room for unfiltered content underneath it. Capabilities of new media cannot, however, get evaluators around the problem of conceptualizing clearly what they consider to be success in public journalism.

Operationalizing Public Journalism

In interviews of community members, any single evaluation indicator falls short of representing the entire richness of the goal or quality that is at stake. Just as a survey researcher might sample a few knowledge items to estimate impact on public knowledge, it is common to sample even fewer indicators of, say, interpersonal discussion or organizational activity. An evaluator is presumably interested in all serious discussion that is stimulated by public journalism, but it is almost never practical to gather complete evidence. The same is true of psychological constructs such as feelings of political efficacy or cynicism. An educational psychologist might administer a battery of 50 items to classify a single person in terms of an important attribute such as intelligence or introvertedness. In an interview of the same length to assess the many possible effects of public journalism we might instead ask five questions to get at each of 10 concepts. Although reliability of measurement is much lower with so few items, statistical tests can take random error into account when drawing conclusions about large numbers of people and events in the aggregate.

Rarely in evaluating public journalism is a single questionnaire item meant to represent the entire goal in question. (An exception is the typical measure of voting turnout, "Did you vote in the election?") When we do find statistically significant evidence consistent with the proposition that the journalistic intervention stimulated, say, interpersonal discussion, voting turnout, or neighborhood participation, it is not taken literally as positive evidence of effects of the program. But it is evidence against the null hypothesis, that the program had no effect. No one type of evidence could suffice to support a conclusion that it succeeded in all intended respects.

Civic participation is one general goal, and it offers many manifestations that might be incorporated into an evaluation. But one can rapidly get into arguments about the quality of participation that is desirable versus that which is superficial and trivial. In choosing criterion indicators, project evaluators must acknowledge that what *can be* measured is not always what *should be* measured. Researchers should derive operational measures based on careful explication of normative and theoretical concepts that, as a set, do justice to the goals of the program. Too many researchers have a favorite tool, which they are likely to push as *the* way to evaluate a public journalism project. One should avoid reliance on a method that merely happens to be convenient, An evaluation should be as innovative as the public journalism effort itself.

Evaluators, Participants, and Evaluator–Participants

As with any program evaluation, the relationship between evaluators and public journalism participants needs to be negotiated carefully. Paralleling our general internal–external distinction are two distinct roles, evaluator–participant[19] and the more remote evaluator.[20]

The evaluator–participant approach is internal in that the researchers involve themselves in the evaluation alongside direct participants. They might ask journalists or citizens whether they think the program was a success, a procedure that in effect invites participants to share in evaluating the program as they have experienced it. Community evaluation is also built into the practice of public journalism, in the form of various consultations and focus groups. An evaluator–participant can absorb people's reactions without conducting a lot of formal interviews.

The more external evaluator remains outside the community for the most part, and attempts an "objective" evaluation that is more standard-ized than the autobiographical study an evaluator–participant might write. When this is done, several public journalism projects can be evaluated in parallel, using an audience survey in which predetermined questions are asked of individuals randomly sampled throughout a community without regard to their connection to the particular intervention. Our studies described later are of this character. We consider them complementary to the evaluator–participant study that was conducted alongside ours at each site. The advantage of a standardized instrument is that comparisons can be made between projects, to get some idea of what works and what does-n't in a comparative perspective.

A public journalism program is evaluative from the start. It usually begins with one or more news media in a community, which undertake to define a local problem of high public concern that lends itself to realistic solutions via journalistic efforts.[21] Here we will not deal with this ascertain-ment phase, in which the research methods are mostly qualitative and idio-syncratic. We will also not describe in any detail the field interventions car-ried on by local newspapers, radio, and television stations. Our work on these projects began when they were well under way in each community. In this respect, our studies are akin to "summative evaluation" as distinct from the earlier "formative evaluation" research that is more integral to designing and improving the program itself.[22]

Two Projects: Madison, San Francisco

To illustrate our methods of external evaluation we describe two recent public journalism projects, conducted in Dane County, Wisconsin, and San Francisco, California.[23] We refer to these as the Madison and San Francisco projects; the newspapers and other media that undertook them are based in those cities even though they serve wider regions.

In Madison, We the People/Wisconsin began in 1992. This ongoing community entity undertakes at least four projects a year including in 1996 the efforts regarding land use that we evaluated. Participating media include the *Wisconsin State Journal* (the area's largest circulation newspa-per), WISC-TV (the area's only VHF television station), statewide public television and radio systems, and a public relations consulting firm. Among the events were a community forum that citizens could attend and address, broadcast debates, and numerous news features designed to edu-cate citizens about land use issues. The general goal was to inform citizens and to increase public debate on land use, a major public problem in a county in which rich farmland is steadily being converted to urban pur-poses.

San Francisco, the diverse and busy hub of the nation's fifth largest media market, is a challenging site for public journalism because so much seems to be going on there. But within this international tourist mecca there is a local community with a vibrant city government. The project we evaluated concerned a city issue, the 1995 election campaign for mayor. Voice of the Voter, as the civic journalism program was called, was carried regularly on the "op-ed" page of the *San Francisco Chronicle,* largest circulation newspaper in the region; on its NBC affiliate KRON-TV; and via the public radio station KQED-FM. The program included candidate debates, polls, and targeted neighborhood reporting. It also sought citizen participation via e-mail, voice mail, and a hotline.

Our study strategy was the same in each community. A commercial survey research firm was hired to draw a random sample of adult residents (18 or older) and interview them. Perfectly representative sampling is impossible, but we specified the same procedures (random digit dialing and eight callbacks) in each site. To take advantage of this comparative feature of the overall set of studies, we wrote a large battery of "common" questions, which were the same in every site. Then, in each community, we added a number of "local" questions intended to estimate exposure to the public journalism project and the extent to which the respondent might have been affected in the particular ways intended.

We tested media effects by correlations between measures of exposure to each public journalism project and both the common and local indicators of program goals. This method is admittedly far from foolproof. Correlation is only one element of a cause–effect inference; our data cannot address questions of time order nor fully rule out (even with control measures) alternative explanations. It is important to recognize, though, that a null correlation is a powerful method for *falsifying* an inference of media effects. If one finds no statistical correlation between an independent variable and a hoped-for effect, there is little point in further empirical tests; in the absence of raw correlation, further investigation of causation becomes moot. A survey that measures many variables that one considers relevant to evaluation is thus an efficient way of testing the viability of a number of effects hypotheses at one time. Those inferences that survive such tests can be the focus of more elaborate investigation, such as field experiments, in future research.

Estimating Exposure

The standard method of measuring exposure to any mass communication source is self-report questioning. Our first items asked about the newspaper and broadcast stations the person used. This behavioral report is relatively objective, and it gives each study a quasi-experimental character because there was in each city a rival newspaper that did not participate in the public journalism intervention.[24] The same was true of the broadcast stations. We generally ask about "attention" to media in line with research showing that questions about sheer exposure tend to undervalue electronic media.[25] Self-reports of attention to the specific campaign in the media invite an upward bias due to "demand characteristics" of the interview; it is impossible to ask about a person's attention to, say, Voice of the Voter without also suggesting that such attention might be a good thing. If everyone overstated their attention to the public journalism project equally, this would not affect the correlation coefficients much, because they are estimates of covariation around the mean level on each of two measures. But some kinds of people are more likely to overstate than others. Highly educated respondents, for example, and those who think of themselves as public minded, are prone to inflate their self-reports of activities that might be expected of educated, public-minded citizens. Many college-educated people also understate their television viewing, a pastime that is discrepant with the image they like to project. A less distortable method of estimating exposure to the media's public journalism efforts is needed.

To supplement the self-report measures, we separately assessed exposure by measuring *knowledge of the public journalism project*. Most respondents will try to score well on a knowledge test, but they cannot willfully exaggerate on such a test in the way they might on a self-report of interest or attention. Typically, a local educational effort involves many news stories, and often these include unique informational content that citizens would not usually get from other sources. Our questionnaires included a number of local items testing knowledge of this specific nature, based on content analyses of the media programs. In line with Price and Zaller,[26] we assume that citizens who possess information about the public journalism project have probably been exposed to it, even if they might not remember it by name or claim to have paid great attention to it.

Like any particular news item tested across a broad cross-section of citizens, our public journalism knowledge questions tended to be difficult to answer. An index composed of the total number of correct answers nonetheless provided an undistorted indicator of exposure to the public journalism project. In most evaluations of public campaigns, grounded as they are in the mass-communication model of effects, knowledge derived from the project is thought of as a major dependent variable. Often, in fact, knowledge gain is the only effect that can be demonstrated. It makes sense, though, for us to treat knowledge gained as part of the independent variable, given that a public journalism project aims at much more than didactic instruction. Imparting information is at best a by-product of a journalistic effort whose larger purposes lie beyond, in community participation and civic values. This demanding view is characteristic of public journalism, whereas traditional libertarian journalism would be relatively satisfied to demonstrate informative effects on citizens.

General Effects

A number of general goals of public journalism should be assessed in evaluating any project. These have to do with the qualities of citizenship public journalism works to foster. Our first-order evaluation, accordingly, concerns the extent to which such general outcomes appear to have been affected by each project. With minimal variation in wording from site to site, we asked the same self-report questions about these global behaviors and mental orientations. For example, we looked for evidence that those heavily exposed to the project were more prone to engage in political discussion, or to participate in local civic organizations. We also investigated several aspects of psychological response.

Our results were consistent with the expectation that these interventions would affect citizens in Madison and San Francisco.[27] That is, self-reported attention to We the People/Wisconsin or Voice of the Voter was significantly correlated with higher levels of cognitive involvement, organizational activity, and interpersonal discussion (including a separate measure of initiating discussion) regarding the topic. Both perceived political efficacy and attitudes toward discussing civic affairs were also associated with self-reported attention to the public journalism programs in the media. Only political cynicism remained clearly unaffected. These positive correlations held up in multiple regression analyses in which we controlled statistically for the individual's levels of exposure to news in general and partisan political involvement, plus standard demographic variables. Thus a case could be made that each program had an impact on the quality of citizen participation in its community.

But we also found reason to question this conclusion, in at least some respects. In every test our measure of knowledge of the public journalism intervention, which we take as indicating exposure to the program, produced less evidence of effects. Each correlation coefficient involving this kind of measure and a criterion variable was lower than the corresponding correlation for the self-reported attention measures. In San Francisco, in fact, only for frequency of civic discussion did we find a positive correlation with knowledge of Voice of the Voter. In Madison, though, all the knowledge-to-impact correlations testing for effects on these global measures were positive and statistically significant.

This pattern of results led us to several immediate conclusions. First, effects in Madison seem robust whereas those in San Francisco were more limited. Second, our method of estimating "exposure" by knowledge about the project, as well as by self-reported attention, proved useful in sorting out possibly spurious evidence. Finally, the hypothesis that intended effects occurred remains viable in both interventions; this invites a closer look at the details within each community.

Effects on Local Measures

Because each local public journalism project dealt with a different topic, we created in each site criterion measures that reflected specific aspects of the goals we assessed via the general measures. For example, we created measures of cognitive involvement and active participation related to land use issues in Madison, and to the election campaign in San Francisco. In each locale we also used criteria that would not be applicable elsewhere. In San Francisco for example, one important outcome was whether the person had voted in the mayoral election; this question would be meaningless with respect to land use in Madison.

Results for these local measures parallel what we found with the general measures. First, the evidence of impact was stronger in Madison than in San Francisco. We found significant correlations between self-reported attention to We the People/Wisconsin, and measures of interest in and opinions about land use. We also found positive correlations with two indices that were not specific to land use but that bear upon citizen connection to the community: participation in solving a neighborhood problem and positive feelings toward Madison. These correlations all remained strong when control variables were added to the equation.

The coefficients were generally weaker in San Francisco, but self-reported attention to Voice of the Voter did predict greater interest, and voter turnout, in the mayoral election. Attention was also correlated with participation in civic life of the person's neighborhood and in solving a community problem. Our most encouraging findings in San Francisco concerned effects on specific kinds of citizens. The likelihood of voting in the mayoral election appears to have been enhanced by Voice of the Voter, especially among citizens who had not lived long in the city, were non-white, or were not involved in community organizations. We interpreted these interaction effects as evidence that Voice of the Voter succeeded in "closing gaps" in political participation that would otherwise have continued to exist in San Francisco. Socialization to politics of people who are new to a community is a potential benefit of a public journalism project that is rarely explicit but which an evaluation could make manifest.[28]

It is important in evaluating a public journalism project not to be hypercritical based on rough evidence from a standardized survey such as we conducted in these two instances. We should be wary of inferring no effect when there in fact has been one, just as the careful researcher avoids making a positive inference when a correlation is spurious. We found that exposure to each public journalism program had effects above the direct effects of our control variables and also beyond these variables' indirect effects via attention to the program. This test may be overly stringent; a program can influence people's civic activity without their remembering much about the stimulus itself, just as commercial advertisements can influence consumer purchases without recall of the ad itself.

Our evaluation reminds us that public journalism interventions are not all of a piece. The Madison intervention seems to have had more impact than the one in San Francisco, perhaps due to differences in communities, or in topics. San Francisco is a more diverse and mobile community than Madison, so it is probably harder to get people discussing a particular problem with one another. Also, land use is an engaging long-term topic for a farm-belt community like Madison, whereas a mayoral election is a relatively brief episode in a metropolitan city's life.

Overall, our empirical findings establish a presumptive case for the proposition that public journalism interventions can affect the broad range of people in a community in ways that are consistent with some hoped-for goals. In none of our tests, even using the rigorous knowledge test of exposure and the many control variables, was that conclusion literally falsified. But these results at their best take us only a few steps toward evaluating the broad range of goals to which public journalism aspires.

Community Institutions

A full evaluation of the impact of a public journalism project would surely call for a separate study of local organizations. Did citizens create any new institutions, or expand the mission of an existing agency, to address the civic problem highlighted in the project? Did organizations that already dealt with this problem experience membership growth, or a measurable surge in activity? Were there neighborhood meetings? Were petitions brought to local governmental bodies? Did aspirants for public office bring the issue into their campaigns? All these are questions that survey research based on aggregating a few hundred individual cases cannot address effectively.

In Madison and San Francisco we asked a large number of questions about the respondent's activities in specific kinds of organizations, but this exercise produced little evidence that we could aggregate into community-level measures. Even in these two reputedly "activist" communities, organizational leadership is rare, and increases in participation may be too ephemeral to be detected with standardized batteries of survey questions. A more penetrating unit of study to estimate public journalism effects on community institutions would be the organization or agency, not a blanket survey of residents selected randomly from the population at large. An evaluation at that level would need to include evidence of changes in both the composition and the activities of organizations that might be linked to the public journalism program.

The Press and Public Journalism

Public journalism finally ends where it begins, with the press. An important part of evaluating a public journalism project is to examine journalists' reactions to it. And an important audience for the evaluation consists of those same professionals. One central purpose of the movement is to affect how journalism is practiced, and an evaluation should be designed to demonstrate to a skeptical professional corps what works, and what good it can do.

Our field studies have been accompanied by parallel interviews with journalists,[29] which indicate that many experienced news workers consider public journalism an unnecessary slap at their professionalism. Even as some editors welcome budgetary resources that they can direct toward these kinds of projects, others view the public journalism movement skeptically. This chapter is not the place to review their reasons, but clearly journalists themselves should be part of any thorough evaluation.[30]

Controversy among journalists is viewed by some advocates as itself a positive outcome of the public journalism movement. The very broaching of the subject stimulates debate within the profession about what its mission is, raising many questions about values that journalists might otherwise not consider seriously as they work through their busy days. Public journalism is composed of a number of arguable assertions that professionals (and their critics) might well ponder. We suspect that issues raised about civic participation by the media mask divisions between the metropolitan and the smalltown press, between professional aspirations of reporters and editors, and between liberal and communitarian models of citizenship. Airing these cultural, economic, and philosophical divisions is one purpose of public journalism, and whether it occurs is a subject worthy of research in itself.

Local media also invite study in terms of their manifest content. One evaluation question is whether news coverage on the topic of the public journalism intervention spreads to other media, and whether the increase is sustained after the project itself comes to an end. In Madison, one might look, for example, not only for sustained coverage of land use issues in participating media (e.g., the *Wisconsin State Journal* and WISC-TV) but also in their competitors who did not participate in the project (e.g., *The Capital*

Times and WKOW-TV). An intervention that affects a community as a whole would in the long run manifest its influence by raising attention via the media—and for that matter, among people who had not themselves been directly exposed to the project.

Conclusion

Evaluations of public journalism projects need to be approached with modest expectations. A community typically identifies a particular local problem as important in part because it has been dealing with it (however unsuccessfully) for a long time. No project conducted via only a few local media reaches everyone; the newspapers and broadcast stations we have studied face local competition. Moreover, every community includes many people who, for various reasons, cannot be engaged in media coverage of local issues. To have made an apparent dent is not a trivial achievement by any means. Indeed, it is difficult to imagine conditions under which a very deep impact on a total community could be achieved, and it would be even more difficult to design a study that could provide unarguable evidence of that impact even should it occur. For now, we conclude that these kinds of programs appear to be effective, and to merit the full array of investigative methods that the scholarly community can bring to bear on them.

Notes

1. For a general discussion on the linking of normative goals to operational measures, see Steven H. Chaffee, *Explication* (Newbury Park, CA: Sage, 1991).
2. See Commission on Freedom of the Press, *A Free and Responsible Press* (Chicago: University of Chicago Press, 1947).
3. Social responsibility of the press is described in Frederick Siebert, Theodore Peterson, and Wilbur Schramm, *Four Theories of the Press* (Urbana: University of Illinois Press, 1963).
4. See Commission on Freedom of the Press, *A Free and Responsible Press.*
5. For a discussion of the tradition of journalistic autonomy, see John C. Merrill *The Imperative of Freedom* (New York: Hastings House, 1974).
6. For insight on the "marketplace of ideas" metaphor, see Rodney A. Smolla, *Free Speech in an Open Society* (New York: Vintage Books, 1993).
7. Siebert et al., *Four Theories.*
8. For an analysis of factors that affect the quality of political dialogue, see Kathleen Hall Jamieson, *Dirty Politics: Deception, Distraction, and Democracy* (New York: Oxford University Press, 1992).
9. On the problem of ruling out alternative explanations for supportive evidence, consult Thomas D. Cook and Donald T. Campbell, *Quasi-Experimentation: Design and Analysis Issues for Field Settings* (Chicago: Rand-McNally, 1979).

10. Cook and Campbell, *Quasi-Experimentation.*

11. For evidence on this point, see Xinshu Zhao and Steven H. Chaffee, "Campaign Advertisements versus Television News as Sources of Political Issue Information," *Public Opinion Quarterly,* 59,1 (1995): 41–65.

12. The importance of the primary group as a setting for political discussion is demonstrated in studies such as Elihu Katz and Paul Lazarsfeld, *Personal Influence: The Part Played by People in the Flow of Mass Communications* (Glencoe, IL: Free Press, 1955); and Michael McDevitt and Steven H. Chaffee, "Second Chance Political Socialization: Trickle Up Effects of Children on Parents," in *Engaging the Public: How Government and the Media Can Reinvigorate American Democracy,* eds. Thomas J. Johnson, Carol E. Hays, and Scott P. Hays (Boulder, CO: Rowman & Littlefield, 1998).

13. The knowledge gap concept is explored in Phillip Tichenor, George Donohue, and Clarice Olien, "Mass Media and Differential Growth in Knowledge," *Public Opinion Quarterly,* 34 (1970): 158–170; and Cecilie Gaziano, "Forecast 2000: Widening Knowledge Gaps," *Journalism and Mass Communication Quarterly,* 74,2 (1997): 237–264.

14. For example, see Thomas E. Patterson, *Out of Order* (New York: Knopf, 1993).

15. For a critical perspective on the communitarian impulse in press reform, see Ralph D. Barney, "Community Journalism: Good Intentions, Questionable Practice," *Journal of Mass Media Ethics,* 11,3 (1996): 140–151.

16. For a thoughtful discussion on the implications of journalistic objectivity, see Robert A. Hackett and Yuezhi Zhao, "Journalistic Objectivity and Social Change," *Peace Review,* 8,1 (1996): 5–11.

17. See David L. Protess, Fay Lomax Cook, Jack C. Doppelt, James S. Ettema, Margaret T. Gordon, Donna R. Leff, and Peter Miller, *The Journalism of Outrage: Investigative Reporting and Agenda Building in America* (New York: Guilford Press, 1991).

18. See, for example, Smolla, *Free Speech.*

19. The evaluator–participant role is exemplified in Esther Thorson and Lewis A. Friedland, "Civic Lessons: Report on a 1996 Evaluation of Four Civic Journalism Projects Funded by the Pew Center for Civic Journalism," presented to the Pew Charitable Trusts (1997).

20. Chaffee et al., "Citizen Response," exemplifies the more remote approach to evaluation of public journalism programs.

21. For an overview of implementation issues, see Arthur Charity, *Doing Public Journalism* (New York: Guilford Press, 1995).

22. Michael Scriven, "The Methodology of Evaluation," pp. 39–83 in *Perspectives of Curriculum Evaluation* (AERA Monograph Series on Curriculum Evaluation, No. 1), ed. Ralph W. Tyler, Robert M. Gagne, and Michael Scriven (Chicago: Rand McNally & Co., 1967).

23. Chaffee et al., "Citizen Response."

24. Although in each city the participating newspaper is dominant in circulation, each of them is tied in a joint operating agreement to a second newspaper with which it shares business functions such as advertising, production, and delivery.

25. Steven H. Chaffee and Joan Schleuder, "Measurement and Effects of Attention to Media News," *Human Communication Research,* 13 (1986): 76–107.

26. The distinction between news exposure and reception is explored in Vincent Price and John Zaller, "Who Gets the News? Measuring Individual Differences in Likelihood of News Reception," *Public Opinion Quarterly*, 57 (1993): 133–164.

27. Chaffee et al., "Citizen Response."

28. Political socialization is usually thought of in terms of young people, who are rarely an explicit target of public journalism or its evaluation. Interpretation of public journalism projects as political socialization agents was suggested to us by Elissa Lee.

29. See Thorson and Friedland, "Civic Lessons."

30. One of the coauthors of the companion report to ours (Thorson et al., 1997) was Frank Denton, editor of the *Wisconsin State Journal*. See Frank Denton, Esther Thorson, and James Coyle, "Effects of a Multimedia Public Journalism Project on Political Knowledge and Attitudes," presented to the Mass Communication and Society Division, Association for Education in Journalism and Mass Communication (1995).

Reinventing the Press for the Age of Commercial Appeals
Writings on and about Public Journalism

Hanno Hardt

University of Iowa
University of Ljubljana

The decline of journalistic authority in the United States remains a serious social and cultural issue that is only too often dismissed as the erosion of an elitist notion whose public credibility has vanished long ago. Instead, turning to public opinion has become a favorite gesture to capture the attention of the media with promises of change, if not salvation. Similarly, debates about the ignorance of the masses have been replaced by hopes for the wisdom of the public and its desire for enlightenment. At the same time, technological change and economic necessities have pushed the practice of journalism beyond traditional expectations. As a result, the prevailing commercial interests of the media in an increasingly more competitive environment have begun to transform status and skills of the work force and to undermine its authority, while mass audiences have moved beyond the reach of a traditional press to be replaced by the potential of an affluent, middle-class clientele with specific information needs. These develop-

Parts of this appendix originally appeared in H. Hardt, "The Quest for Public Journalism," *Journal of Communication,* 47,3 (Summer 1997): 102–109. Copyright 1997 by the Oxford University Press. Reprinted by permission.

ments are a reminder of a historical process in late capitalism that subordinates journalism as a cultural practice to the economic rationale of marketing and new information technologies. They are also the historical context for a number of projects that address the crisis of journalism by focusing on the relationship between journalistic practices and public reception.

For some time, American newspaper journalism has been confronting its own crisis of lackluster performances and sagging circulation figures with a second look at its traditional, self-defined practice of public service, egged on by press critics and the realization that readers may well cancel their subscriptions and forego local newspaper services in favor of a host of "free" media services, ranging from television news to shopping guides.

Supported by the financial resources of several foundations, a crusade for responsive journalism recently united academics and press management to change the ways of local news coverage with the help of the public. At the center of these activities are the Project on Public Life and the Press, funded by the John S. and James L. Knight Foundation (together with the Kettering Foundation, the American Press Institute, and the New York University Department of Journalism), and the Pew Center for Civic Journalism, funded by the Pew Charitable Trusts (together with the Poynter Institute for Media Studies). The former focus on the making of "public" journalists and "public" journalism; the latter advocate "civic" journalism, both in the most recent effort to turn around the fortunes of American journalism. Their collective judgment calls for public participation in a joint endeavor to restore proximity and relevance to the press and its reporting practices.

These current initiatives by two major foundations, together with the more pervasive activities of the Freedom Forum, constitute a major effort to shape the future of journalism (and journalism education) in the United States. Their agendas for media reform focus on operationalizing ideas that have a potential for consensus and a tendency to produce pragmatic solutions; they also signal an alliance between journalism and foundations that would have been inconceivable several years ago. Indeed, it has been a long road from the editorial fallout of the 1947 Hutchins Commission Report to the partial success of these projects of public involvement in the future of 1990s journalism. Although the press ignored the 1947 report, or denounced its authors, the recent calls for public or civic journalism have produced a range of responses from tales of cooperation and civic approval mixed with professional skepticism to outright rejection for fear of jeopardizing the traditional sense of editorial autonomy. There has been no objection to the cooperation between academics and professionals with the goal of translating suitable ideas into journalistic practices.

As a result, there has been a lively debate of public journalism in professional journals, among academic experts, and in various reports from the field without much apparent concern, however, about the expanding role of foundations in shaping public policy, including their impact on the future of journalism. In fact, the prominence of media foundations as powerful institutional forces in various professional and educational arenas of public life has never been raised as a political issue with potentially undesirable influences on the process of journalism or journalism education. Instead, over time considerable numbers of journalists, editors, and educators, as well as their institutions, have participated in the organized activities of several foundations and profited from their support of specific, university-based programs. At a time that industrial interests are met with increasing regularity by universities eager to obtain private funding to offset shrinking state support, journalism education, in particular, has become vulnerable to the specific agendas of media interests as articulated by their foundations. At stake is the definition of journalism and its role in contemporary society, the nature of professional work, and the future of journalists. Ultimately, the campaign for public or civic journalism demonstrates the institutional power of media foundations as shapers of press policies. The attempt to establish a new raison d'être for the American press as a commercial concern should be reason enough for uneasiness among journalism faculties about the industrialization of higher education and the potential impact of specific media interests on the location, size, and content of journalism education in the United States.

∗   ∗   ∗

Discussions of public or civic journalism, as documented in some recent publications, address the practice of journalism in contemporary society. They appear as a rhetoric of change that claims neither theoretical depth nor historical consciousness but insists, nevertheless, on the need for a new understanding of journalism. The result is a collective appraisal of the relationship between journalists and their publics that appeals to commonsense solutions without a sense of history. There is no consideration of contextual issues, such as major social and economic changes in the relations between publics and their media or the reaction of media ownership to social and economic shifts in society. Instead, there is a preoccupation with the surface phenomena of content matter and topical concerns, rather than with structural constraints due to the changing objectives of media enterprises that may have contributed to the demise of newspaper journalism over the last 30 years. Missing is a critical examination of the underlying assumptions of journalism, professionalism, and freedom of expression, particularly in light of historical social, political, and economic developments that continue to deconstruct traditional views of journalism and are leading to a different understanding of the role of journalism in American society.

Thus, in the face of major institutional changes that have redefined notions of "the public" and the idea of "work" among journalists, the proponents of public or civic journalism promote a new definition of journalism to respond to the demands of the public and the desires of the industry with a combination of positively endowed concepts (public and journalism) to project the scope of their undertaking. After all, journalism has always been considered public, in the public interest, or for the public good, whereas journalists have always been defined as members of a fourth estate, privately employed and protected by the First Amendment. Yet, there are limitations to the definition, which does not encourage the pursuit of public interest journalism under new forms of ownership and public participation, or a new understanding of professionalism that frees journalists from editorial controls and acknowledges their professional independence. Instead, it remains ideologically committed to approach journalism as a business that relies on the satisfaction of its particular consumer community, which constitutes the extent and nature of the public, redirects journalistic practices accordingly, and offers a recipe for temporary relief from the symptoms of a deeper social and economic crisis.

It is no accident that *Doing Public Journalism* traces the theoretical foundations of public journalism to the writings of a public opinion pollster, because polling itself constitutes a familiar (American) approach to identifying contemporary problems and formulating immediate solutions. There is no room for the potential of a historical explanation to reflect on a series of complicated probable causes. The author describes the rise of public journalism based on social–scientific insights into the process of making "stable, responsible" choices on issues that matter and proceeds to produce an upbeat account of public journalism. He makes no attempt to offer historical insights into the reasons for an alienated, misunderstood, or misguided public and its conditions of illiteracy, poverty, or intellectual competence. Likewise, there is no response to the failure of journalism and the occupational dilemma of journalists as newsworkers to respond successfully to a public need for information and enlightenment. Instead, journalists become public journalists, and journalism rises as public journalism to engage with an interested public in addressing common concerns. The goal is a practice of journalism that "ought to make it as easy as possible for citizens to make intelligent decisions about public affairs, and to get them carried out."

Consequently, public journalists must not only be "experts in public life" but also "civic capitalists" and "full-time citizens"; in other words, they are the "clear-eyed pragmatists that conventional journalists only pretend to be." They are also experts in understanding the needs of their respective communities and are advised that "the final word on a public journalist's news choices can never come from the publisher, colleagues, or the Pulitzer Prize committee, but only from what happens or doesn't happen in the community as a whole." Guided by the principle that "journalism should advocate democracy without advocating particular solutions," finally, journalists will have no choice but to engage in public relations for the benefit of an emerging patronage press. The book concludes with a description of journalistic practices from newspapers around the United States which participate in the project and report a modicum of success as "fair-minded" participants in their respective communities, reflecting confidence and optimism in the professional response to public journalism.

Civic Journalism: Six Case Studies, which offers insights into a project involving newspapers, radio, and television stations, provides more evidence of changing journalistic practices with the aid of foundation support. Its goal was to make news coverage more meaningful and to stem "cynicism and alienation" in society with the objective to improve both journalism and community life. As a result, a variety of news organizations report on becoming sensitized to the concerns of their audiences as citizens by providing mechanisms for interaction between institutions and individuals. The examples demonstrate the success of cooperation among media, the continuing need for professional investigative reporting and its effectiveness, and the consequences of providing public access.

The previous reports offer examples of how public or civic journalism has been operationalized, whereas *Public Journalism: Theory and Practice* offers a short argument for public journalism because "if changes are necessary for America to meet its problems and strengthen its democracy, then journalism is one of the agencies that must change." The question is how and at what cost? The authors obviously think that it must be done and that journalism will survive. Therefore, they challenge journalists to redefine their standing in the community and to "take responsibility for helping to support and even create (a vibrant public culture)." This need for renewal also extends to traditional journalistic practices, like the reporting of facts, sharing ideas, encouraging debate, and promoting consensus. All the while, "reviving public life while dealing with the realities of the popular marketplace" is a plausible, coexisting task of public journalism, which wants to emerge as a new philosophy of action. Rejecting the idea that public journalism turns into public relations or civic boosterism (two perfectly plausible explanations), the authors rather envision a form of populism that relies on the presence of a socially mobilized middle class, media leadership, and a charismatic connection between community and journalism.

Getting the Connections Right provides a more detailed theoretical basis for the promotion of public journalism "to help revive civic life and

improve public dialogue—and to fashion a coherent response to the deepening troubles in our civic climate, most of which implicate journalists."
The author suggests that journalists, prone to spreading cynicism, "drop
the devastating illusion of themselves as bystanders" and rejoin "the American experiment." His solution is the practice of public journalism, which
frees the journalist from charges of bias and lack of professionalism. As
impressive as these charges may be, there is little to suggest that the bias of
journalists as community workers will help revive civic life or produce professionalism.

The author agrees with most observers that the conditions of contemporary journalism have deteriorated to a point of disconnection and
mutual disenchantment between the press and the public, fueled by a general feeling of separation and alienation in society but he fails to address
the root causes of this development which are not restricted to journalism
or the press. Although he briefly acknowledges six particular "alarms"
(economic, technological, political, occupational, spiritual, intellectual) of
American journalism, he misses an opportunity to address the changing
conditions of newswork and their consequences for individual journalists.
Instead, he sees no reason why public journalism cannot succeed in providing values, giving directions, and promoting activism among journalists
that translate into community service.

Answering critics of public journalism, whose charges range from
reducing journalism to a marketing tool, surrendering professional judgments to audience opinions, to creating a partisan press, he concedes the
potential dangers of this approach to traditional notions of journalism and
its place in society, but expresses an overriding need for change that is supported by the actual work of practitioners. The book challenges the growing detachment of journalists at a time when the economic goals of the
press to achieve "audience production at the lowest possible cost" constitute a formidable obstacle to the kind of journalism that celebrates community by practicing democracy. It also challenges traditional understandings of the role of journalists in society, including their claims of autonomy
and the meaning of professionalism by rejecting traditional notions of
expertise among journalists in favor of building community relations.
Although there is much to be said for efforts to reinvent the best of traditional American journalism and for the positive response from some
media organizations, the book advocates a new direction in American journalism with significant consequences for the definition of work and the
role of the press in society.

In fact, these accounts of public or civic journalism are reminiscent of
progressive ideas about the need for change in an effort to improve the
conditions for democracy. Unfortunately, however, those conditions seem
to have worsened, and it turns out that the problems of journalism are the

problems of society. Thus, disillusionment among journalists and their reported cynicism are symptoms of widespread alienation and disbelief, while dissatisfaction with work (and pay) in the face of shifting requirements concerning the type and quality of intellectual labor in the media industries is a sign of fundamental social and economic changes in society and their effects on the workplace. To blame journalism for the demise of civic life and the failure of the great community or the good society is simplistic at best and cynical at worst, when solutions to the dilemma of journalism must address the social, political, and economic dimensions of journalists and their publics. There is a concomitant need to retrace the historical ties between journalists and the public and to consider the existential conditions of journalists vis-à-vis media institutions, when professional judgments, editorial decisions, and freedom of expression clash over controversial public issues.

Indeed, in a society in which property rights have been far more protected historically than other rights, including the right of free expression, media ownership still dictates the type and quality of journalism as well as its purposes. The drive for public journalism fails to examine the prerequisites of journalistic practice, for example, the nature of newswork and ownership of the means of production, and the consequences of changing conditions of labor for the future of newsworkers, when it seems appropriate (and necessary) to question the practices of those in control of the means of communication. Instead, the advocates of public journalism appeal to the civic conscience of individual journalists or, with management support, ask for compliance with their new rules of civic engagement.

In addition, the creation of public or civic journalism anticipates a community that is capable of responding to its own desire for information or to institutional propositions to articulate collective interests. After all, the presence of "civic capital" depends on a socially and politically active, culturally aware, and economically stable public and describes the activities of the middle class. Because public journalism refers mainly to the constituents of a political culture, there is not much room in these discussions for a notion of culture as a way of life in which issues of communication and participation become crucial elements of a complex social existence. Nevertheless, what emerges from the rhetoric of public or civic journalism is a new press for a new age in which journalism will become oblivious to Joseph Pulitzer's words, "always oppose privileged classes and public plunderers, never lack sympathy with the poor, always remain devoted to the public welfare." Consequently, it may make sense to think in terms of aligning the middle-class concerns of audiences with the commercial intent of the media to better represent those class interests, but it remains questionable whether an alienated, fractured (middle-class) public can be restored to its ideal function by changing the practices of journalism. What is lost in these grand schemes to improve journalism for the benefit of society is an opportunity to broaden the spectrum of public communication by empowering journalists as intellectual workers and privileging the concerns of the underprivileged.

*   *   *

Public Journalism and Public Life is an autobiographical account of American journalism that provides professional insights into the promotion of public journalism as a desirable alternative to traditional notions of journalism. Based on his experiences since the 1960s, the author argues for a redefinition of journalism that requires "mental shifts" among journalists to act on the relationship between journalism and public life according to the social and cultural realities of society. In a curious and frequently anecdotal manner, journalism emerges as a professional activity that relates to the inadequacy of traditional norms and its failure to appreciate the importance of becoming part of a public concern. Unfortunately, the book does not problematize the condition of the public, the predicament of newsworkers, or the impact of corporate media ownership on both the public and its journalists. Instead, the author acknowledges the presence of "corporatism" as an economic reality, notes its impact on the mobility of editors, in particular, and moves on with his discussion of "non-resource-based" changes to arrive at a definition of public journalism that requires "individual consciences and judgments" from journalists in their dealings with the public. There is not much new in the argument that the strength of tradition, objectivity, or news for the sake of news, inhibits the contemporary practice of journalism, except that this book reinforces a growing tendency to blame journalists for a variety of public conditions, including the circumstances of their own practice, and to claim that journalists can actually help improve the dismal conditions of society. However, it is particularly unfortunate that the author, a prominent editor, disregards the possibility that conditions of employment, smaller staffs, increasing and diversified tasks, and the demands of rising profitability direct the process of change by defining journalism according to the perceived needs of the industry. Instead, the book confirms the suspicion that journalism (and journalism education) is not defined by journalists but by management interests.

However, there are other perspectives on the dilemma of public communication. For instance, *The Conversation of Journalism* offers a more differentiated response to the plight of the press; by building on traditional understandings of journalism to reinvigorate and renew its contributions to society, the authors focus on its central function, the communication of ideas. They not only provide an argument for change but offer strategies for journalism and journalism education that connect historically with the role and function of the press in American society.

Under present conditions journalism is unlikely to retain its "current preoccupation with narrow definitions of detachment, news 'coverage,' complete objectivity, and market-oriented decision-making," if it wants to participate in a democratic dialogue. Since people, by their very nature, want to be included in the deliberative process of society, the authors see journalists as imminently qualified to serve as conduits for ideas that appeal and are relevant to the public debate. The challenge for journalism is to become a "responsive social force" while realizing that "insight and outreach are mutually reinforcing."

The guiding metaphor of this argument is the notion of conversation, grounded in a philosophical discourse that ranges from the pragmatism of Dewey and Mead to the work of Gadamer, in which dialogue becomes a basic human practice. Such practice also includes the art of listening and the responsibility for understanding the other; it suggests the proximity of community life with its own demands for moving beyond disseminating information to telling stories. However, conversation requires an ability to communicate; it constitutes a changing partnership based on language and education that cannot be taken for granted. In fact, journalists often dominate the public sphere with monologues because there are no shared meanings, no common ground, and no reasons to respond for those who are culturally impoverished and incompetent to communicate in their alienated and decimated environments. The assumption of equality in conversation may offer false hopes but, once recognized, places additional responsibilities on journalism to initiate and lead those conversations in unconventional and creative forms and languages that capture the attention of the inattentive and challenge the imagination of the disenchanted.

Mixed News: The Public/Civic/Communitarian Journalism Debate promises to "offer strong voices on several sides of the complex debate" involving the public journalism "movement." Based on a project supported by the Ethics and Excellence in Journalism Foundation, several authors share their insights into the consequences of communitarianism and the prospects of public journalism. Although the notion of communitarianism offers an intriguing approach to dealing with the relationship between journalism and society and provides a potential answer to the critique of contemporary journalism, the book only devotes a few chapters to the debate over the potential of communitarianism in the context of public or civic journalism and the consequences of a collective approach to journalism and public life.

By relinquishing traditional ideas of individualism and replacing Enlightenment liberalism with an ideology of common interests and a pursuit of the common good (without abandoning the individual), a communitarian perspective recognizes the changing historical conditions and places journalism squarely within a public context, in the service of public life and responsible to the community. As such, communitarianism provides a theoretical explanation for public journalism that is based on an alternative view of human relations. It is a view, however, that encounters (predictable) resistance, if not opposition by several authors, whose libertarian and liberal–pluralist representations of the role of individualism in American society celebrate not only the individualism of practicing journalists but also the power of journalism as a form of private enterprise.

Communitarianism, on the other hand, challenges not only preconceived notions of journalism as individual expression but also the nature and purpose of information and the production of media content by stressing the importance of acting in the public interest. Indeed, there is much to be said for shifting attention toward a collective model of society by emphasizing the primacy of "community" and the binding force of communication, but the problem of communitarianism in the context of media studies, as opposed to the potential of critical theory, for instance, resides in its failure to address the institutional conditions of economic or political control of communication, the idea of property, and the social consequences of private ownership. Instead, communitarianism extends the liberal–pluralist arguments of the role and function of the media by addressing the decline of individualism in the United States without endangering the goals of capitalism. It is about social evolution and, therefore, helps confirm the observation that public or civic journalism as a form of social engineering serves to realign and strengthen the existing ideological framework without much hope for fundamental changes that are based on the promises of alternative models of human relations.

The complexity of relations between journalists and the public emerges more fully from *The Crisis of Public Communication,* whose authors address the consequences of their previous work on politics and communication. Although this book may seem peripheral to the debates over public journalism, it appeals to readers interested in a holistic explanation of change in the shifting relationship between politicians, journalists, and their respective institutional interests in the context of confronting "an increasingly disaffected and fragmented audience/public/citizenry." In fact, the book offers insights into the conditions of public communication that help explain the position of journalists between special interests and public apathy. Recast in the light of demands for public journalism, the authors address the need for public engagement in the political discourse by providing a sociopolitical explanation of journalism and politics. The cumulative findings of their research projects over the last 30 years suggest significant trends in the organization of public communication, ranging from the professionalization of political advocacy by politicians to the response of journalism, which may help explain the noted cynicism among journalists as well as their frequent references to a disenchanted public.

The authors describe a "crisis of communication for citizenship" after important shifts of media practices, which have created political space for experts whose only responsibility is to their own political causes, while journalists retreat into representations of stereotypes and characterizations of politics as a game. The result has been the emergence of journalism as an oppositional force in a political dialogue that excludes the public.

The authors also cite efforts by citizens/voters and the positive response by media to provide a voice for ordinary citizens as evidence of a popular move to participate constructively in the process of civic communication. But they suggest, at the same time, that the restoration of ordinary individuals as active participants with a substantive agenda for public communication could set up a populist form of discourse that responds to politics as spectacle and fails to replace older forms of political communication. Indeed, the authors sense that the crisis of public communication has deeper structural roots buried in the "massification" of Western societies and exposed in the manipulative control of public communication by professionalized politics. This book serves an as excellent example of a contemplative social scientific practice that understands the importance of rendering judgments that reflect on a much larger social and political totality.

There is agreement among various authors about the current crisis of public communication and its challenge to democratic societies and about the place of journalism and the role of the public in addressing the consequences of a failing dialogue. But it also becomes clear that the notions of public or civic journalism are theoretically and historically tied to notions of society, and democratic societies in particular. Thus, journalistic practices are affected by social and economic developments that redefine the place and function of the media as society adapts to the aftermath of modernization and the public reconstitutes itself under new conditions of the marketplace.

There is much to be said for dialogue and conversation in a democratic system that values authentic communication, which includes the capacity to believe and the courage to disagree. But as long as commercial considerations dictate the nature of journalism and direct the discourse in society, many publics will remain silent and without representation and many journalists will surrender to the demands of a patronage press.

In fact, *Market-Driven Journalism: Let the Citizen Beware* provides a more recent account of commercializing journalism, in which the author concludes that "audience-building values" are replacing journalistic selection and reporting criteria. In an atmosphere of intense commercialization, the promotion of public or civic journalism qualifies as a legitimation of audience-building practices; journalists lack neither creative nor intellectual skills and understand the nature of professional demands. Their engagement in the production of news is complicated by constraints on time and resources, instead, which discourage or prevent the kind of meaningful and responsive journalism that inspires readers and shapes communities. When journalists have conspired with readers in their surveillance of the public sphere, they have done so for specific reasons, voluntarily, and typically in the public interest. In this sense, their journalism has been public with a sense of civic responsibility that goes with good journalism.

These discussions of public or civic journalism, as they relate to the American experience in particular, are based on ideological perceptions of journalism and society that ignore questions of economic and political power and understand the institutional crisis of journalism as a predicament of individual practices without analytical depth; they also fail to assess the social conditions of society and the place of journalism in the discourse of culture. Instead, the reigning assumption about the public relies on the commercial appeal of the press to the economically privileged and constitutes citizenship through audience participation.

Furthermore, by separating journalists from society by a critique of their traditional practices, only to reunite them with their publics by new demands on their skills, the advocates of public or civic journalism create a convenient fiction that undermines the possibility that the failures of journalism are the failures of society. After all, the experience of alienation and fragmentation in a hostile, institutional environment cuts across the everyday life of society. At the same time, these writings express a sense of confidence in the future of journalism that reflects a belief in the ability to adjust to the demands of the marketplace at the expense of journalists and their freedom to determine the position of their craft vis-à-vis the social and political realities of commercialization. In fact, the debate about public journalism occurs by and large without the participation of rank-and-file journalists who stand accused of having lost public credibility or a sense of community service, while definitions of journalism and questions of work remain topics of conformist academic speculation and management decrees.

In their enthusiasm for reinventing journalism in the United States, these writings share an intense, if not exaggerated, belief in the importance of the press and its power as an agent of social change. They construct a vision of public journalism that reflects the hegemonic force of old ideas, which reinforce the centrality of a liberal–pluralist understanding of communication in society and confirm the desire for a new practice of the press that integrates the social and economic consequences of a market-driven media system into a new definition of journalism. But above all, they signal the end of traditional explanations of journalism, including the role of journalists, in the process of societal communication.

Books Cited

Anderson, Rob, Robert Dardenne, and George M. Killenberg. *The Conversation of Journalism: Communication, Community, and News.* Westport, CT: Praeger, 1996.

Black, Jack, ed. *Mixed News: The Public/Civic/Communitarian Journalism Debate.* Hillsdale, NJ: Erlbaum, 1997.

Blumler, Jay G., and Michael Gurevitch. *The Crisis of Public Communication.* London and New York: Routledge, 1996.

Charity, Arthur. *Doing Public Journalism.* New York: Guilford Press, 1995.

McManus, John H. *Market-Driven Journalism: Let the Citizen Beware.* Thousand Oaks, CA: Sage, 1994.

Merritt, Davis "Buzz." *Public Journalism and Public Life. Why Telling the News Is Not Enough.* Hillsdale, NJ: Erlbaum, 1995.

Rosen, Jay, and Davis Merritt Jr. *Public Journalism: Theory and Practice.* Occasional Papers. Dayton, OH: Kettering Foundation, 1994.

Rosen, Jay. *Getting the Connections Right: Public Journalism and the Troubles in the Press.* New York: Twentieth Century Fund, 1996.

Schaffer, Jan, and Edward D. Miller, eds. *Civic Journalism: Six Case Studies: A Joint Report by the Pew Center for Civic Journalism and the Poynter Institute for Media Studies.* Washington, DC: Pew Center for Civic Journalism, n.d.

A Selected
and Annotated Bibliography

This annotated bibliography is intended as a conceptual road map for locating articles and books that address the core issues of public journalism, as well as work that provides a theoretical foundation for developing and deepening the rationale of public journalism. We divide the readings into three sections: "Definitions and Critiques of Public Journalism," "Work Related to Journalism and Communication," and "Social and Political Theory." The annotated sections are followed by an alphabetical list of all the readings we have included.

In keeping with our focus on the *idea* of public journalism, we have omitted articles and books that describe and evaluate specific projects. For works of this type, readers should consult the annotated bibliographies included in Arthur Charity's *Doing Public Journalism* (1995) and Jay Black's (ed.) *Mixed News: The Public/Civic/Communitarian Journalism Debate* (1997). Additional sources and resources are described by Edmund Lambeth in "A Bibliographic Essay on Civic/Public Journalism," *National Civic Review,* 85,1 (1996): 18–21.

Definitions and Critiques of Public Journalism

Black, Jay, ed. *Mixed News: The Public/Civic/Communitarian Journalism Debate.* Mahwah, NJ: Erlbaum, 1997.
    Essays from practitioners and critics who address issues that animate the debate about public journalism. Philosophical questions are discussed within

---

Compiled and annotated by Elissa Lee, Michael McDevitt, and Karin Wahl-Jorgensen.

the context of the daily routines of news production to explore how journalism might contribute to public life.

Broder, David S. "Campaign '92," *Quill*, March 1992, pp. 8–9.

Describes *The Washington Post's* attempts to identify readers' concerns by initiating discussions with people in the community. Discusses citizens' need for substantive reporting beyond horse-race campaign coverage.

Calvert, Clay. "Clashing Conceptions of Press Duties: Public Journalists and the Courts," *Communication Law and Policy*, 2 (Autumn 1997): 441–475.

Compares public journalism's claims about the role of the press with the press practices and goals the judiciary is willing to support and protect. Concludes that "public journalists and the courts have two distinct pictures about the roles and responsibilities of a free press."

Charity, Arthur. *Doing Public Journalism.* New York: Guilford Press, 1995.

An overview of the basic principles and assumptions of public journalism, including case studies of a variety of public journalism projects. Develops and applies public journalism as an idea that can improve journalism throughout the newsroom.

Coleman, Renita. "The Intellectual Antecedents of Public Journalism," *Journal of Communication Inquiry*, 21,1 (1997): 60–76.

Traces the evolution of public journalism to the debate of the early 20th century on the proper role of media in a democracy. Argues that the problems and potential of public journalism are best understood in a historical and philosophical context.

Ettema, James S., and Limor Peer. "Good News from a Bad Neighborhood: Toward an Alternative to the Discourse of Urban Pathology," *Journalism and Mass Communication Quarterly*, 73 (Winter 1996): 835–856.

Analyzes the language through which journalists comprehend the nature and meaning of urban affairs reporting. Promotes a "vocabulary of community assets" consistent with public journalism's interest in having the press develop better ways to establish relationships with its readers and their communities.

Glasser, Theodore L., and Stephanie Craft. "Public Journalism and the Prospects for Press Accountability," pp. 120–134, in Jay Black, ed., *Mixed News: The Public/Civic/Communitarian Journalism Debate.* Mahwah, NJ: Erlbaum, 1997. Excerpted in *Journal of Mass Media Ethics*, 11,3 (1996): 152–158.

Argues that the press fails to recognize itself as a distinctly public institution bound by the same standards of accountability expected of other public institutions. Suggests that editorial pages have been for too long a lost opportunity for newspapers to identify, explain, and defend their news judgments and policies.

Glasser, Theodore L., and Stephanie Craft. "Public Journalism and the Search for Democratic Ideals," pp. 203–218, in Tamar Liebes and James Curran, eds., *Media, Ritual and Identity.* London: Routledge, 1998.

Reviews and critiques public journalism's disarray as a normative theory of the press. Examines contradictory claims concerning public opinion, agenda setting, public discourse, and press structure and control. Wonders about the prospects for a public purpose for a private press.

Hackett, Robert A., and Yuezhi Zhao. "Journalistic Objectivity and Social Change," *Peace Review,* 8,1 (1996): 5–11.

Public journalism champions itself as a partisan of a particular form of politics rather than a particular cause. Yet this raises questions: Where does it stand in relation to power elites and dominant values in a community? Will public journalism promote democratic decision making or is it more likely to gloss over fundamental conflicts and forge a false consensus?

Heikkilä, Heikki, and Risto Kunelius. "Public Journalism and Its Problems," *Javnost– The Public,* 3,3 (1996): 81–95.

Examines the theoretical underpinnings of public journalism. Focuses mainly on John Dewey and Hannah Arendt and their treatment of the concepts "public," "action," and "storytelling."

Hodges, Louis W. "Ruminations about the Communitarian Debate," *Journal of Mass Media Ethics,* 11,3 (1996): 133–139.

Discusses public journalism as a reflection of the revival of communitarian thinking, focusing on communitarianism as presented in *Good News: Social Ethics and the Press* (1993). Concludes that communitarianism does not threaten liberal democracy but holds promise for regaining the liberal ideal.

Lambeth, Edmund, and David Craig. "Civic Journalism as Research," *Newspaper Research Journal,* 7 (1995): 149–160.

Argues for civic journalism as an opportunity for academics and journalism practitioners to work together in building a tradition of performance assessment. Describes examples of projects and defines the goals of civic journalism as an effort to probe beneath the surface of events and cover all issues, as well as have experts speak clearly to the public.

Merritt, Davis. *Public Journalism and Public Life: Why Telling the News Is Not Enough.* Hillsdale, NJ: Erlbaum, 1995.

Illustrates the changing environment of journalism through a narrative of the author's career. Discusses the need for a vocabulary that addresses the idea of the press as the "fair-minded participant" in a quest to revitalize public life.

Merritt, Davis. "Public Journalism—Defining a Democratic Art," *Media Studies Journal,* 9,3 (1995): 125–132.

Because journalism must be performed under severe restrictions of time and space, requiring adherence to professional norms that have, over time, hardened into cultural traits, public journalism should work toward developing a new set of reflexes for the purpose of reinvigorating public life.

Meyer, Philip. "Defining Public Journalism: Discourse Leading Solutions," *Investigative Reporters and Editors Journal* (November/December 1995): 3–5.

Argues that anyone prepared to defend public journalism should be specific about what is being defended. Defines six goals worth defending. Describes how the absence of a well-formed theory makes public journalism vulnerable to being used as camouflage for special interests.

Parisi, Peter. "Toward a 'Philosophy of Framing': News Narratives for Public Journalism," *Journalism and Mass Communication Quarterly,* 74 (Winter 1997): 673–686.

Focuses on the importance of fostering press narratives by recognizing journalists' interpretive role. Examines the prospects for a journalism that truly deserves the name "public."

Raines, Howell. "The Fallows Fallacy," *New York Times*, 25 February 1996, sec. 4, p. 14.

Editorial page editor of *The New York Times* replies to James Fallows's *Breaking the News*. Responds to Fallows's call to limit personality coverage and horse-race journalism by arguing that "public policy missionaries" are equally dangerous and that citizens are not just choosing a bundle of policies, but a person.

Reider, Rem. "Public Journalism: Stop the Shooting," *American Journalism Review* (December 1995): 6.

Argues that the polarization between traditionalists and advocates of public journalism is eased by overlapping values, including the belief that news must go beyond official agendas and sources; the commitment to reporting that reflects the complexity of reality; and the focus on how news coverage can help a community to solve problems.

Rosen, Jay. "Making Journalism More Public," *Communication*, 12 (1991): 267–284.

Suggests how journalism might become more public and argues that a public cannot exist if it is not seen as such by journalists, officials, and intellectuals. Discusses corporate encouragement of public journalism, the effects of increased community connectedness on circulation, and the need for corporations to be more public.

Rosen, Jay. *Community Connectedness: Passwords for Public Journalism*. St. Petersburg, FL: Poynter Institute for Media Studies, 1993.

Argues that traditional notions of responsible journalism must be expanded to include the role of the press as "a support system for public life." Discusses community connectedness as a manifestation of public discussion and civic involvement and suggests that "public time" is essential to a healthy democracy.

Rosen, Jay. "Making Things More Public: On the Political Responsibility of the Media Intellectual." *Critical Studies in Mass Communication*, 11 (December 1994): 363–388.

Focuses on the problem of "the public" in communication studies. Argues that journalists and intellectuals alike should work to assist and legitimize the democratic process. Argues that scholars perform a public service by working to form a common culture and values across public life, not just among intellectuals.

Rosen, Jay. *Public Journalism as a Democratic Art*. New York: Project on the Public Life and the Press, 1994.

Portrays public journalism as an experimental movement in the tradition of American pragmatism. Argues that the movement seeks to "make journalism whole again" by stressing the neglected values of civic participation, dialogue, cooperative problem solving, and community responsibility.

Rosen, Jay. *Getting the Connections Right: Public Journalism and the Troubles in the Press*. New York: Twentieth Century Fund, 1996.

Introduces central ideas and principles of public journalism and addresses criticisms. Develops the argument that the press can do much more than it has previously done to engage people as citizens, to improve public discussion, to help communities solve problems, and to assist in creating a workable public life.

Rosen, Jay, and Davis Merritt Jr. *Public Journalism: Theory and Practice.* Dayton, OH: Kettering Foundation, 1994.

First section discusses basic principles of public journalism and ways to redesign coverage so that politics becomes the common responsibility of journalists, politicians, and citizens. Second section reviews the dynamics of democratic communities and what they require to function properly.

Woo, William F. "As Old Gods Falter: Public Journalism and the Tradition of Detachment." Press-Enterprise Lecture Series, No. 30, University of California, Riverside, February 13, 1995.

Acknowledges the potential for public journalism to achieve community cohesiveness and ties but questions the rejection of traditional values. Argues that although the public voice is important, journalists should not automatically make the town consensus their own.

Related Studies of Journalism and Communication

Anderson, Rob, Robert Dardenne, and George M. Killenberg. *The Conversation of Journalism: Communication, Community, and News.* Westport, CT: Praeger, 1994.

Argues that journalism, to fulfill its responsibilities and its potential, must adopt a wider and more dialogical role in public life—becoming, in essence, a "commons" for public conversation in addition to reporting what it defines as news.

Altschull, J. Herbert. *Agents of Power: The Media and Public Policy.* 2d ed. New York: Longman, 1995.

Asserts in this update of his 1994 book that news media in all press systems are agents of those who exercise political and economic power. The interdependence of mass media and politics precludes the possibility that news has a kind or independent character, or that stories tell themselves.

Bennett, W. Lance. "A Policy Research Paradigm for the News Media and Democracy," *Journal of Communication,* 43,3 (1993): 180–189.

Calls for a broadening of research frames to study communication processes in which the press, government, and the public interact through the news. Argues that we need to compare complex cases to identify general conditions that affect the quality of political debates in the news.

Blumler, Jay G., and Michael Gurevitch. *The Crisis of Public Communication.* London: Routledge, 1995.

Argues that political communication must be understood as an institution in its own right, with characteristic influences, constraints, and problems. A highly complex web of relationships among politicians, professional advisers, and journalists leaves little room for citizen involvement.

Broder, David S. "Campaign '92," *Quill* (March 1992): 8–9.

Describes *The Washington Post*'s attempts to identify readers' concerns by initiating discussions with people in the community. Discusses citizens' need for substantive reporting beyond horse-race campaign coverage.

Carey, James W. "The Press, Public Opinion, and Public Discourse," pp. 373–402, in Theodore L. Glasser and Charles T. Salmon, eds., *Public Opinion and the Com-*

munication of Consent. New York: Guilford Press, 1995. Also in *James W. Carey: A Critical Reader*, pp. 228–257, Eve Stryker Munson and Catherine A. Warren, eds. Minneapolis: University of Minnesota Press, 1997.

Assesses the cultural, economic and historical dimensions of the relationship between the press and the public. Argues that the "expansion of individual rights" and the "erosion of common judgment" make it difficult to sustain a "meaningful notion of public life."

Carey, James W. "Community, Public, Journalism," pp. 1–15, in Jay Black, ed., *Mixed News: The Public/Civic/Communitarian Journalism Debate.* Mahwah, NJ: Erlbaum, 1997.

Examines the meaning and viability of a "republican community" and assesses the social, political, and Constitutional forces working against it. Discusses the difficulty of honoring "interdependence without sacrificing individuality."

Christians, Clifford G. "Social Ethics and Mass Media Practice," pp. 187–205, in Josina M. Makau and Ronald C. Arnett, eds., *Communication Ethics in an Age of Diversity.* Urbana: University of Illinois Press, 1997.

Contends that international audiences are viewed by companies as an exploitable resource, and a one-way flow of information ignores the value of indigenous programming. Media giants have organized themselves in a moral vacuum, without resistance, despite the rise of ethnicity as an elemental force in the upcoming global order.

Christians, Clifford G., John P. Ferré, and P. Mark Fackler. *Good News: Social Ethics and the Press.* New York: Oxford University Press, 1993.

Critiques the rampant individualism of libertarianism and proposes a vision of journalism based on a communitarian understanding of the human condition. Emphasizes that "community cannot be resuscitated without the leadership of the press" and that fundamental changes are needed in the press's view of itself and the world it covers.

Entman, Robert M. *Democracy Without Citizens: Media and the Decay of American Politics.* New York: Oxford University Press, 1989.

Argues that the press should enhance democracy by stimulating the citizenry's political interest and by providing specific information to hold government accountable. Explores various aspects of news, public opinion, and democracy.

Ettema, James S., and Theodore L. Glasser. *Custodians of Conscience: Investigative Journalism and Public Virtue.* New York: Columbia University Press, 1998.

Assesses and critiques investigative reporting as a form of social and moral inquiry, focusing on the contradictions and tensions that characterize modern American journalism. Examines the importance of understanding how facts implicate values and why the future of news requires a deeper appreciation for the connection between human knowledge and human interest.

Fallows, James. *Breaking the News: How the Media Undermine American Democracy.* New York: Pantheon Books, 1996.

Argues that present practices and values of journalists undermine the credibility of the press and distort the democratic process by which leaders are chosen and society is governed. Focuses on the behavior of the Washington press corps and the acceptance of journalists into the world of the elite. Explores efforts at reform, including public journalism.

Fuller, Jack. *News Values: Ideas for an Information Age.* Chicago: University of Chicago Press, 1996.

Seeks to understand the underlying public values a newspaper serves and the implications of those values for journalists' behavior. Argues that for newspapers to survive changes in the way information is delivered, they must retain a commitment to providing comprehensive and coherent daily information for use in an increasingly complicated world.

Glasser, Theodore L. "Communication and the Cultivation of Citizenship," *Communication,* 12 (1991): 235–248.

Discusses the differences between liberal and communitarian forms of community and communication. Underscores the importance of narrative as a means to sustain community and cultivate citizenship.

Graber, Doris A. *Processing the News: How People Tame the Information Tide.* New York: Longman, 1988.

Argues that classic theories about the role of citizens in democratic societies are based on flawed assumptions about citizens' interest and knowledge in political matters. Calls for a better understanding of information processing, which can provide the basis for constructing more viable theories about democratic participation.

Harwood Group. *Citizens and Politics: A View from Main Street America.* Dayton, OH: Kettering Foundation, 1991.

Identifies groups and actions that people claim alienate them from politics. Concludes that although citizens participate when they perceive an opportunity to have impact, American politics is dominated by technical experts and shallow interactions.

Harwood Group. *Meaningful Chaos: How People Form Relationships with Public Concerns.* Dayton, OH: Kettering Foundation, 1993.

Citizens say they prefer news delivered in a way that allows them to become involved in an undefined dialogue with connections to other issues rather than news that is narrowly packaged. Discusses citizens' need for ambivalence to explore their beliefs about public concerns.

Lambeth, Edmund B. *Committed Journalism: An Ethic for the Profession.* 2d ed. Bloomington: Indiana University Press, 1992.

Argues that the professional interest of journalism—and the public interest—requires unrestrained ethical dialogue in newsrooms. Offers criteria by which to evaluate news media leadership and journalistic storytelling and shows how the narrative and interpretive power of news stories can foster moral dialogue within communities.

Leonard, Thomas C. *News for All: America's Coming-of-Age with the Press.* New York: Oxford University Press, 1995.

Examines the historic role of the American press in the making of a democratic reading public. Concludes that there was no age of innocence for the American press; the history of newspaper production and circulation does not point simply in the direction of civic high-mindedness.

Page, Benjamin I. *Who Deliberates? Mass Media in Modern Democracy.* Chicago: University of Chicago Press, 1996.

Investigates how public deliberation in America works through media. Describes circumstances in which the public is enlightened, and occasions when it is fooled, by mediated discussion of political issues. Argues that deliberation is compromised when media rely too heavily on official sources for news and commentary.

Patterson, Thomas E. *Out of Order.* New York: Knopf, 1993.

Rather than bringing candidates and voters together, election news drives a wedge between them. By focusing on campaign strategy over substantive issues, the press depicts campaigns as more chaotic, manipulative, and combative than they actually are.

Protess, David L., Fay Lomax Cook, Jack C. Doppelt, James S. Ettema, Margaret T. Gordon, Donna R. Leff, and Peter Miller. *The Journalism of Outrage: Investigative Reporting and Agenda Building in America.* New York: Guilford Press, 1991.

Finds that investigative journalism effects public policy independent of manifest changes in public opinion or interest group pressure. Policy reform appears to be a direct result of collaboration between journalists and officials in a process that bypasses the public.

Schudson, Michael. *The Power of News.* Cambridge, MA: Harvard University Press, 1995.

Argues for a view of journalism as a cultural system and suggests how individual reporters and their personal values fit into this system. "The News Media and the Democratic Process" is a particularly relevant chapter to public journalism.

Neuman, W. Russell, Marion R. Just, and Ann N. Grigler. *Common Knowledge: News and the Construction of Political Meaning.* Chicago: University of Chicago Press, 1992.

Combines surveys, in-depth interviews, learning experiments, and content analysis to examine how citizens make sense of politics. Focuses on the connections made, and connections missed, between citizens' interests and the language of public discourse in the news.

Peters, John Durham. "Distrust of Representation: Habermas on the Public Sphere," *Media, Culture and Society,* 15 (1993): 541–571.

Traces in Habermas's work the lineage of current debates about active versus passive media audiences. Emphasizes the theoretical value of the public sphere but argues as well that the insistence on rationality fails to acknowledge the possibilities for participation that might derive from narrative, rhetoric, and other forms of communication.

Peters, John Durham, and Kenneth Cmiel. "Media Ethics and the Public Sphere," *Communication,* 12 (1991): 197–215.

Argues that the media's preoccupation with professionals and experts is one consequence of the "lack of a vigorous public sphere in our society and imagination." Reviews political theorists' models of the public sphere and applies these concepts to media ethics and democratic participation.

Underwood, Doug. *When MBAs Rule the Newsroom: How the Marketers and Managers Are Reshaping Today's Media.* New York: Columbia University Press, 1993.

Contends that the profession is in danger of losing its "journalistic soul" due to the emergence of market-driven approaches to news reporting. Warns about the possibility of public journalism degenerating into marketing.

Yankelovich, Daniel. *Coming to Public Judgment: Making Democracy Work in a Complex World.* Syracuse, NY: Syracuse University Press, 1991.

Argues that journalists are effective during the beginning phase of public opinion formation when the news raises public consciousness about a pressing issue. But journalists must learn to help people take the next steps, to confront and commit to solving pressing issues.

Social and Political Theory

Barber, Benjamin R. *Strong Democracy: Participatory Politics for a New Age.* Berkeley: University of California Press, 1984.

Argues that liberalism has created a crisis of democracy, characterized by plummeting electoral turnout, distrust of politicians, and pervasive apathy. "Strong democracy" does not assume that community exist prior to, or independent of, politics; creation of community is one of the chief tasks of political activity.

Bellah, Robert N., Richard Madsen, William M. Sullivan, Ann Swidler, and Steven M. Tipton. *The Good Society.* New York: Knopf, 1991.

Maintains that the individual is realized only in and through community, but contemporary Americans have trouble seeing how this applies to their lives. Argues that we need to renew conversations about our collective life, in contrast to liberalism's conception of autonomous voters acting as consumers out to protect their interests.

Calhoun, Craig, ed., *Habermas and the Public Sphere.* Cambridge, MA: MIT Press, 1992.

Collection of essays focuses on the relationship between state and civil society, the origins and prospects for democracy, and the impact of media. Contributors deal with themes addressed by Habermas, including the origin of rationality and conditions for critical debate.

de Tocqueville, Alexis. *Democracy in America.* Ed. J. P. Mayer. Trans. George Lawrence. New York: Harper & Row, 1969.

Describes the passion of 19th-century Americans for engagement in civil life and argues that associations unite the energies of divergent minds and direct them toward a clearly indicated goal.

Dewey, John. *The Public and Its Problems.* New York: Holt, 1927.

Addresses challenges of democratic realists such as Walter Lippmann, who exposed the shortcomings of the press and a bewildered citizenry. Argues that Lippmann dismissed too readily the potential for newspapers to engage the public as attentive citizens.

Dionne, E. J. Jr. *Why Americans Hate Politics.* New York: Simon & Schuster, 1991.

Asserts that Americans have lost faith in democratic institutions over the past three decades and view politics as a "spectator sport." Argues that liberals and conservatives falsely frame political issues as a set of polarized choices and thus prevent the public from settling troubling questions.

Evans, Sara M., and Harry C. Boyte. *Free Spaces: The Sources of Democratic Change in America.* New York: Harper & Row, 1986.

Argues that "free spaces," although conceptually complex and ambiguous, are real enough and are crucial to the process of social change. Describe a "vast middle ground of communal activity," between private life and large institutions, that nourishes civic virtue and responsibility for the common good.

Fishkin, James. *Democracy and Deliberation: New Directions for Democratic Reform.* New Haven, CT: Yale University Press, 1991.

Examines the problem of deliberation given that the idea of democracy was based on populations of several thousand in a Greek city–state. Proposes a "deliberative opinion poll" as a mechanism for combining political equality with deliberation.

Fowler, Robert Booth. *The Dance with Community: The Contemporary Debate in American Political Thought.* Lawrence: University of Kansas Press, 1991.

Looks at community as a "contested concept" and considers a diversity of images of community, including participatory, republican, global, traditional, and religious models. Concludes that the prevalence of community as a concern in American political emerges from a dissatisfaction with modern liberalism.

Matthews, David. *Politics for People: Finding a Responsible Public Voice.* Urbana: University of Illinois Press, 1994.

Argues that Americans' conception of politics is too narrow; people feel estranged from the formal political system but they do participate in communities. Stresses the importance of public forums and public dialogue as institutions that allow people to come together as a more responsible public.

Sandel, Michael J. *Liberalism and the Limits of Justice.* Cambridge, MA: Cambridge University Press, 1982.

Challenges the liberalism of Kant and of much contemporary political philosophy, arguing for a deeper understanding of community than liberalism allows. Argues that liberalism puts the self beyond the reach of politics.

Schudson, Michael. *The Good Citizen: A History of American Civic Life.* New York: Free Press, 1998.

Argues that citizenship has changed but not declined. Traces the history of American citizenship from the "politics of assent" in the early years of the republic to the "politics of party affiliation" in the 19th century to the "politics of rights" that today characterizes an enlarged and more inclusive domain of politics.

Taylor, Charles. *Multiculturalism and "The Politics of Recognition."* Princeton, NJ: Princeton University Press, 1992.

Offers a philosophical perspective on what is at stake when people demand recognition of their particular identities by public institutions. Commentary from Susan Wolf, Steven C. Rockefeller, and Michael Walzer, who suggest new ways of conceiving the relationship between our personal identities and political practices.

Alphabetical Listing

Anderson, Rob, and Robert Dardenne, and George M. Killenberg. *The Conversation of Journalism: Communication, Community, and News.* Westport, CT: Praeger, 1994.

Altschull, J. Herbert. *Agents of Power: The Media and Public Policy.* 2d ed. New York: Longman, 1995.

Barber, Benjamin R. *Strong Democracy: Participatory Politics for a New Age.* Berkeley: University of California Press, 1984.

Bellah, Robert N., Richard Madsen, William M. Sullivan, Ann Swidler, and Steven M. Tipton. *The Good Society.* New York: Knopf, 1991.

Bennett, W. Lance. "A Policy Research Paradigm for the News Media and Democracy," *Journal of Communication,* 43,3 (1993): 180–189.

Black, Jay, ed. *Mixed News: The Public/Civic/Communitarian Journalism Debate.* Mahwah, NJ: Erlbaum, 1997.

Blumler, Jay G., and Michael Gurevitch. *The Crisis of Public Communication.* London: Routledge, 1995.

Broder, David S. "Campaign '92," *Quill* (March 1992): 8–9.

Calhoun, Craig, ed. *Habermas and the Public Sphere.* Cambridge, MA: MIT Press, 1992.

Calvert, Clay. "Clashing Conceptions of Press Duties: Public Journalists and the Courts," *Communication Law and Policy,* 2 (Autumn 1997): 441–475.

Carey, James W. "The Press, Public Opinion, and Public Discourse," pp. 373–402, in Theodore L. Glasser and Charles T. Salmon, eds., *Public Opinion and the Communication of Consent.* New York: Guilford Press, 1995.

Carey, James W. "Community, Public, Journalism," pp. 1–15, in Jay Black, ed., *Mixed News: The Public/Civic/Communitarian Journalism Debate.* Mahwah, NJ: Erlbaum, 1997.

Charity, Arthur. *Doing Public Journalism.* New York: Guilford Press, 1995.

Christians, Clifford G. "Social Ethics and Mass Media Practice," pp. 187–205, in Josina M. Makau and Ronald C. Arnett, eds., *Communication Ethics in an Age of Diversity,* Urbana: University of Illinois Press, 1997.

Christians, Clifford G., John P. Ferré, and P. Mark Fackler. *Good News: Social Ethics and the Press.* New York: Oxford University Press, 1993.

Coleman, Renita. "The Intellectual Antecedents of Public Journalism," *Journal of Communication Inquiry,* 21,1 (1997): 60–76.

Craig, David. A. "Communitarian Journalism(s): Clearing Conceptual Landscapes," *Journal of Mass Media Ethics,* 11,2 (1996): 107–118.

de Tocqueville, Alexis. *Democracy in America.* Ed. J. P. Mayer. Trans. George Lawrence. New York: Harper & Row, 1969.

Dewey, John. *The Public and Its Problems.* New York: Holt, 1927. Dionne, E. J. Jr. *Why Americans Hate Politics.* New York: Simon & Schuster, 1991.

Entman, Robert M. *Democracy without Citizens: Media and the Decay of American Politics.* New York: Oxford University Press, 1989.

Ettema, James S., and Theodore L. Glasser. *Custodians of Conscience: Investigative Journalism and Public Virtue.* New York: Columbia University Press, 1998.

Ettema, James S., and Limor Peer, "Good News from a Bad Neighborhood: Toward an Alternative to the Discourse of Urban Pathology," *Journalism and Mass Communication Quarterly,* 73 (Winter 1996): 835–856.

Evans, Sara M., and Harry C. Boyte. *Free Spaces: The Sources of Democratic Change in America.* New York: Harper & Row, 1986.

Fallows, James. *Breaking the News: How the Media Undermine American Democracy.* New York: Pantheon Books, 1996.

Fishkin, James. *Democracy and Deliberation: New Directions for Democratic Reform.* New Haven, CT: Yale University Press, 1991.

Fowler, Robert Booth. *The Dance with Community: The Contemporary Debate in American Political Thought.* Lawrence: University of Kansas Press, 1991.

Fuller, Jack. *News Values: Ideas for an Information Age.* Chicago: University of Chicago Press, 1996.

Glasser, Theodore L. "Communication and the Cultivation of Citizenship," *Communication,* 12,4 (1991): 235–248.

Glasser, Theodore L., and Stephanie Craft. "Public Journalism and the Prospects for Press Accountability," pp. 120–134, in Jay Black, ed., *Mixed News: The Public/Civic/Communitarian Journalism Debate.* Mahwah, NJ: Erlbaum, 1997.

Glasser, Theodore L., and Stephanie Craft. "Public Journalism and the Search for Democratic Ideals," pp. 203–218, in Tamar Liebes and James Curran, eds., *Media, Ritual and Identity.* London: Routledge, 1998.

Graber, Doris A. *Processing the News: How People Tame the Information Tide.* New York: Longman, 1988.

Hackett, Robert A., and Yuezhi Zhao. "Journalistic Objectivity and Social Change," *Peace Review,* 8,1 (1996): 5–11.

Harwood Group. *Citizens and Politics: A View from Main Street America.* Dayton, OH: Kettering Foundation, 1991.

Harwood Group. *Meaningful Chaos: How People Form Relationships with Public Concerns.* Dayton, OH: Kettering Foundation, 1993.

Heikkilä, Heikki, and Risto Kunelius. "Public Journalism and Its Problems: A Theoretical Perspective," *Javnost–The Public,* 3,3 (1996): 81–95.

Hodges, Louis W. "Ruminations about the Communitarian Debate," *Journal of Mass Media Ethics,* 11,3 (1996): 133–139.

Lambeth, Edmund B. *Committed Journalism: An Ethic for the Profession.* 2d ed. Bloomington: Indiana University Press, 1992.

Lambeth, Edmund, and David Craig. "Civic Journalism as Research," *Newspaper Research Journal,* 7 (1995): 149–160.

Leonard, Thomas C. *News for All: America's Coming-of-Age with the Press.* New York: Oxford University Press, 1995.

Matthews, David. *Politics for People: Finding a Responsible Public Voice.* Urbana: University of Illinois Press, 1994.

Merritt, Davis. *Public Journalism and Public Life: Why Telling the News Is Not Enough.* Hillsdale, NJ: Erlbaum, 1995.

Merritt, Davis. "Public Journalism—Defining a Democratic Art," *Media Studies Journal,* 9,3 (1995): 125–132.

Meyer, Philip. "Defining Public Journalism: Discourse Leading Solutions," *Investigative Reporters and Editors* (November–December 1995): 3–5.

Neuman, W. Russell, Marion R. Just, and Ann N. Grigler. *Common Knowledge: News and the Construction of Political Meaning.* Chicago: University of Chicago Press, 1992.

Page, Benjamin I. *Who Deliberates? Mass Media in Modern Democracy.* Chicago: University of Chicago Press, 1996.

Parisi, Peter. "Toward a 'Philosophy of Framing': News Narratives for Public Journalism," *Journalism and Mass Communication Quarterly,* 74 (Winter 1997): 673–686.

Patterson, Thomas E. *Out of Order.* New York: Knopf, 1993.

Peters, John Durham. "Distrust of Representation: Habermas on the Public Sphere," *Media, Culture and Society*, 15 (1993): 541–571.

Peters, John Durham, and Kenneth Cmiel. "Media Ethics and the Public Sphere," *Communication*, 12 (1991): 197–215.

Protess, David L., Fay Lomax Cook, Jack C. Doppelt, James S. Ettema, Margaret T. Gordon, Donna R. Leff, and Peter Miller. *The Journalism of Outrage: Investigative Reporting and Agenda Building in America*. New York: Guilford Press, 1991.

Raines, Howell. "The Fallows Fallacy," *New York Times*, February 25, 1996, sec. 4, p. 14.

Reider, Rem. "Public Journalism: Stop the Shooting," *American Journalism Review* (December 1995): 6.

Rosen, Jay. "Making Journalism More Public," *Communication*, 12 (1991): 267–284.

Rosen, Jay. *Community Connectedness: Passwords for Public Journalism*. St. Petersburg, FL: Poynter Institute for Media Studies, 1993.

Rosen, Jay. "Making Things More Public: On the Political Responsibility of the Media Intellectual," *Critical Studies in Mass Communication*, 11 (December 1994): 363–388.

Rosen, Jay. *Public Journalism as a Democratic Art*. New York: Project on the Public Life and the Press, 1994.

Rosen, Jay. *Getting the Connections Right: Public Journalism and the Troubles in the Press*. New York: Twentieth Century Fund, 1996.

Rosen, Jay, and Davis Merritt Jr. *Public Journalism: Theory and Practice*. Dayton, OH: Kettering Foundation, 1994.

Sandel, Michael J. *Liberalism and the Limits of Justice*. Cambridge, MA: Cambridge University Press, 1982.

Schudson, Michael. *The Good Citizen: A History of American Civic Life*. New York: Free Press, 1998.

Schudson, Michael. *The Power of News*. Cambridge, MA: Harvard University Press, 1995.

Taylor, Charles. *Multiculturalism and "the Politics of Recognition."* Princeton, NJ: Princeton University Press, 1992.

Underwood, Doug. *When MBAs Rule the Newsroom: How the Marketers and Managers Are Reshaping Today's Media*. New York: Columbia University Press, 1993.

Woo, William F. "As Old Gods Falter: Public Journalism and the Tradition of Detachment." Press-Enterprise Lecture Series, No. 30, University of California, Riverside, February 13, 1995.

Yankelovich, Daniel. *Coming to Public Judgment: Making Democracy Work in a Complex World*. Syracuse, NY: Syracuse University Press, 1991.

Index